The Dream That Failed

THE DREAM
THAT FAILED

*Reflections on
the Soviet Union*

WALTER LAQUEUR

New York   Oxford
OXFORD UNIVERSITY PRESS
1994

Oxford University Press

Oxford   New York   Toronto
Delhi   Bombay   Calcutta   Madras   Karachi
Petaling Jaya   Singapore   Hong Kong   Tokyo
Nairobi   Dar es Salaam   Cape Town
Melbourne   Auckland   Madrid
and associated companies in
Berlin   Ibadan

Published by Oxford University Press, Inc.
200 Madison Avenue, New York, New York 10016

Oxford is a registered trademark of Oxford University Press

Library of Congress Cataloging-in-Publication Data
Laqueur, Walter, 1921–
The dream that failed : reflections on the Soviet Union /
[Walter Laqueur].
p.   cm.
Includes bibliographical references and index.
ISBN 0-19-508978-2
1. Soviet Union–History–Philosophy.
I. Title.
DK266.L336   1994   947.084–dc20   94-14539

2 4 6 8 9 7 5 3 1

Printed in the United States of America
on acid-free paper

Preface

Leopold von Ranke, the great German historian, once asked whether anyone would bother to study history but for the dramatic impact of current events; the number of students would certainly be small. But for the breakup of the Soviet Union, there would be no rethinking now of the Soviet experience and of Communism. The year 1991 saw the end of a whole historical epoch and the beginning of another, the contours of which are as yet only dimly discernible. Not only the heritage of Marx and Lenin, but the wider issues of socialism and nationalism in the modern world have to be reconsidered. Why did the Soviet system collapse, and why were the signs ignored?

Where should the rethinking start? A reasonable case can be made in favor of encompassing in a postmortem most of Russian history, for that history has been in many ways sui generis, different from that of other European nations. If the question of a *Sonderweg*, a particular "way" of development, has preoccupied students of Germany for some considerable time, this applies even more strongly to Russia. History, as frequently observed, is a seamless web: Gorbachev and Yeltsin cannot be understood without the preceding "period of stagnation," which in turn can be explained only with reference to the era of Stalinism. If one wishes to discuss the revolution of 1917, it can be done, needless to say, only in conjunction with the state of affairs in Russia under Nikolai II.

I do not take the arrival of the Vikings in Russia in the ninth century as a starting point, but some comments on Russia on the eve of the revolution are called for. The circumstances of the downfall of the Soviet empire are well remembered. The early, "heroic" period of Soviet Communism, though, is now all but forgotten; yet it is essential to recall that there was a time when enthusiastic belief in and mass support for the system existed. A small group of professional revolutionaries seized power in a giant country, but it is unlikely that but for wider support Communism would have prevailed in the civil war of 1918 to 1921. The question why the Soviet system stayed in power for some considerable time is as pertinent as the questions concerning its decline and fall.

The second part of this inquest concerns Western interpretations of developments in the Soviet Union. Great events in history, especially if they happen suddenly, are seldom predicted with any kind of accuracy even by those closest to and most knowledgeable about them. No one has blamed French political scientists for not predicting in 1788, or early 1789, the storming of the Bastille, let alone subsequent events. Sovietology,[1] however, has come under fire for two valid reasons. In 1789, the study of contemporary France was not an academic discipline; it had no systematic theoretical underpinning, research institutes, courses of study, or countless publications. It did not claim to have a reliable body of knowledge about the mood of France, the state of society, and the economy. At the same time, few thinking Frenchmen of the late eighteenth century maintained that radical change was altogether unthinkable. They did not rule out violence; as Mirabeau wrote; "I never believed in a great revolution without bloodshed."[2]

The claims of mainstream political scientists specializing in Sovietology, with some notable exceptions, were far more ambitious. Many practitioners of this discipline believed in the stability of the regime almost up to the end. For this reason, the record of this discipline raises searching questions concerning the validity of much of contemporary social science. The failures would have been less pronounced if the claims had been less far-reaching and confident.

Comments on the present state and the future prospects of Russia should be made in a spirit of caution. The failure of the Soviet system now seems as obvious an outcome as the failure of Jacobinism must have appeared to the French after Thermidor in 1794. The effects of the French Revolution did not end then and there, however, even with the rise of Napoleon—or his fall. A mere five years had passed in 1794 since the days of the Bastille, and the social transformation had been infinitely less than in the case of Russia. But the consequences of 1789 shaped French history for almost a century—until a new equilibrium emerged in the 1870s with the rise of the Third Republic. Even then, there was no real ending to the French Revolution; seen in retrospect, it was only in the 1980s, at the time of the preparations for the celebration of the bicentenary of the revolution, that it ceased to be a divisive factor in French politics.[3]

The consequences of the October Revolution of 1917 are bound to be equally lasting, as a new equilibrium is not even in sight. Euphoria prevailed for only a brief moment after the fall of Communism; in the words of a semi-respectable song of the pre-*glasnost* period of Odessa provenance - "nedolgo muzika igrala," the music did not play for long. The economic future is, at best, uncertain; the political prospects are as murky as ever; and violent national conflict persists. Communism failed to "solve" the nationality question, but then it could be argued that all attempts to bring about a peaceful coexistence between the various nationalities were bound to fail, in Eastern Europe as much as in the former Soviet Union. "Proletarian internationalism" was never a reality in the

Soviet Union; much of the time, it was no more than a fraud. Future historians, however, may reach the conclusion that it caused less harm than does open, unbridled chauvinism. The appeal directed to the proletarians of all countries to unite was utopian, but on balance it did less damage than appeals that they should fight one another.

Where is Russia heading? It is unlikely that, outside the circle of Communist hardliners, the October Revolution will again be hailed as the most wonderful achievement in human history, nor will Stalin be given high marks for his achievements. But as the attempts to establish a stable, effective, and free political system in Russia are not successful, there is bound to be even more nostalgia for the good old days, when the streets were reasonably safe and vodka was cheap. As French historian Alphonse Aulard wrote many years after the event: "Que la république était belle sous l'Empire!" Future historian may paraphrase Aulard: How beautiful was freedom under Soviet oppression![4] Following the loss of empire, Russia is in search of a new role in the world, and the idea of a national renaissance is bound to figure high on its agenda. In the circumstances, the past days of national greatness (and superpower status) acquire new respectability.

In the sections that follow, I have tried to give at least tentative answers to some of the questions that have preoccupied me and many of my generation, "professionals" and "laymen" alike, concerning the October Revolution of 1917, the essence of the Soviet regime, the reasons for its downfall, and why the shortcomings and weaknesses of the system were ignored.

Some of the debates of past years have to be wound up: about Stalin's allegedly progressive role, the great economic and social achievements of the Soviet system, its (partly) democratic character, and so on. But I hesitate to agree with those who believe that the race between a planned economy and capitalism is over and that it has ended with the victory of capitalism, unless, of course, we restrict our purview to North America and Europe. In a long-term perspective, the prospects of socialism (not Marxian, not "scientific") could have improved once it got rid of the Communist incubus. The historical competition between Soviet Communism and the democratic societies has ended. But history does not consist of races in which only the winners qualify for the next round, as in the Olympic Games. It consists of contests at irregular intervals according to rules that tend to change. Some competitors are eliminated; others reappear under different guises. Victory on past occasions means nothing in conditions that perpetually change. No one can say as yet with any confidence what political, social, and economic system will supplant Soviet Communism.

Willi Muenzenberg, the most gifted propagandist of the Communist International, in 1934 asked a number of leading intellectuals (among them André Gide and H. G. Wells) for their comments on the planned economy. A typical answer was given by Klaus Mann, the son of the famous writer and not a member of the Communist party:

The state of our civilization under the rule of capitalism is so pitiful that everyone knows and feels that it cannot go on like this. Everyone knows that the economic system is responsible for the catastrophe and the shameful confusion. This is to say that the economic system has to fall, and it is to be succeeded by what we call socialism. He who does not believe in socialism and a planned economy has given up the hope that mankind will ever be better off, he despairs of the future.[5]

Klaus Mann's views were widely shared at the time, not only on the left. There is a wider lesson to be drawn from the danger of sweeping, confident predictions in the realm of economies and politics. It is a mistake to bury Communism too early; in one guise or another, its heritage could be with us for a long time to come, and for the emergence of an American- or a -West European–style system one may have to wait even longer. If within a few years even in eastern Germany and Poland, former Communists re-emerged as a substantial political force, if as in Ukraine and White Russia they never really lost power, it was perhaps no surprise that the nationalist–Communist camp should show such strength and staying power in Russia. Even some of those who had initially welcomed the breakdown of the Soviet system turned back from the new order in anguish or anger. At a time of economic, social, and political crisis, the urge for strong leadership resurfaced with a vengeance. While Communism had been a failure, it had at least safeguarded survival at a very low level of substance.

Under the new conditions in Russia, few prospered while the majority was badly off. Within a very short time, the very terms "democracy" and "democrats" acquired a pejorative meaning. As Vadim Kozhinov, one of the gurus of the Russian right, wrote, the true dividing line in Russia is not now between Communists and anti-Communists but between "patriots" and "anti-patriots"[5] – that is to say, those who do not share the ideology of the far right. A relapse appeared a distinct possibility, perhaps a certainty. But a relapse to what? If the Communist establishment had a soft landing, Communism as an idea and an ideal had suffered irreparable damage. It could no longer be revived; the ideological and political alternative is a hotchpotch of a strongly nationalist regime with pronounced state-capitalist (or state-socialist) elements, a fatal mixture, new perhaps to Russia, but experienced at their cost in one form or another by other European countries in the past.

My interest in Communism and Soviet affairs goes back to the awakening of my interest in politics in general in the 1930s and my first Russian lessons in the early 1940s. Traveling in Russia was almost unthinkable at the time, and it was not until the 1950s that I first visited the country. It was not very hospitable, and as a critical observer from abroad, I certainly did not imagine at the time that one day my work would be published in Moscow.

But my involvement in Soviet affairs was not total. I edited *Survey*, specializing in this field from 1955 to 1964, and I wrote a historical survey of Soviet studies.[7] Russian culture intrigued me at least as much as Soviet politics, which, especially in the 1960s and 1970s, were not a subject of great intellectual fascination. When I realized that I had to force myself to read Russian political literature and when visits to Russia brought diminishing returns, my work shifted to other directions, until in the 1980s I again became interested in the dramatic and unexpected developments in the Soviet Union.

This book, an inquest rather than an attempt to pass a final verdict, is the summing up of many years of learning and thinking about Russia and Communism, the dream that turned into a nightmare. As an ideological challenge, Communism ceased to exist many years ago. But it still was a great force in the real world. The fact that the Soviet Union became a superpower had a great impact on the thinking of many contemporaries. After all, not so long ago almost one-third of mankind lived under Communist rule: surely, there must have been a reason why a political system made such spectacular progress over such short time. Since human memory is notoriously short, some of those who thought of the Soviet Union as the wave of the future now claim that it was a mirage from the beginning, lacking ideological appeal, and was in later years a colossus with feet of clay that should never have been taken seriously. To them, the whole preoccupation with the Soviet Union and Communism now appears unintelligible and indefensible.

Such views seem to me unpersuasive. There was a time when Communism did cast a powerful spell, and among those who were attracted were not the worst and the most stupid of their generation. To dismiss Communism as if it were never of consequence shows neither good sense nor historical understanding. At the same time, writing under the immediate impact of the collapse of the Soviet Union, I find it unhelpful to draw conclusions from the Communist debacle, which could well be premature. In my own writings on the subject, I have been critical of Soviet politics to a greater degree than it was fashionable at the time. Such skepticism seems correct in retrospect, but having been prematurely right does not necessarily add to one's popularity. However, these considerations did not appear to me of consequence at the time, and they seem even less important now.

An earlier and shorter version of Chapter 3 appeared in the *Journal of Contemporary History* (July 1993); abridged versions of Chapters 7 and 8 were published in installments in *Novoye Vremya* (Moscow) throughout 1993. I have benefitted from exchanges with various colleagues and would like to express gratitude in particular to Karl Dietrich Bracher for discussing yet another time the issue of totalitarianism as it appeared in 1993; to Igor Birman for reviewing the facts, figures, and opinions that appear in Chapter 2; and to Nikolai Rudensky for discussing interethnic relations and for some material he helped to obtain for me. I also wish to thank David Augustyn and Marek Michalewski.

Washington, D.C.   W.L.
March 1994

Contents

The Dream That Failed

1

The Age of Enthusiasm

Communism was the great ideological divide of our time: some countries were more acutely affected by the challenge than others, but none was passed by. It was much more than a political or an economic confrontation; few people would have gone on the barricades for the sake of either a market or a planned economy. The conflict was in essential respects cultural and religious in character. The Communists were not a political party like others; they promised not just good government and a thriving economy but a new world of freedom, justice, and happiness for all. While they were not religious believers, their vision strongly resembled that of paradise, the Greek Elysium, the Muslim seventh heaven, and similar ideas in other religions: a place in which there would be neither sin nor death. In this earthly Eden, freed from the shackles of oppression and exploitation, each individual (and society as a whole) would be able to develop to its full capacity. At long last, human beings would become fully human. The ascent to this glorious haven would be long and arduous. It would lead mankind (as it had Dante) through the inferno and purgatory. At times, there would be dark night, and the sight of the stars would be lost. But then, a signpost would be reached reading *Incipit Vita Nova –* "Here begins the new life."

I deal in this book with the decline and fall of Soviet Communism and its attempt to build this new world, and the failure on the part of those with a special interest in this new world to see the unfolding disaster in time. This failure was by no means restricted to one group of people; academic experts were as much involved as diplomats and journalists. The case of East Germany shows that the same misapprehensions that beclouded understanding of the Soviet Union could be found in conditions when a realistic appraisal should have been much easier.[1] Or did the catastrophe

3

occur like a bolt out of the blue without warning signs that could be discerned? Lastly, I shall briefly deal with the heritage of Communism and the possible consequences for the countries that have gone through purgatory without ever reaching heaven.

It is impossible to write the end of this story without referring to its beginning. It is easy now to point to the many causes of Soviet decline and to the reasons that so many outside observers were confused and misled. It is far more difficult in the present psychological climate to explain the great magnetism that Soviet Communism once exuded. But without this, Communism does not make historical sense. If it was no more than a combination of a planned economy, propaganda, and terror, why did it last so long and why was it for a long time seemingly so successful?

For those who became interested in the Soviet Union in the 1960s and 1970s—including those who took a positive view—Communism was a tedious subject: a stagnant society guided by a boring ideology, the Soviet Union was the very antithesis of the revolutionary impulses that had once been so characteristic for the "socialist sixth" of the world. This expression was coined in the 1930s, before Communism expanded and became the socialist third—or even half—of the globe. By the 1960s, however, the monolith had split, and to the extent that Soviet Communism grew in power, it lost dynamism and appeal. Its ideological attraction was limited in recent years to the most backward part of the globe. Its well-wishers among diplomats, journalists, and academic experts in the West were motivated by a variety of motives and attitudes, but there was no John Reed, no Raymond Robbins, no Lincoln Steffens among them, to recall only a few of the enthusiasts of an earlier period. The Soviet system seemed to work, better in some respects than in others, but it was no longer regarded as the wave of the future. Only a very few earnest scholars took Leninism seriously anymore. On the contrary, there was a certain condescension. Communism had been appropriate—probably inescapable—in Russia, but no one in his right mind wanted to live in such a system.

For a considerable time, Communism had been the great hope, the great temptation, and, later yet for many, the great enemy in Europe and even beyond. In my own generation were young men and women who fought and died for Communism—fine, selfless people and great idealists. This may not be easy to understand for a younger generation. When Raymond Aron wrote his "Opium of the Intellectuals," in 1955, the attraction of Communism was already on the wane, except perhaps in France. When J. F. Revel wrote his "Totalitarian Temptation" in 1975, he focused more on the decay and weakness of the West than on the health of Soviet society.[2]

To understand the faith Communism inspired once upon a time, we ought to recall a distant period. Before World War I, there was increasing sympathy for democratic socialism in most civilized countries. It corresponded with the sense of fairness and social justice, and its indirect impact—resulting in social legislation—was even greater. It also corresponded with another strong tradition—the idea of progress, the belief that man and society could be greatly perfected and that utopia was not an impossible dream but one that the human race could gradually attain. Edward Bellamy's *Looking Backward* (describing Boston in the year 2000) and George Bernard Shaw's play *Back to Methuselah* (which takes place in the year A.D. 31,290) were not Marxist tracts, but expressed the optimism underlying Marxism that was shared by many millions.

In several European countries, the Social Democrats were the strongest, or one of the strongest parties, and France had its first socialist minister well before 1914. There was little sympathy for extremism and violent revolution, however. Even the advocates of general strikes and other such mass action thought of it as the exception rather than the norm. In the nineteenth century, the socialist movement had rejected Blanquism, the theory and practice of armed insurrection by a few conspirators, just as it rejected anarchist terrorism in later years. Such opposition was pragmatic as well as principled. It was pragmatic because the application of violence was thought to antagonize wide sections of society. Furthermore, violence would probably be unsuccessful against the state monopoly of armed force, which had become progressively stronger—even Friedrich Engels had said so. In any case, there seemed to be a good possibility of approaching the socialist ideal in an evolutionary way. There was steady progress in the strength of left-wing parties and trade unions. Even the practice of the parties that had officially embraced Marxism—for which the idea of revolution was a central tenet—had become reformist. They were still ridiculing Fabianism, with its vision of a welfare state, but in their political practice they were becoming gradualists.

It was also a matter of principle because the overwhelming majority of socialists were democrats and had misgivings about a revolution that would bring a dictator (or a group of little dictators) to power. True, Marx had written in a letter in 1875 about the "dictatorship of the proletariat," but he had never elaborated the theme. It was clear that he regarded it as an emergency measure, not, as Lenin later described it, "a particular form of government during a whole historical epoch." Marx had even argued that he did not mean by "dictatorship" the abolition of democracy, although he did not make it clear how the two opposites could be combined—perhaps he was not a consistent Marxist. Those who gave the issue more than passing thought knew, of course, that such an impersonal dictatorship was a mere abstraction. Political power in such a case would not be in the hands of a social class but in the hands of an individual, or a group of leaders, claiming to act on behalf of the working class. Such a contingency was thought to be highly undesirable because it would result in tyranny, however well intentioned. Hence the misgivings uttered even by orthodox Marxists such as Karl Kautsky and Rosa Luxemburg vis-à-vis the Bolsheviks virtually from the day they seized power: "A dictatorship not of the proletariat but of a handful of politicians . . . such conditions must inevitably cause a brutalization of public life: attempted assassinations, shooting of hostages etc."[3] If the German extreme rightists had not murdered her, Stalin would have killed Rosa Luxemburg in 1937 at the latest.

In brief, the idea that violence was both inevitable and desirable was limited in the West to a few eccentrics such as Georges Sorel, who found more readers among future fascists than from the left. True, there was general agreement among democrats that the tsarist regime would have to go. But it was a far cry from this recognition to Lenin's idea, first developed in "What Is to Be Done" (1902),[4] that what Russia needed was a small highly organized group of professional revolutionaries: "Give us an organization of revolutionaries, and we will overturn Russia!" Lenin assumed that by itself the working class could not be trusted, for it would never rise for any length of time beyond the level of "trade union consciousness." As Lenin saw it, the "vanguard" would carry out the revolution not only against the state, but also against the bourgeois democrats. As he envisaged it, the uprising would not be just a political revolution, but a social and economic turning point, the beginning of a new era in the history of mankind.

What would happen after the revolution? In his Zurich exile, Lenin reached the conclusion that the state was always and everywhere the instrument of the ruling class. As long as the state apparatus existed, true freedom was impossible. The state would have to be dismantled and wither away.

Lenin's belief in "scientific socialism" was second to none, but with this pronouncement utopianism reached its climax. We do not know whether he meant what he wrote; if he did, his ideas were as radical as they were unreal. Moreover, Lenin was to believe in later years that this vision was the shape of things to come, not only in Russia, but all over the world—hence the idea of "world revolution." With beliefs like these, Lenin was bound to remain outside the mainstream of the socialist movement. True, he gained a temporary victory inside Russian social democractic circles, but only at the price of splits and more splits, which pushed his group into virtual isolation.

It was only as the result of World War I that the Bolsheviks got their chance. Even in 1917 and 1918, however, there was no enthusiasm for their cause in Russia—and even less outside it.

We knew that when the storming of the Bastille became known in 1789, there was jubilation all over Europe; strangers embraced in the streets from London to far-away St. Petersburg. The citadel of tyranny had fallen at long last. It was bliss to be alive at this new dawn of mankind! But in Petrograd, the citadel had fallen six months earlier, and all the Bolsheviks did was to suppress the other political parties, including the socialists.

The Leninists had very few foreign supporters, and even apologies were pronounced without great conviction: there had been anarchy in Russia, and as the democratic parties had failed, was it not natural that the Bolsheviks should take over? It was the only party to have a clear program and sufficient self-confidence. When asked whether any movement felt capable of leading the country out of the crisis, Lenin responded, "There is such a party."

Lenin's answer became famous. It was quoted incessantly for seventy years and eventually came to haunt the Bolsheviks, who were certain that socialism could be built as the result of a jump or by legal enactment, as Kautsky had put it.

Against all prophecies, the Bolsheviks kept power and gradually sympathy for their cause increased. What were the reasons? Initially and above all, they were aided by the violent reaction against World War I, its senseless slaughter of millions and its horrible destruction. The Leninists had been among the first and most consistent opponents of the carnage. Little did it matter that their theoretical explanation of the mechanism that had allegedly caused the war was wrong or, at best, only partly right: the economic conflicts between the imperialist powers that (they claimed) had triggered the war were not really of decisive importance. What did matter was that the Bolsheviks had opposed the war, had unilaterally ended it in 1917, and promised that the proletarian world revolution would be the last and decisive fight. After that, mankind would live forever in peace and harmony.

There had been great hope in most countries that after the war everything would be different and better. Instead, in some countries, unprecedented inflation occured. All were affected by the Great Depression after 1929, with many millions unemployed. A mood of hopelessness descended on Europe and America. While the rise of fascism gave new hope to some, it caused fear and despondency among others. "Bourgeois" parliamentary democracy seemed to have failed to cope with the great political, social, and economic problems of the 1920s. "Parliamentary" became a synonym for "ineffectual," and democracy was discredited. Since capitalism seemed so obviously doomed, there was great interest in all kinds of social and economic planning and, above all, in the greatest planning experiment—the Soviet Union. The question why so many foreigners became well-wishers and admirers of the Soviet Union in these years will continue to preoccupy us. Naïveté may explain the reaction of some but by no means all foreign visitors. Not all were fools eager to be deceived by Potemkin villages shown on carefully prepared guided tours.

Why did the Bolsheviks retain power? It was one thing to seize some key positions in Petrograd and other major cities by surprise at a time of virtual chaos. It was another, far more difficult enterprise to gain victory in the face of White Russian armed resistance, peasant rebellions, and foreign intervention and to make the state apparatus work. It was not just superior organization: the Bolsheviks had no experience in this respect. Nor was it mainly terror: there were not enough commissars in leather jackets to make the soldiers shoot and the peasants sow and harvest. In any case, there was a great deal of violence in both the Red and the White camps. The Red military leaders were not military geniuses, and the leaders of the White armies were not ineffective bumblers. Nor were the White generals aristocrats divorced from the people; Anton Ivanovich

Denikin was the son of a poor peasant, and the others (with the exception of Wrangel) did not belong to the nobility either.

What, then, made the Red soldiers fight better and with greater persistence? The Bolsheviks were more united than their enemies, as Richard Pipes, the most recent historian of the revolution, rightly notes.[5] Luck also played a considerable role. But the moral factor was probably decisive. Seen in retrospect, the Red Army was more highly motivated than its enemies. Once the civil war ended, the true difficulties—famine and, generally speaking, economic ruin—had still to be faced.

Propaganda and terror alone would not have achieved this aim. Those ruling Russia had to persuade at least substantial segments of the population that they were capable of leading the country toward a better future. The Russian people had unquestioningly obeyed the tsars for centuries—would they not show similar obeisance toward the new masters? This was by no means certain, for the old establishment had grown roots over the centuries, whereas the new rulers had to establish their legitimacy. Their ideology was wholly unfamiliar and in most respects not in line with Russian traditions. Although the majority of the population, workers and especially peasants, remained passive throughout the 1920s and 1930s, they did passively cooperate. To achieve minimum readiness, the party leadership needed enthusiasts and militants. At this stage, a new class with a vested interest in the perpetuation of the new order would not have been sufficient, for something more than class interest was needed. Such a class did come into existence eventually, but only in later years.

In the 1920s Soviet power rested on the presence of hundreds of thousands—perhaps millions—of enthusiasts, mainly young, whose imagination had been fired by the Bolshevik vision. This was the generation of the battle of Perekop and of Chapayev, of *How the Steel Was Forged* and the *subbotniki*.[6] These were not the "children of the Arbat" (referring to the 1987 novel by A. Rybakov, dealing with Moscow in the 1930s) but the previous generation, the children of Dnyeproges, Magnitogorsk, and Komsomolsk, on the Amur—the great industrial enterprises of the first Five-Year Plan. Those were the people who helped to build the Moscow metro, went to teach in isolated villages, took crash courses to gain a higher education—for according to the slogan of those days, there were no heights Communists could not conquer. They volunteered for paramilitary organizations (such as the Ossoviakhim) and were believing atheists, trying to persuade the peasants that there was no God and that the churches had to be closed. Some became "Red professors;" others, officers in the army or the secret police. They were idealistic, aware of the miserable condition of their country but firmly convinced that the situation would quickly improve because their party had both the wisdom and the determination to tackle all the difficulties. They knew that the future belonged to Communism—capitalism, the system of oppression and exploitation, was in its death throes. Even foreign visitors hostile to Communism, even some of the émigrés, had to admit that the Communists had been able to win over the vanguard of the young generation–and thus hopes for a quick collapse of the Soviet regime faded. For these young militants, the "best sons and daughters of the fatherland," it was a time of hope, hope in the midst of misery, and even of innocence. They were killing, but they were so deeply convinced that they were right and that it was necessary that doubts never bothered them.

Today the enthusiasm and revolutionary romanticism of the 1920s has become a matter of ridicule, but at the time the pathos did not sound hollow. Even the unpolitical Boris Pasternak wrote long poems about the revolution (as Aleksandr Blok and Sergei Esenin had done before). Even Gorky, who had been so critical of Lenin and the Bolsheviks in 1917, decided to return to Russia, and Vladimir Mayakovsky (especially in *Charasho*) reached new heights of optimism. Even Ilya Ehrenburg, the old skeptic, came from his Paris exile to describe the new mood in *Den Vtoroi* (*The Second Day*).

The work of poets of the generation of Komsomol (the Communist Youth organization),[7] bears evidence of the sanguine mood of that period. Paradise seemed just around the corner, and even if they did not live to witness it, what did it matter? There was the great satisfaction of being a member of an army fighting for a great cause–the highest ideals of mankind: true liberty, social justice, the creation of a higher man. This was the time when it was solemnly announced that mental disease had been conquered in Russia and crime was about to disappear. The spirit of sacrifice, of selfless devotion to the cause, was preached. While these young men and women did not become saints in their daily life, many of them lived modestly and frugally, gave much of their energy and time to Communism, and were optimistic and happy. Perhaps the best description of this new spirit came from a German student visiting Russia from 1929 to 1931. As he saw it, a great number of the new Russian students felt themselves responsible for the future of their country–fighters "in the great army of the nation."[8] They had been raised from nothing to head the nation and were told every day that they were the advance guard of a new era, the creators of a new humanity: "They feel that they have to fight the whole world, that they can be victorious only if they stand up for each other"–all for each and each for all:

A moral code for fighters exacting such great sacrifice and discipline from every single person that but few can do justice to it; a moral code that remains great, even if those believing in it should fail.[9]

Owning property meant nothing for this vanguard. They have an unshakable sense of superiority: it is the superiority felt by a healthy man among a crowd of sick, by one who can see among a crowd of blind, the superiority felt by a man who is convinced that he alone had a clear course before him, while all the rest are moving senselessly towards insanity.[10]

But, alas, this elite did not forever stay healthy; they exhausted themselves quickly. In Nikolai Ostrovsky's novel, there is a dialogue between two such very sick veterans not yet aged thirty:

There is no taking life easy nowadays, it simply won't work. How nice it would be to take a little rest, just to catch your breath. After all, I am not as young as I was. . . . But it's no use. The more powerful the machine, the faster the wheels run, and with us the speed increases every day, so that we old folk simply have to stay young.

The hero is then told by another old timer (aged twenty-six or twenty-eight) that although he had suffered a lot—his affliction included blindness—he had lost none of his enthusiasm, "and that is the main thing."[11]

The optimistic spirit of the period emerged from the plays and above all, the films of the period. This refers not only to those that invoked the heroic days of the revolution and civil war, but also those on new themes like "socialist reconstruction," such as Valentin Katayev's novel *Vremya Vperyod* or the movie *Road to Life*, describing the redemption of the *bezprizorny*, vagrant children who had grown up without shelter and control. Did it not show that there was no limit to the improvement and perfectability even of young criminals? These plays and films were quite effective and generated great interest among foreigners. Even Goebbels said that *Battleship Potemkin* was the most effective film ever made. The political and social revolution had taken place, and now a cultural revolution was following it.

It was in its poems and songs that this heroic age found its most perfect expression. Anatole D'Aktil's "March of the Enthusiasts" proclaims:

> We are always right in our daring
> There are no obstacles for us on land or on sea,
> we fear no ice, no clouds.
> We achieve in a year the work of a century,
> happiness we take as of right,
> We carry the banner of our country
> through the whole world and all ages.

According to a song by Bezymensky, the young guard of workers and peasants was rushing into the struggle so that labor would become the master of the world and unite all as one great family. "Youth led us into battle," Bagritsky wrote, looking back, so that a new young generation would emerge out of the bones of the fallen heroes. "We are born to make a new reality out of fairy tales," announced the song of the young aviators, written by Pavel German.[12]

Reference has been made to the enthusiasm of youth. But youth is not a social class or a political party. Could Communism have lasted but for the support of the workers? Great social changes took place under Soviet rule. The old ruling stratum and the middle class were eliminated and replaced by a new elite. These new men and women had every reason to favor the new order, which had given them a privileged position in society. Among the younger members of the new intelligentsia, it could be heard that it was quite unthinkable that in any other society young people of poor background would have received a higher education. The Communist party certainly invested a great deal of propagandistic effort among the workers, whom they thought their most reliable supporters. There was much less agitprop in the countryside; the leaders were no doubt aware that the effort required would be even greater and the political result meager.

How successful was the Communist indoctrination among those who did not rise in society but remained manual workers? They had to persuade the workers that they were the most important, the most honored, members of society; that there was no exploitation, as existed in other societies; that they lived better than workers in the rest of the world; that life was getting better every year; and that they had social services of which workers under capitalism could not even dream.

The results were mixed. Official propaganda was partly believed. Workers marched in the demonstrations on May Day and on November 7; Stalin was not unpopular, nor were his henchmen, such as Mikhail Kalinin, Sergei Kirov, and even Lazar Kaganovich. The workers did not strike, but there was no spectacular rise in productivity. There was more apathy than enthusiasm—the song about workers walking "like masters in their native country" always sounded hollow. The workers gave their passive support during the 1930s and the war, but in the postwar period, it became less and less as time went by, eventually turning into alienation.

The Bolsheviks never succeeded in winning over a majority of the older generation, but given the dictatorial system there was no need to. Their success with the younger generation is one of the keys for an understanding of the revolution, civil war, and the events of the 1920s. If the Bolsheviks were just a bunch of half-mad foreign gangsters, they could not have inspired the people to undertake such tremendous efforts and undergo such deprivations.

There is no rational explanation for the Communists' achievements in these early days, unless one accepts the obvious: that a significant part of the young generation—and by no means the worst among them—sincerely believed in Communism, often with a fanatical faith. Communism was a secular religion with its pope, ritual prayers, saints, confessions, promises of reward and punishment. It satisfied spiritual needs—it was a myth, one of the most powerful of all time.

Communism was not the only secular religion that had a hypnotic effect on millions of people, especially the young. Fascism was equally, in some respects even more, effective. There is no way to measure popular enthusiasm, but there is much reason to assume that support for National Socialism in Germany (and to a somewhat lesser extent for fascism in Italy) was spontaneous and genuine. The Nazis did not have to employ political commissars in peace and war as the Russians did, nor did they have to impose a system of political control as thorough as that of the Russians. In daily life, ideology played a much lesser role. In many cultural and social fields, the ruling party did not intervene except when it removed "racially undesirable elements." There was no jamming of foreign broadcasts in

Germany or Italy; the Nazis and fascists felt so sure of success that this was thought to be unnecessary.[13]

Fascism was in many respects an anti-movement. Its enemies figured more centrally than its aims. This explains its considerable electoral support—for instance, in Germany in the early 1930s. Like Italian fascism and the other fascisms, Nazism never made a great effort to win over the intellectuals, whom, by and large, it despised. Its ideal was the *Tatmensch*, the man of action, not the intellectual. Communism, too, did not think much of the wavering, inconsistent intelligentsia—very much in contrast to the faithful, reliable working class. But at least Communism in its doctrine was not openly and proudly irrational.

Fascism, like Communism, looked for the support of the young generation. It was a movement of youth—the Italian anthem was "Giovinezza" ("Youth"). The German government after 1933, like the Soviet government of the 1920s and 1930s, consisted of people in their thirties. Goebbels was head of the Nazi organization in Berlin at twenty-eight and minister of propaganda and one of the most influential people in the Third Reich at thirty-six. Himmler became head of the SS at twenty-nine, and some of the other key figures were even younger. In Italy, Ciano became foreign minister at thirty-two. Balbo became a minister at thirty-three; Grandi, at thirty-four. Degrelle, Codreanu, and José Antonio Primo de Rivera became leaders of the fascist movements in Belgium, Romania, and Spain in their twenties. In the Soviet Union, Tukhachevsky was an army general at twenty-six. Viacheslav Molotov, Sergo Ordzhonikidze, Sergei Kirov, Anastas Mikoyan, and Lazar Kaganovich, all Stalin's young men, were in their early thirties when they became secretaries of the party Central Committee or government ministers. Even in the 1930s, many a newly appointed minister had just turned thirty; for example, Gromyko was made ambassador to the United States at thirty-four.

Nazism's and fascism's appeal to youth was not based on terror. Elsewhere I have quoted the evidence of a young idealist German who had previously not been a Nazi:

> National Socialism offered all that a young man in his most secret and proudest imagination would desire—activity, responsibility for his fellows, and work with equally enthusiastic comrades for a greater and stronger fatherland. It held official recognition, and careers that had been unthinkable before; while on the other side there were only difficulties and dangers, an empty future and doubts in the heart.[14]

Such a confession could have come from a young Communist in 1925 or 1930. Young people were given chances they did not have before. What latter-day Sovietologists wrote about "upward mobility" in Stalin's Russia was equally true with regard to Nazi Germany and Fascist Italy. As Aldous Huxley noted at the time, Communism and fascism appeal for the support of youth and youth alone. In Rome and Moscow, age had been disenfranchised.

The careers of members of the new elite quite apart, there was a feeling among young Communist enthusiasts that the collective was infinitely more important than the individual. The "fear of freedom" as a negative motive was frequently invoked as an explanation in later years, but equally there was the feeling that their country, Europe, and the world were facing a great crisis and that strong leadership and iron discipline were needed to confront the challenges.

It was obvious that a price had to be paid for the system of regimentation, but many did so gladly. If Stalin had liquidated unemployment, engaged in giant economic projects, and made his country powerful and respected—or at least feared—in the world community, so had Hitler. Despair had given way to a climate of optimism. In particular, 1935 and 1936 were good years for the dictatorships: progress seemed obvious all around, in stark contrast to the old, helpless democracies in their decay. Quite manifestly, the future belonged to young peoples such as Germany, Italy, and the Soviet Union. It is instructive to watch documentaries showing the May Day or November 7 rallies in Moscow—and the Nuremberg party rallies and the Olympic Games of 1936. The enthusiasm was genuine, nor was it primarily militaristic in inspiration; no one but Hitler and a few confidants thought in 1936 about great wars of conquest and the German domination of Europe. The great majority welcomed the fact that Germany's rightful place in the world was gradually restored. For this, as everyone knew, a strong army was needed. The mass slaughter of later years was beyond the imagination of the young generation. They were indoctrinated to believe in the ideal of being a soldier. But this was rather abstract, and the connection between soldier and war, strange as it may appear, was seldom made. The appeal of fascism for the young remains a subject to be investigated and pondered by historians and psychologists.[15]

What was the impact on a young believer in Communism of the forcible collectivization of agriculture, the purges and the terror, and the repulsive cult of Stalin forever increasing in intensity? How could youthful enthusiasm have survived the cruelty, obvious mendacity, and regimentation that became stronger all the time? Certain changes did take place under the surface—1935 was probably the last more or less peaceful year for many people in the Soviet Union. Life became better, as Stalin had promised; there was more to eat and a greater selection of consumer goods. There was also a new constitution, the freest in the world. Nineteen thirty-four was the year of *Veselye Rebyata (Merry Children)*, a very popular movie, and of celebrating how beautiful life had become. Again there was the motive of conquering space and time: to quote one of the hit songs, "We shall achieve and discover everything, the cold polar region and the blue firmament, and if the country will give us the order to be heroes—everyone will be a hero." With 1935 came "Song of the Fatherland," another message that with every day life was becoming more joyous and proclaiming, "I do not know any other country in which people breathe as freely."[16] To get a sense of how people were feeling, or at least how they were expected to feel, one ought to watch popular movies of those years such as *Circus* and *Merry Children* – an instructive and shattering experience at a distance of fifty years. "Song of the Fatherland," having served for decades as the anthem of Radio Moscow, became an often-quoted bitter joke under *glasnost*. But this was much later. At the time, there was nothing funny or ironic about these songs and their message.

After 1935, a far-reaching change took place. There still was support for Stalin and his cohorts. It would appear that a substantial part of the population believed even the most absurd accusations in the Moscow trials, or at least gave Stalin the benefit of the doubt. Perhaps the accused were guilty of crimes other than those charged, which could not be mentioned; but guilty they were.

Above all, there was the growing danger of war. Could there be any doubt about who was right and who was wrong in the Spanish Civil War? And was it not clear that Europe – indeed, the whole world – was rapidly moving toward a new war? In these circumstances, Stalin could count on the support of a large proportion of the people, certainly in the cities. There was not much affection for Stalinism in the countryside, as the advancing Nazi armies found in the summer of 1941.

But the erstwhile enthusiasm had disappeared. Some astute observers realized this first in 1936 at the time of Stalin's greatest triumphs. Georgi Fedotov, the émigré religious historian and philosopher, wrote in 1936 that previously the decay of the revolution had been covered up by revolutionary enthusiasm.[17] In earlier years, a minority, the revolutionary youth and the militants, had possessed a "monopoly on truth"; their optimism had been Russia's saving grace. Their enthusiasm had been genuine, not something staged by Moscow theatrical producers. Generations of young enthusiasts had burned themselves out, their lives and their consciences, on the bonfire of the revolution. They had committed horrible crimes, but their willingness to sacrifice themselves made one able to forgive them much. Despite undoubted Soviet achievements, despite satiety, satisfaction, and the increasing outward signs of civilization, the spirit of enthusiasm had disappeared. The country was changing. Now everyone had to lie; the system of police provocation was corrupting not only the government and the party, but the whole people.

This could be regarded as a natural process. Revolutionary impulses do not last forever: for a command economy, a command society is needed. Discipline and unquestioning obedience were now far more in demand than enthusiasm. As traditional idols who had been removed in the 1920s were restored to the Russian pantheon, enthusiasm became suspect, and spontaneity became a crime. Stalin distrusted everyone and everything he could not control.

Where the authorities tried to generate enthusiasm – in industrial and agricultural production – the attempts were disingenuous and unsuccessful. There was nothing spontaneous about the Miner Aleksei Stakhanov and the tractor driver Pasha Angelina. They were not enthusiasts, but well-trained puppets. Their exploits were carefully prepared, and all such heroes were consigned to limbo after a little while.

Even in the earlier days it had always been easier to generate and sustain enthusiasm in a demonstration or the field of battle than at the workplace. Manual labor is not a receptive soil for revolutionary enthusiasm, except during short, hectic periods. A good example is Dziga Vertov's documentary film, appropriately called *Enthusiasm: "The Symphony of Donbas"* (1930),[18] which was a huge success in view of its avant-garde techniques—but not inside Russia and in front of working-class audiences, where its pathos would not have gone down well. It dealt with the efforts of miners in the Don region to overfulfill the first Five-Year Plan. It was a breathless cinematic tour de force, and it had nothing to do with real life and work. And it was typical of a whole genre of newspaper reports, books, and films of the time.

In the cultural field, this process can be traced back with considerable accuracy. In the 1920s interesting books and movies appeared, and the painters and composers also had some artistic freedom. But subsequently, absolute regimentation took over, and even books like Mikhail Sholokhov's *Quiet Flows the Don*, Yuri Olesha's *Envy*, and Leonid Leonov's *The Thief* could no longer have been written in the 1930s. There was no room for passion, under "socialist realism." As Olesha had predicted in *Envy* (1927), this wonderful new breed of man would no longer be capable of love and compassion.

But human beings do not live by culture alone. There was always the classical cultural heritage to fall back on, and the Soviet people survived the years that followed even without great new symphonies, novels, and pictures. The fact that the regime was not overthrown during the early years of World War II was owing to Stalin's appeal to Russian patriotism (Communist slogans were more or less shelved for the duration). The barbaric behavior of the Nazis made it appear soon enough that they had not come as liberators but as enslavers and exterminators. If Hitler had played the liberate-Russia-from-Communism-and-let's-be-friends card, the outcome of the war could have been different, but then Hitler would not have been Hitler.[19] Furthermore, the army command was faithful to Stalin, and there was always the NKVD (later the KGB) to heighten their enthusiasm whenever needed.

Once the war ended, the enormous task of rebuilding the economy absorbed all energies, and successive governments persuaded their people that harsh measures were needed to carry out this giant task. Furthermore, the imperialist wolves were ready to jump at any time, waiting for a moment of weakness and flagging attention to invade and rob the country: hence the need for a continued state-of-siege mentality, despite all the victories and territorial expansion. The new achievements had to be guarded, and to this end, an extra effort was needed.

It is exceedingly difficult to generalize with total confidence about the attitude of Soviet people toward their own government during the war and after.[20] Many collaborated in the areas occupied by the Nazis. Many more would have collaborated had the Germans made any serious effort to find allies among the local population, as they did in other countries. True, there was also resistance against the invaders. Some young members of the Komsomol went underground. Former party secretaries and NKVD officials took to the woods—they had nothing to expect from the Germans but the firing squad. In later years, a few instances of resistance, such as the case of Zoya Kosmodemyanskaya, the young resistance heroine, became myths, embellished and magnified every year. But in truth, there was little partisan activity during the first eighteen months of the war, when the Red Army would have needed it most; it became a factor of some military and political importance only after the winter of 1942–1943, when the tide of war had turned.

It is difficult to determine the attitude of the Russian people, partly because Soviet society was divided, like most others, into a majority wholly preoccupied with the challenges of daily life, lacking the initiative and energy to concern itself with issues beyond this, and a minority at least potentially active in public life. The Russian people had always been very obedient, willing to put up with more hardships than other peoples, provided the bare minimum needed for their existence was safeguarded. This characteristic operated in favor of every ruler, tsar or commissar. True, there was also an anarchist tradition, the *bunt* led by Pugachev and Stenka Razin, whose acts of rebellion often seemed senseless and purely destructive. But these had occurred only infrequently, and it was believed that anarchism had been beaten, first by the tsars, later by the Bolsheviks. Paradoxically, the inclination toward anarchism was occasionally adduced as an argument against democratization, even by those who fought against despotism: How could one give full freedom to the masses, who would only abuse it, engaging in another senseless orgy of destruction? Democracy, many thought, was not for Russia, at least not for a long time to come. Until that time, the most one could hope for was the "inner freedom" that had been evoked for generations by writers from Pushkin to Dostoevsky and Blok.

One hesitates to generalize even on the attitudes of the minority, a forever changing mixture of sentiments of which people were seldom fully aware. Given the strict controls, feelings had to be hidden not just from one's family, friends, and neighbors, but sometimes even from the self.

There were a few uncompromising enemies of Communism; no one knew them because outwardly they, too, had to conform. A greater number unquestioningly accepted the party line, however absurd. The great majority, party members and otherwise, were with some reservations in favor of the system—some more so, others less—until the time when the general mood of the country turned to skepticism and even pessimism.[21]

A kind of internal dialogue was going on inside individuals and society as a whole: "The situation is bad," said one inner voice. "We face many deprivations; there is much injustice."

"Yes," said the other inner voice, "but it is getting a little better every year. We need patience. Think of the ravages of the war."

"What happened to the old ideals, to the hope that after the war Russia would be a freer and happier country?"

"Perhaps our hopes were too high," said the other voice, "but look at the situation in other countries–unemployment and misery in the West. At least we do not have these extremes of obscene wealth side by side with abject poverty. Why give up hope? Is there not a self-correcting mechanism? The last years of Stalinst repression were followed by a thaw. After the thaw, there was another wave of repression, but less harsh. One day, there will be a second thaw. As the Russian proverb says, 'There will be a holiday also in our street.' "

"We have been waiting too long," the critical voice would say. "Our masters are stupid and lack new ideas. There is no progress. We are falling behind the rest of the world. Life is full of unnecessary irritations–personal life, work, public life. Can we live like this forever? Conditions deteriorate, and so do individual people–it is the fault of the system."

"There is no alternative," the other voice would say. "Socialism is here to stay for better or worse. We shall improve it, in certain respects, but there will be no radical change. It is the best, the only system for our country. This is your home. Anywhere else you will be a stranger. Adjust yourself as well as you can in the house that has been built and that will stand for many generations to come."

Most Soviet people were torn between these two kinds of sentiments. There was a substantial stratum of people, the new class, from the upper reaches of the *nomenklatura*, with its many privileges, to a body of petty *nachalniks*, or bosses, who had a vested interest in the survival of the system. Some benefited more, others less. There was a great deal of envy, competition, and in-fighting among the lower echelons, but their overall attitude was favorable to the regime, because they could not be certain they would keep their place in society in case of change. It is also true that inside this group there was growing criticism; Gorbachev's reforms came from within the *nomenklatura*.

Life was infinitely harder for those who had to stand in line for everything and did not belong to the *nomenklatura*, but somehow the system worked. There was no happiness and little satisfaction. Instead of enthusiasm, there was massive, constant indoctrination. True, no one believed everything broadcast by official propaganda, but few dismissed it altogether. Something always stuck, as the old Latin proverb says. Society was to a considerable degree atomized, so there was always room for illusions: perhaps life was somewhat better in other parts of the Soviet Union.

Until the 1970s, only a handful of people had been abroad, and afterward only a trickle. The fact that other countries were making more rapid progress than the Soviet Union was only slowly sinking in. There was always the "Moscow kitchen" as an outlet–the intimate conversations in a small circle, tolerated by the KGB as long as no attempt was made to communicate these discussions to others.

For a long time after the war, many Soviet people subscribed to mutually exclusive sets of belief, torn between hope and despair. And in the meantime they worked, made love, read books, ate and got drunk, and sought happiness on weekends at their dachas or watching football games. Not much more was expected from them. The mobilization of the masses in the early days of the regime had turned into their demobilization. The virtues of an ideal member of this deeply conservative society were quietness, obedience, patriotism, and trust in authority.

There never was a Thermidor in Russia, as Trotsky and other enthusiasts of the 1920s, thinking in historical stereotypes, had feared. There had been no coup by counterrevolutionaries. The revolution had gradually transformed itself into a rigid, unchanging system that worked continually to expand its influence. The only revolutions that were still acceptable were those imposed from above—which was, of course, how the Bolsheviks had come to power originally. The young enthusiasts of the 1920s had been utopians. The strong utopian sentiment was shared by Stalin, even to a certain extent by Khrushchev, but it was an inspiration very different from the spirit that had motivated the young enthusiasts of the 1920s. After Khrushchev, it disappeared altogether.

The system still had a fairly broad base of support, but the mentality of the ruling stratum was strictly orientated toward the preservation of the status quo. Their catchwords—like "order," "work," and "patriotism"—were those of Marshall Pétain and General Franco, not those of the early revolutionaries. The last thing the system wanted was revolutionary enthusiasm, spontaneity, and utopian longings. These were kept for the rituals at the high holidays of the Communist year, and they were less and less in evidence even on these occasions.

II

When the dust had settled after the breakdown of the Soviet system, a growing number of people in Russia were asking why so many foreigners either had been deceived by the Communist regime or had deceived themselves: "We could not have known to what extent our system was based on corruption and deception, how mendacious its claims were, how unreal its achievements. But those abroad must have known and probably did know. If so, why did they keep silent, or worse, why did they praise a regime that was both inhuman and inefficient?"

The question, asked time and time again, came from both the extreme right and the liberals. The extreme right in the persons of academician Igor Shafarevich and critic Vadim Kozhinov discovered a dangerous plot. Their argument ran, very briefly, as follows: there had been a deliberate conspiracy of silence. Leading Western intellectuals such as Lion

Feuchtwanger, Henri Barbusse, Shaw, Sidney and Beatrice Webb, Romain Rolland, Theodore Dreiser, Thomas Mann, and Einstein had actually approved of Stalin and Stalinism, even though, unlike the Russian intelligentsia, they had not been forced to support the regime. In fact, they had continued to support the Soviet regime up to the last months of Stalin's life, when the doctors' trial was prepared. They had turned against the Soviet Union only when most of the inmates of the gulag were released— when conditions in Russia improved.

All this showed to the satisfaction of the spokesmen of the far right that these "liberal" Western intellectuals approved of Communism. When Russia became more nationalistic and militarily too powerful, they had turned against it. In other words, they became enemies of Russia, not of Leninism and Stalinism. And they had acted in unison, according to a preconceived master plan.

Similar questions, shorn of the paranoid element, were asked by Russian democrats. One literary critic described in detail how as a child during the war, while evacuated to Novosibirsk, he had watched *Mission to Moscow*[22] and similar movies in the local Mayakovsky cinema. In later years, he studied the works of Western writers and thinkers from Herbert Marcuse to Graham Greene. He apparently made a special study of the politics of American and British thriller writers—he mentioned in considerable detail John Le Carré, Len Deighton, Robert Ludlam, Martin Cruz Smith, and Frederic Forsyth.[23] Why had Western writers legitimized Stalin and later Mao, Kim Il Sung, and still later Andropov? Why had they taken at face value the empty human rights declarations of the tyrannies? Why had they discovered openness and a human face, even Western standards of freedom and democracy, where there were none?[24]

For Western writers free of such delusions, it is not easy to answer these questions, even with the benefit of hindsight. One could dismiss the thriller writers as of no consequence, for no serious person in the West would look for political and moral inspiration in *Gorky Park* or *The Spy Who Came in from the Cold*.[25] Or it could be argued that there were others in this genre who made a comfortable living out of depicting Communist villains; Ian Fleming was an obvious case, but he took politics far less seriously. And it is also true that the thriller writers expressed something of the zeitgeist as it was perceived in influential circles in the West in the 1970s.

The wider issue is, of course, not the politics of the thriller writers. The Soviet system had admirers abroad from an early date; so had Italian fascism in the 1920s, less so Nazism in Germany. Communism was perceived in the early days as a radically socialist (hence humanist), anti-imperialist—even pacifist—movement aspiring to build a new world out of the ruins and inequities of the old. Support in the early days came almost exclusively from the left, from socialists and radical liberals. But as Soviet power became more repressive, as it banned all left-wing groups in the Soviet Union and exiled, imprisoned, or executed their leaders, Western Social Democrats, some of whom had been instinctively anti-Communist from the beginning, finally turned their backs on the Soviet Union. It has seldom been noted that after the mid-1920s as the "heroic age" of the revolution ended, very few socialists were supporters of the Soviet Union.

Many of those who went to Moscow and returned idolizing Stalin and his system were politically naïve people who gravitated toward the maintenance of order and other traditional values. The Webbs and Thomas Mann are obvious examples; they could not have supported Russia in the age of Lenin and Trotsky, whereas under Stalin it became considerably easier for them. The great majority of "fellow travelers" were not "intellectual friends of Communism,"[26] as some latter-day Western historians tend to believe, but friends of the Soviet Union. This may appear a contradiction in terms, for how could anyone support the Soviet Union without at the same time subscribing to the all-pervasive ideology underlying it? But they could and they did; a division was made between Communist ideology and Soviet achievements. Doctrine was thought to be of relatively little importance. Some thought that Communism was a reincarnation of progressive Christianity. One example is the "Red Dean" of Canterbury. Others believed that Stalinism represented a specific Russian road to democracy. Whatever the explanation, it would be difficult to find prominent Western sympathizers who, as the result of visits to Moscow, engaged in a serious study of dialectical materialism, let alone understood and accepted all its tenets. Even Rolland and Feuchtwanger did not read Lenin and Stalin except perhaps for a few of their speeches. A few of the French and American fellow travelers regarded the Russian Revolution as an extension of the French and American Revolution. These were the exceptions. In retrospect, such belittling of the ideological inspiration of the Soviet system seems almost inconceivable. But men and women do live with contradictions, and this was one such case.

What attracted Western fellow travelers to the Soviet Union? Above all, the apparent decline of the West, as manifested in the Great Depression, and the seeming inability of Western governments to cope with it. Later it was the threat of fascism, and still later the alliance with the Soviet Union in World War II. The growing interest in the Soviet planned economy as a reaction against the failure of irrational and chaotic capitalism has been described in the memoirs of many contemporaries. In Russia, living standards were low, but at least the minimal demands of the people (all people!) were fulfilled. No one was unemployed, and the situation was said to improve every year.

The impact of Hitler was even greater. Between Hitler and Stalin, the choice was a foregone conclusion. This was the age of the popular front and the civil war in Spain, which made collaboration with Moscow much easier. Stalin was not merely an ally in the struggle against Hitler, but the best hope of the camp of freedom. While British Prime Minister Chamberlain and successive French governments were trying to appease the fascist dictators, only Stalin could be relied upon, because he took a principled antifascist stand.[27]

Stalin did not make it easy for his admirers. In Spain the Communists used the civil war to eliminate their opponents in the democratic camp, which quite often meant their murder. More important, the Moscow trials, the "cult of personality," the harsher rule inside the Soviet Union, and the growing resemblance of the Soviet regime to fascist regimes could not be ignored by fellow travelers.

The charges against the accused in the Moscow trials strained the imaginations of even the most gullible foreign visitors, but perhaps there had been other, even deeper plots that could not be mentioned in public? Perhaps some innocents had perished in the process? But what was the alternative for Western progressives? To express doubts, to stab Stalin in the back and thus "objectively" help Hitler?

Later-day Soviet and Western students of the phenomenon of fellow traveling have had difficulty finding rational explanations. How could sophisticated Western visitors have misjudged the real situation in the Soviet Union so profoundly? Were they not bound to know the truth?

Such assumptions fail to take into account the full historical context. Stalin seemed to many a staunch antifascist at least up to 1939, and even the treaty with Hitler was justified by some as a purely tactical maneuver (if not a stroke of genius), made inevitable by the British sellout at Munich.

Present-day Soviet writers usually tend to overrate the extent of knowledge and judgment of these friendly visitors. Hardly any of them knew Russia or spoke Russian. They were in no position to judge whether what they were told by their translators in the course of a conducted tour (or by Stalin or Gorky in person) was the truth or a monstrous lie. They came for a week, or two or three at the most, and it was easy to believe what they were told. It was far more difficult for the refugee Communists from central Europe then residing in Moscow to keep their faith – they knew the realities of Soviet life, the mass arrests and the executions. And yet most of them kept faith.

The Webbs, Shaw and Wells, Rolland, Feuchtwanger, and Heinrich Mann were gifted people, reasonably well informed about conditions in their own surroundings. Had they talked or written nonsense on this subject, someone would immediately have put them right. About the world outside their country, they knew little; about the Soviet Union, next to nothing. They were educated people. Shaw knew about Wagner, and Rolland about Beethoven and Empedokles, but it is doubtful whether even one of them had ever read a history of Russia. Their political judgment was at best mediocre, and quite often they lacked elementary common sense. Some of them were plainly gullible. An example is Joseph Davies of *Mission to Moscow* fame, who later declared that there was no fifth column in Russia because Stalin had shot them. In fact, Stalin had not shot potential traitors but supporters, and there was more collaboration with Germans in Russia than in most other occupied countries during the war. The idea that Westerners "must have known" the truth persists in Russia to this day, as does an exaggerated view of their political wisdom and influence.[28]

Unfortunately, the word of many of the well-known Soviet sympathizers carried considerable weight because it was assumed that people
outstanding in one field of achievement would also be gurus in other
disciplines. Their political influence should not be overrated, however. It
is doubtful that many people in authority in the West were influenced by
the writings and speeches of prominent fellow travelers. Perhaps the
media were influenced to some extent—but the media did not carry much
weight at the time.

III

The question of how much was generally known outside the Soviet Union
remains to be explored in detail. It was, of course, impossible to seal off
hermetically such an enormous country, although Stalin and his successors attempted to do so. For more than twenty years after 1935, it was
virtually impossible for foreign tourists to visit Russia, and for another
twenty-five years only a few did come. In addition, large parts of the
country remained out of bounds for foreigners. Diplomats and a few
foreign correspondents were stationed in Moscow, but they could not travel
freely. They had to apply for permission for any trip even a few miles
outside Moscow, and usually their requests were turned down. In contrast,
citizens of Nazi Germany and Fascist Italy could travel freely abroad up to
the outbreak of the war, and hundreds of thousands of foreign tourists
visited these two countries. In fact, even during the war, thousands of
Germans visited Switzerland and Sweden on business and even as tourists.
This is not to say that the fascist regimes were less repressive. It simply
tends to show that their self-confidence was greater.

How did the handful of foreigners in Moscow obtain their information
about events in the Soviet Union? They were subject to the strictest
control; their phones were tapped; they lived in houses allocated to foreigners only, and were cut off from the rest of the population in every
possible way. Police followed them wherever they went. The better their
Russian and the greater their knowledge of Soviet conditions, the more
closely they were watched and the more likely they were to be expelled.
Some had Russian wives and were hostages to the regime. It was impossible
to maintain close relations with Soviet citizens. It was impossible for
foreign residents to subscribe to local newspapers published outside Moscow.[29] Foreign observers were reduced to getting information from Soviet
radio (and later television), the central newspapers, official announcements, and occasional guided tours of such places as the Lenin Library
and perhaps the occasional showcase *kolkhoz* (collective farm). They could
go for strolls in the cultural parks, visit the museums and cemeteries, and
watch movies and attend concerts, but in the main they were talking to one
another. Later on, beginning in the late 1960s, a few courageous Russian

dissenters would occasionally meet a foreign correspondent; sooner or later, they were arrested.

There still would be some chance meetings with strangers in public places, and visitors would learn about social conditions from watching people in the street, in restaurants, or in lines in front of the shops. Even this could be misleading, for in many respects Moscow was not typical, but the show window of "really existing socialism." Furthermore, their observations could teach them nothing about the workings of Soviet politics.

Even the best informed foreigners did not know for many years after the war how many Soviet citizens had been arrested or executed, or how well (or how badly) the Soviet economy performed. Even thirty years after the event, no one in the West knew what had become of Karl Radek, or of Isaac Babel or Osip Mandelstam, who had disappeared in the late 1930s. Once the satellites were orbiting the globe, American military intelligence could start counting nuclear and other military installations. But there was no certainty even in this respect, and, in any case, what was truly important—such as decision making in the Politburo—could usually not be quantified.

No mention has been made of those who left the Soviet Union temporarily or forever: the many prisoners of war, the Russian workers in Germany who later defected, the Poles who were permitted to leave in 1942 and 1943, and the thousands (among them many Jews) who escaped during the general disorder immediately after the end of the war. By 1946 the curtain came down again and remained firmly shut for a long time thereafter. A few hundred—sometimes a few thousand—were permitted annually to leave the country in later years within the framework of family-reunion schemes. They went to Israel, Germany, and other countries. But great care was taken to prevent the departure of anyone with the knowledge of anything of importance, be it the Soviet economy, Soviet science, or Soviet defense, defined in the broadest possible way. If those who left had been submitted to thorough and systematic debriefing, an interesting picture of the state of Soviet society would have emerged. But there were neither the resources nor the desire in the West to find out, and those who had stories of interest to tell complained in later years that no one had ever wanted to listen to them. Those who had left Russia were considered unreliable sources by many Western experts. They obviously did not like the Soviet system; otherwise, they would not have left the country. The judgment and even the observations of such disaffected people could not be trusted. Thus the West lost the opportunity to avail itself of one of the few important sources at its disposal.

The same was true, a fortiori, with regard to defectors and Western "renegades." There had been renegades from the Communist movement all along. Ultimately, there were many more of them in the West, especially among the intelligentsia, than actual party members. They had believed in Communism and loved it. They had served the movement, often for many years, until they reluctantly reached the conclusion that they had been mistaken from the very beginning or the great cause had betrayed them. It was always a most painful experience. For years it had been their duty as party members to denounce traitors. Now all of a sudden, they became traitors in the eyes of yesterday's friends and comrades.

Among these men and women there were experts on Communism and things Russian. They had been in leading positions in the party. They had visited Russia, and even if they did not know Russian, they had an instinctive understanding of how Communists would behave, which others – unless they had devoted years to the study of Soviet affairs – would not have and would never acquire.

The evidence of the renegades was not, of course, altogether ignored. Some of their books were widely read, but there were reservations about them. Anti-Communism was never as fashionable as antifascism, partly, no doubt, because among the anti-Communists there were people such as Hitler and Senator Joseph McCarthy. Even a renegade of the 1960s, Guenther Zwerenz, argued that his generation could not rely on what Ignazio Silone and Arthur Koestler, of the previous generation of "renegades," had said.[30] The former Communists certainly made no impact on the fellow travelers; on the contrary, they only made them angry.

Many non-Communists complained in the postwar period about the excessive shrillness of the anti-Communists and their obsessive preoccupation with the subject of Communism. Thomas Mann wrote that there was something "superstitious and childish in the fear of the bourgeois world of Communism." He found something distasteful in the renegades, whereas the fact that his brother Heinrich had called Stalin the incarnation of an intellectual did not bother him. For the fellow travelers, the former Communists were traitors and fifth columnists,[31] objectively, if not intentionally, serving Hitler and Nazism.

Many ex-Communists did not want to be identified as anti-Communists. Richard Crossman, who edited *The God That Failed* (1949), perhaps the best-known book on defection, wrote in his introduction that there had been no intention whatsoever to add to the "tide of anti-Communist propaganda." But as Koestler conceded in 1984, this had been precisely the intention; only a Member of Parliament or the Labour party could not openly say so.

The negative attitude was even more pronounced with regard to Soviet defectors. The case of Viktor Kravchenko was probably the most famous because of the trial in Paris in 1947 and the whole literature it produced. He was considered not only by Communists but by all fellow travelers to be a base creature, a despicable traitor who had been bought by the Americans and was spreading calumnies and lies against his own country.

Defectors in the years that followed included intelligence agents as well as some artists, for they were among the few classes of Soviet citizens who were permitted to travel. What the Soviet spies could tell the West was no doubt of considerable interest, as far as the structure and activities of the KGB were concerned. But about the Soviet Union as such, even about the personalities of the leaders–their views and the relations among them–they knew little or nothing. It was a highly compartmentalized society in which each member knew little more than he or she needed to know.

None of this excuses Western ignorance over a period of decades, specially among those who had expertise of one kind or another in Soviet affairs and should have known better. But that is not to say it was easy to know what went on inside the Soviet Union. There was a veil of secrecy not just around the defense sector, but around all important issues, political, economic, social–even relations among the nationalities. There were very few people inside the Soviet Union who had a reasonable knowledge of the state of affairs except in their own immediate surroundings. The heads of the secret police should have known, but if the East German example can serve as a guide, the men in the field were frequently reluctant to stick their necks out by conveying an unvarnished picture to their superiors. The higher echelons did not want to jeopardize their careers by transmitting alarmist information. It was the same in the economy and most other fields. Everyone in the Brezhnev era knew that the system was corrupt, but few knew the full extent of corruption.

Even in these circumstances, a far truer picture should have prevailed in the media and among experts in the West. We shall deal with the poor performance, by and large, of Sovietology and "Germanology" in the last two decades of the existence of the regime. While a considerable body of knowledge was available, it was rejected because it did not suit preconceived beliefs. In certain respects, this syndrome resembled the rejection during World War II of the knowledge of mass murder committed by the Nazis in Eastern Europe. The facts were widely known, but for a variety of reasons their full implications were not accepted.

Ignorance of things Russian was by no means always the main reason. Among the foreign nationals who left the Soviet Union in the 1930s and 1940s and who had first-hand knowledge of the system, many were very critical of the regime. But some still supported Communism despite bitter personal experience–a few even became leading Sovietologists. This phenomenon, too, remains to be investigated.

The Russian emigration to France had been predominantly anti-Soviet before World War II, and émigrés always closely followed events in the Soviet Union. But in 1944 and 1945, they fell over one another in paying their respects to Stalin and his representatives. Thousands applied for Soviet citizenship. Berdyayev said it was the moral duty of a Russian émigré to do so (even though he himself did not). Others were wining and dining the Soviet ambassador, expressing all along their undying devotion to the Soviet system, which they had denounced in the harshest terms before 1944. Among these prodigal sons, those of the right and leading churchmen who had only yesterday denounced godless Communism were prominent. It took them years to regain their equilibrium, and some never did. Many of them had never been democrats in the first place, and for this reason it was perhaps not too difficult to embrace Stalin. What was the difference between the situation in 1940 and that four years later? The Soviet Union had defeated Germany in the war.

It was, of course, Russian patriotism that blinded émigrés with regard to the true character of the regime. With regard to others, the motivation was quite different. If many French intellectuals became pro-Communist in the postwar period, it had to do partly with their bad conscience. Like Jean-Paul Sartre, whose plays were performed under German occupation, and Paul Eluard, they had not been active resisters, they detested America, and they were quite ignorant of events inside Russia, which they mistakenly regarded as the vanguard of progress and freedom. They kept silent even during the harshest years of Stalinist terror (1949–1953) because "we must not disillusion the workers." Anti-Communism, as Mounier (and even Camus) argued at the time, was the beginning of a fascist dictatorship; there was no real choice between Hitler and Harry Truman. Thus it came to pass that Koestler's *Darkness at Noon* was a huge success in France (selling more than 500,000 copies) but had little impact on the intelligentsia. Solzhenitsyn's *Gulag Archipelago*, published thirty years later after the Communist tide had abated, had a tremendous influence, even though it was a mere enumeration of facts–most of which had been known before. In the 1970s, there was a willingness to accept facts; in the late 1940s, there was not.

For similar reasons, there was great enthusiasm in Italy for things Soviet. The record of leading Italian writers and filmmakers under Mussolini had not been a shining example of courage. In Italy, however, the disappointment with Soviet Communism set in earlier; if Palmiero Togliatti criticized the Stalin period, the fellow travelers could not lag behind. In America, Britain, and Germany, there was initially much less pro-Soviet enthusiasm than in France and Italy, but at the time of the student revolt and the Vietnam War, a marked upsurge of Marxist and neo-Marxist thought occurred, the effects of which can be felt in some circles to this day.

However, on the whole, it became more and more difficult to justify Stalinism in the postwar period. Once the fascist danger was no longer present, America was painted with the fascist brush, but this was never quite convincing–there was no dictatorship in America, no censorship, no concentration camps. As a result, defections from the Communist camp took place far more often (and much more rapidly), especially in France, than in the prewar period: to be a renegade was no longer a disgrace; there were too many of them.

The circumstances that tended to becloud the judgment of not a few Soviet experts in the West will be discussed later. Partly it was a generational problem; as the Cold War generation (including a fair number of former Communists) passed from the scene, it was replaced by younger people whose outlook on the world had been shaped by Vietnam and the general ferment of the late 1960s. There were other reasons, such as academic fashions among historians, sociologists, and political scientists.

Some revolutions run out of steam earlier, some later. The phenomenon has been known to students of history for a long time: What happens when the original impetus fades and the charisma becomes routinized, when prophecy fails and utopian hopes disappear? This stage was reached in the Soviet Union in the mid-1930s, but the appeal to patriotism and the defense of the fatherland against the outside enemy replaced Communist romanticism, at least to some extent.

After the war, the urgent need for rebuilding the country served for a number of years as the ideological cement. In the meantime, a new class had emerged with a vested interest in the survival of the regime. There was also an ideology of sorts—national socialism—which served to legitimize the system. It was not exactly a novel mixture, but it could still have worked for a longer time if it had adapted itself to changing conditions.

However, the problem confronting the Soviet Union was not only the vanishing idealism of the early Soviet period, but a sclerotic process that prevented innovation. Nationalism was in principle a powerful stimulus, but since there was no Soviet nation, it did not make much sense in a multinational empire. On the contrary, it added to the latent conflict between the nations. The internationalist and revolutionary impulses had petered out long ago, and references to a "classless society" were irrelevant in view of the fact that the presence of classes in the Soviet Union was only too manifest. True, there still was social mobility, but this also existed in nonsocialist societies.

A leading historian wrote in 1993 that there were no basic differences of opinion in the 1970s concerning the state of Soviet society between the Soviet dissidents and the party leaders and KGB officials.[32] The only difference was that the dissidents wanted change, whereas the party leadership preferred to perpetuate the prevailing state of affairs.

If one had been able to present a new non-Marxist social and political system under which the *nomenklatura* could have kept its status and privileges in society, this elite would, in all probability, have accepted it. In the absence of such a perspective, the majority of the leadership opted against innovation until the difficulties facing Soviet society and its economy had aggravated to such an extent that some leaders voted for a reform course. Being optimists, they thought that the regime could be reformed.[33]

2
1917: The Russia We Lost?

The Russia We Lost, a television documentary watched by many millions of Russians in 1991 and later shown in the cinemas, created a considerable stir. It was written and produced by Stanislav Govorukhin, one of the masters of this genre, well known for the film *This Way We Cannot Live*, which was screened a year earlier, a moving and depressing account of the many social ills afflicting his country. Govorukhin's new film depicted prerevolutionary Russia, a country making good progress, allegedly producing more wheat than Canada, the United States, and Argentina combined.

The film opens with scenes showing men and women skiing in the suburbs of St. Petersburg, well-nourished peasants working in the fields, and giant factories. A ninety-year-old woman relates how well people lived before the revolution. We are shown the pictures of several dozen substantial individuals and couples, all looking well dressed and happy. These pictures could be of people in any other European country or in America. The scene then shifts to a section of the great Trans-Siberian railway built from 1902 to 1904, one of the technical miracles of the age, and it is revealed that an even more ambitious project was planned by a Russian engineer, connecting Paris with New York by way of Siberia and Alaska. Finally, we see the famous Eliseev food shops in Moscow and St. Petersburg (which still exist, albeit under a different name). Magnificient showpieces of turn-of-the-century architecture, they offered delicacies from all over the world and compared very favorably with Soviet shops of a much later period. A paradise for the rich? By no means: bread was 2 kopeks a pound; sugar, 17; meat, 45. A workman earned 30 rubles a month or more if he did overtime; a physician, 200. In brief, paradise lost, not just for the well-to-do but for every Russian. Why didn't we know about it? Because for seventy years the history of Russia had been written by its killers.

In 1913, the production of coal had grown sixfold over the previous twenty-five years. Seventy percent of the population was said to be literate,[1] and it was thought that by 1925 illiteracy would be stamped out altogether. According to demographic projections, some 348 million citizens would live within the borders of the empire by the late 1940s. Russian social legislation (for instance, with regard to the length of the working day) was more advanced than laws in Western Europe.

True, there were also revolutionaries and terrorists in old Russia and there was repression, but not as much as often thought. Had Stolypin been wrong in retrospect? His philosophy was to give more freedom to the people; however, first a generation of citizens had to be formed, worthy of liberty. And was it not also true that the only answer to the bomb was merciless repression? The country was ruled by the tsar, a man of many good qualities and an exemplary pater familias. In normal times, he would have been a very good senior officer, a colonel perhaps or even a general. In the final analysis, his regime was not overthrown but collapsed because of lack of support.

There is a striking similarity between the sentiments expressed in Govorukhin's film and the recollections of Edmund Burke, almost exactly 200 years earlier, recalling the scene in Versailles when he had first watched Marie Antoinette:

> A more delightful vision had never lighted this orb. I saw her just above the horizon decorating and cheering the elevated sphere she began to move in, glittering like the morning star, full of life and splendor and joy. . . . Little did I dream that I should have seen disasters fall upon her in a nation of gallant men, in a nation of men of honor and of cavaliers. I thought ten thousand swords must have leaped from their scabbards to avenge even a look that threatened her with insult. But the age of chivalry is gone[2]

All in all, Russia in 1913 seemed to be a country of much promise; a French economist even predicted that if economic and social development continued at the same rate, Russia would soon be the leading country in Europe.[3]

Govorukhin's thesis was welcomed with enthusiasm by some and rejected by others. The thesis was not, of course, new; it had been propagated all along by many émigrés, the vanquished of the revolution. It had been propagated in Solzhenitsyn's *Red Wheel* and in a less obtrusive way by several other Soviet writers, especially those extolling life in the Russian village before the revolution. The Russia they conjured up was that of mother and father having tea in their spacious *izba* (peasant hut) with their children playing in sunshine under birch trees, near a lake. This was the Russia of picturesque churches, religious processions, balalaikas, village weddings and dances, a troika hurrying through a majestic forest, and skaters enjoying themselves on a frozen river. In these nostalgic dreams was little room for the reality of village life, with its squalor, poverty, and ignorance.

Govorukhin's figures for literacy in tsarist Russia are almost certainly exaggerated. Half of the urban workers were still illiterate in 1897, and the percentage in villages was higher. Russia had gone through a process of industrialization between 1880 and 1904. The railway network had doubled between 1890 and 1904, and the output of iron and steel had increased tenfold within a mere ten years (1880 and 1900); but labor productivity and per capita income were still very low—about a third of Western Europe's. By 1914, Russia was the fifth largest industrial power in the world, having been the seventh in 1860. Russia had overtaken France as a steel producer, and Russia's oil production overtook that of the United States.[4]

Most of the facts and much of the interpretation of Govorukhin and other spokesmen of the right are derived from a book to which no attention was paid when it first appeared in Munich on the eve of World War II.[5] Its author was S. S. Oldenburg, the son of the famous orientalist, who had also been minister of education in the provisional government of 1917. (The father stayed in the Soviet Union; the son emigrated.) In many ways an excellent book based on much original research, it makes the best possible case for Nikolai II and the monarchy in general. Oldenburg reports enormous progress between 1905 and the outbreak of World War I and not only in agriculture and industry. The national income grew faster than the state budget, public education made great strides, and the number of cooperatives grew sixfold in five years (1907 to 1912). In brief, a new Russia was emerging. A liberal (Prince Trubetskoy) noted that the rise of the standard of living was accompanied by the astonishing growth of a new social order, and a socialist (Bunakov) observed a profound social transformation in the Russian countryside.

The story told by Oldenburg[6] was seldom articulated after the revolution of 1917, certainly not as intelligently or in such detail, and the fact that it was rediscovered and given wide publicity (albeit not always with full attribution) should be welcomed. But it was still not a full account of Russia under the last tsar. In virtually every instance, the achievements made ought to be viewed in a wider context.

Russian industrial production rose between 5 and 6 percent between 1885 and 1914, having started from a very low level. Economic development was particularly strong between 1885 and 1900, and again between 1909 and 1912. But Russian growth rates were by no means exceptional, as Govorukhin and his supporters seem to believe, and these achievements were owing to the vision and energy of a handful of officials, above all Sergei Witte, finance minister and prime minister from 1892 to 1906. The court and the aristocracy were far from enthusiastic about industrialization in view of their fears about political and economic consequences. But since industrialization was equated with a strong, powerful Russia, they had to accept it, just as the aristocracy had to swallow it elsewhere in Europe.

The nobility, many liberals, and all radicals opposed the agrarian reform of Prime Minister Pyotr Stolypin, who aimed at breaking up the old village community, with its egalitarianism and failure of initiative.

Although Russia produced 74 million tons of grain in 1913 to 1914 (out of which one-quarter was exported), the position of the peasant was lamentable – and had deteriorated over many years. As Russia's population grew, the amount of arable land at the disposal of individual peasants shrank. The earnings of an agricultural laborer were miserable, and productivity in farming was low by any standard, especially in the communes, or *mir*, in which the land was owned by the community and cultivated by individual families. These grievances led to widespread unrest, which erupted in the revolution of 1905 to 1906, much to the surprise of the ruling class, which had believed in the limitless patience of the peasantry.

The Stolypin reforms did amount to a fairly radical redistribution of property, even though lands belonging to the nobility were touched only to a limited extent. (There was not much to be redistributed in the first place; the peasants and their advocates had exaggerated notions of the amount of land involved.) However, by the time World War I broke out, some 20 percent of the peasants had left the communes; the rest had stayed, because they either lacked the initiative or preferred the old egalitarianism.

If Stolypin had not been assassinated in 1911, if war had not broken out in 1914, would an independent, free peasantry have come into being, and would economic prosperity and political stability have ensued? These questions have been endlessly discussed. Some historians have argued that the tsarist regime always tended to reject and dismiss far-sighted servants such as Witte and Stolypin; they stood for change and development and were therefore distrusted. This is correct, but it is also true that once Witte and Stolypin did have their way, the changes wrought were irreversible. Others have argued that war was not an accident but an inherent part of the calculations of tsarist foreign policy. But this thesis is not in consonance with what is now known about the aims of Russian policy makers; rather than enthusiasm to go to war, there were considerable misgivings. There was a prewar latent crisis, but from an economic point of view it was not necessarily a fatal one. As one expert has put it: "It seems plausible to say that Russia on the eve of the war was well on the way towards a Westernization, or perhaps more precisely, a Germanization of its industrial growth."[7]

Russian economic progress proceeded fitfully. It was the world's main grain producer, but in the great famine of 1891 to 1892, almost half a million peasants died from starvation and disease. There was another famine in the central Volga region in 1898. Since at the time about 70 percent of Russia's population still lived in villages, these were events of momentous significance, giving great momentum to antigovernment criticism. Some peasants did well, perhaps some 15 to 25 percent, but the majority did not. The debts of the peasantry to the state and private landlords grew every year, and the sale of bankrupt peasant holdings did not have the desired economic effect. After 1905, the tsarist government had no coherent policy.

Although it had been axiomatic that the Russian peasant was passive, obedient, and loyal to the tsar, there had been warning signs, such as the disorders that occurred in 1902 in some parts of Russia. But these did not prepare the rulers for the revolution of 1905, when thousands of "incidents" occurred, beginning in the Poltava and Cherngov districts, when manor houses were burned and forests illegally felled, when the demand was voiced for the abolition of private property in land and the confiscation of all land owned by the church and the imperial family.

Thus came the rude awakening from the fond dream of an idyllic relationship between peasant and landlord, between *muzhik* and tsar. The Russian countryside, where hard-working and virtuous plowmen labored merrily in golden fields and green meadows, where a great calm reigned in stark contrast to the tension, noise, and ugly disharmonies of the cities, appeared to be a figment of the imagination. Revolutionaries like Gorky, who had disputed these notions all along, were dismissed because they had also been critical of the moral character of the Russian villagers. But no such comfort could be drawn from the writings of Chekhov, Vladimir Korolenko, and Ivan Bunin, who were not dangerous revolutionaries but simply realistic writers.

According to official Bolshevik historiography, Russia was not just a backward country prior to 1917; it had no significant industry, no transport infrastructure, no culture. Just about everyone was deprived and miserable; progress came only with Lenin and Stalin. This argument does not deserve to be discussed and refuted in great detail. While Russia was still backward in most respects, it had made significant progress since the 1880s. Those who claim that there was no prospect for peaceful evolution in Russia base this view in the main on social and political arguments.[8]

Many contemporary observers noted even before the revolution of 1905 that all classes of Russian society were in a state of ferment and that an explosion—nay, a general revolution—was probable, if not inevitable.[9] Frequently the analogy with a volcano was invoked.

There is no denying that discontent was widespread in all classes. Peasants were getting poorer, and living conditions of workers were considerably worse than those of Western Europe, which were bad at that time. The middle classes had no political rights, landowners had many complaints, and the importance of the nobility was declining. Students were the most militant part of the opposition. Even among the clergy, the army, and the security forces, there were numerous critics of the regime. Public opinion was in great majority against the system.

Russia was ruled by an autocratic regime, as it had been for the preceding 200 years. While such a system may well have been the only possible one in the eighteenth century, there had been basic social changes since. The cultural level of the population had risen immeasurably. "Society" consisted no longer of a few hundred noblemen, but included a broad stratum of highly trained professionals. Even the bureaucracy was much more efficient in 1910 than fifty years earlier. By not making any political concessions, the autocracy had become an anachronism.

The ruler and most of his advisers and ministers were deficient in many respects. Nikolai II was a man of average intelligence, a bad judge of character, and devoid of vision—a weak man who frequently could not make up his mind. He lived in a world that had little contact with the realities of Russian life. He was dominated by a wife as ambitious as she was stupid. She knew even less of Russia than he did, and she surrounded herself with charlatans and impostors. The courtiers—such men as Plehwe, Goremykin, Sheglovitov, Maklakov, Trepov, and Stürmer—told the sovereign what he wanted to hear. Able and forceful statesmen such as Witte and Stolypin were resented and sabotaged. As the empress later said, Stolypin had committed the unforgivable sin of overshadowing the tsar. Even for honest officials of the second rank, such as Kokovtsev and Krivoshein, there was no room in the long term.

The story of the unfortunate tsar and his family has been told a thousand times. His defenders have reported that he was charming and had nice manners, that he was a hard worker and had a great sense of order and duty, that he was unpretentious, gracious, and loved his family.

And it was also true that under his reign Russia had made great strides. The grain harvest had almost doubled; the output of coal, iron, steel, and other commodities had tripled. But, as noted, this had not been achieved through Nikolai's and Alexandra's efforts; at most it could be said that he did not actively hinder his country's economic development. Even the most sympathetic account of the reign of the tsar concedes that as Nikolai II saw it, there were only two camps: "ours", the "good people," and the evil intelligentsia.[10] Isolating himself even more, the tsar had persuaded himself that he could rule the country relying on "the people"—that is to say, the lower strata—going over the heads of the intermediate classes. This populism of the right, also called *narodnost*, had been an unrealistic concept when it was first conceived in the early nineteenth century. One hundred years later it was altogether out of place. A shy man by nature, the tsar avoided public appearances as much as feasible. The more intelligent men among the Russian right had a poor opinion of the tsar. There is no more devastating account of the immense damage he caused to the monarchy than that given after Nikolai's resignation by Menshikov, the most gifted publicist of the extreme right. Almost anyone else, he wrote, could have saved Russia. Grand Duke Alexander Mikhailovich wrote in 1916 that as he saw it, no one in Russia wanted a revolution, but the court in its shortsightedness and stupidity did the utmost to make it happen.

Seventy years later, Nikolai and his family were beatified and consecrated saints by the Russian Church Abroad. For the right, he again became a hero, but only after the true record had been forgotten. Nikolai's fate was tragic, but this does not diminish his great responsibility for the catastrophe of 1917. To say, as some have done, that the personality of the tsar did not make any difference is to misjudge his freedom of maneuver. It is like saying that since Gorbachev was a member of the Politburo, he was bound to pursue the policy of his predecessors in 1985.

A more enlightened ruler could have done much to overcome the deep divisions in Russian society. He could have made political concessions on the road to a constitutional monarchy, or he could, at least, not have opposed this process. Some on the right of the political spectrum have argued that such an endeavor could not possibly have succeeded in view of the intelligentsia's deep hatred of the tsar and the whole system. But this is far from certain, and in any case the tsar was ruling the country, not the intelligentsia; it should have been up to him to take the initiative.

There was a widespread feeling of impending doom, of sickness and explosiveness among the educated in Russia during the years before the outbreak of World War I.[11] But the same dire forebodings could be found in many other countries, notably Germany–images of railways falling from bridges, earthquakes, tidal waves, and other cosmic disasters dominated German expressionism in literature and the arts. But this phenomenon probably had more to do with cultural discontents such as alienation resulting from the growth of an impersonal urban civilization than with any acute political problems.[12] The feeling of suffocating from intolerable restraints extended well beyond the artistic *avant-garde*. This was the generation of 1914, which went to war with great enthusiasm because it seemed to bring a release from stagnation.

A leading German historian, Hans Delbrück, once wrote an amusing essay entitled "The Good Old Days" ("Die gute alte Zeit"), in which he demonstrated that in every generation as far back as could be traced, there was the belief that in the previous one there had been more virtue and happiness. A similar essay could be written tracing back the belief in the coming of the apocalypse. Aleksander Blok and Dimitri Merezhkovsky (who predicted revolution and apocalypse) thought that their culture was on the eve of a catastrophe, exactly as Nietzsche had done fifteen years earlier in his preface to *Wille zur Macht*. The downfall of tsarism and a revolution had been predicted in Russia for a long time and not only by the revolutionaries. When Georg Brandes, the famous Danish man of letters, returned from a visit to Russia in 1887, he reported that nowhere was there such a lively perception of the great weakness of Russia as in Russia itself. He had heard the wish expressed from more than fifty Russians of all classes, entirely unacquainted with one another, that there should be a decisive Russian defeat in a European war:

> We can scarcely imagine a more instructive symptom of the deep despair which exists as to the present condition of the country. No other possibility of liberation from the predominant misery presents itself than that which is offered in the weakness which an unsuccessful war will entail in the ruling system.[13]

But when war did break out in 1914, the overwhelming majority of the population supported the regime, and dreams about defeat disappeared. Going farther back, one finds the conviction that the tsarist empire would collapse not only among the "Russophobes" of the left but also among professional Prussian diplomats such as Curd von Schlözer, who was in St. Petersburg in the 1850s and 1860s, and even among pro-Russian conservatives such as Joseph von Radowitz, who had been there thirty years earlier.[14] Bismarck was almost the only political figure who thought there was a tendency in the West to underestimate Russia's strength and to overrate the depth of its recurrent crises, but he too had doubts from time to time.

Going back even farther, one finds grave misgivings about Russia's future (in view of the absence of a middle class and for other reasons) among German public figures such as Heinrich von Stein and August von Gneisenau, who had taken refuge in the Russian capital in Napoleon's time.

Some of these forebodings could be dismissed as the posturing of a small group of aesthetes. But it is also true that there was on the eve of war a resurgence of political opposition and social ferment. After the Lena goldfield massacre in 1912, in which about 200 workers were killed by the tsarist police, there was a wave of strikes such as Russia had not witnessed since 1905. Workers set down their tools in the summer of 1914 in the Baku oilfields, St. Petersburg, Moscow, and elsewhere. But there had been mass strikes even greater in France during the years before 1914, and in Germany the Social Democrats (then considered a major danger) had emerged as the single largest party. When Poincaré went to St. Petersburg in July 1914, 200,000 workers went on strike. But if Poincaré had gone to Rome the same month, he would have encountered a country in the middle of a revolution, with whole provinces, such Emilia Romagna, in the hands of the insurgents.

If there was much social tension in Russia, the same was true with regard to the rest of Europe. Politicians, not only those of the center but even those on the left were far more optimistic than writers. The Menshevik Rafael Abramovich wrote in later years:

> As the result of the events of 1905 and the social processes then set in motion, Russia on the eve of the war was well advanced on the path of the evolution towards a modern democratic state. Had the war not intervened, she could have advanced much further, peacefully, through the pressures of the growing labor movement, the liberal middle classes and the socially conscious intelligentsia.[15]

The question as to whether there ever existed the possibility of a peaceful transition in Russia from autocracy to a constitutional regime has been endlessly discussed. One historian has observed that several decades would have been needed before the gigantic restructuring of the traditional agricultural order could have succeeded in eliminating mass rural misery and in developing a healthy, private economy in the countryside, and that success was not assured.[16]

How would these reforms have been financed, and was it not also true that industrial growth could not occur without rapid success on the agricultural front? Such assurances of full success existed in no country.

Nations as well as individuals have succeeded against overwhelming odds, and they have failed when all circumstances seemed to favor them. Those who believe that the cause of greater freedom was bound to fail in Russia must accept the notion that everything was programmed from the very beginning—the fall of tsarism, the February and October Revolutions, and eventually also the fall of the Soviet regime.

But such inevitability does not exist in history. If it had depended entirely on Russia's economic development, there is much reason to believe that but for the war considerable progress would have been achieved under almost any regime—not as much as the most sanguine prophets predicted, but still respectable advances by any standard. There is reason to assume that under a non-Communist regime, Russia would have recovered fairly quickly after World War I—every other country did.

It is much more difficult to speculate on the character of the political regime that would have evolved. Could the Romanov dynasty have been saved? An Anglo-Irish journalist with many years of experience in Russia reported his conversations with Sergei Witte: What if Alexander III had been succeeded by Mikhail, rather than the inept Nikolai?[17] Witte believed that even a talented, statesmanlike monarch would not have been able to do more than prolong somewhat the existence of the autocratic system. This regime was doomed, just like all others in history that had outlived whatever usefulness they had once possessed. But to concede that the prospects for a modern, Western style political system in Russia were less than brilliant in 1913 (let alone in 1917) is not tantamount to saying that Lenin and Stalin were the only alternative. At almost every juncture in the early part of the twentieth century—even after March 1917—events in Russia could have taken another turn. What if the tsar (or Lenin) had died? True, the old system would not have surrendered its position without a struggle. True, there would have been long periods of unrest. But the nobility as a class had lost much of its influence, and among the middle class there was much willingness to make concessions. In 1905, Russia had moved from autocracy to pseudo-constitutionalism (*Schein Konstitutionalismus*, in Max Weber's phrase), but this too was progress of sorts. The powers of the Duma could be whittled down, but the tsar could not simply return to the old way of ruling. In an extreme situation, a military dictatorship might have been established. But an old-fashioned dictatorship would not have lasted very long, and the preconditions for fully fledged fascism did not exist in Russia at the time. A dictatorship of the right would have meant a painful reversal, but it would have caused less damage than the Bolsheviks—if only because the ambition of the right was not to create a radically new social order.

In some ways the situation in Russia was similar to that in Germany, a more developed country with a parliamentary regime of sorts and an autocratic ruler. Wilhelm II and the forces behind him would not have surrendered if it were not for the war. A lengthy struggle would have ensued, probably involving violence. But there can be no doubt that in the end the kaiser would have disappeared, as the tsar did. There would have been crises, perhaps coups d'etat, and periods of suppression. But there is no historical law that predestined the emergence of a totalitarian dictatorship in Germany or in Russia.

Why the talk of the inevitability (or near inevitability) of a Bolshevik victory in later years? Largely because in the 1960s the Soviet Union seemed at the height of its power. This led Western observers to exaggerate the extent of Soviet achievements and their durability.[18] But there were other reasons, and extenuating circumstances could be adduced. At that time, there had been precedents as far as the transition from a dictatorial to a more democratic regime is concerned. Theodor von Laue, a believer in the historical inevitability of a Bolshevik victory, wrote about 1917 that freedom in Russia was bound to destroy itself and that liberal democracy in Russia could never have been more than a transition phase. This was written well before the transition to democracy in Spain, Portugal, Chile, and other countries—and well before the decomposition of Communist rule in Russia and Eastern Europe.[19] Strongly influenced by the zeitgeist, it was easy to believe that the system was to last more or less forever and to forget that there existed an almost unlimited number of possibilities for political change, some, of course, more likely than others. There was a strong temptation to think in terms of extremes—either tsarism (or a similar right-wing autocratic regime) or a near perfect Western democracy, of say, Swiss or British style—and to ignore the great number of possibilities in between.

To return to the theme of Govorukhin's *The Russia We lost*, we have it on the authority of a great many contemporary observers that there was more to Russia before 1914 than poverty, ignorance, and pogroms; it had various attractive features and was not doomed to perdition. Among these observers were academics with no axe to grind, such as Otto Hoetzsch, Anatole Leroy Beaulieu, and Bernard Pares. There were newspapermen like Mackenzie Wallace, students of literature such as Maurice Baring, and seasoned travelers such as Henry Norman.[20] But the idealized Govorukhin version of the old Russia and the nostalgia for the old Russia expressed more recently in the books of right-wing village writers is as wrong as Lenin's and Trotsky's image of tsarist Russia as a place located somewhere at the bottom of the inferno. It reminds one of the Romantics' hankering back to a medieval splendor that never existed. It is a product of fantasy, of dissatisfaction with present-day conditions. It is not historically accurate, and it does not show a way to the future.

II

According to the Communist party line, the October Revolution was the greatest event in Russian, nay in world, history. Only owing to this revolution had the Soviet Union become a great power, established the most progressive social system in the history of mankind, and thus inaugurated a new era in world history. The Bolsheviks had prevailed in the struggle for power in 1917 because they had spearheaded the revolutionary movement, expressing the desires and interests of the people, who wanted peace and land. All other parties had resisted the just demands of the people and were swept aside – this was the irrevocable verdict of history.

This general theme was belabored in many thousands of annual commemorations, speeches, articles, and books that, over the years, became increasingly repetitious.[21] Even some local histories were written several times over, and the party line determined not only the general outline, but even the details. There was no room for reconsideration and new approaches. Furthermore, there was no room for new research. The archives were under the strict control of the security authorities, and the question which sources could be used, and which remained out of bounds, had been decided long before. As far as the "bourgeois" February Revolution was concerned, some differences of opinion began to appear in the 1960s – not so much with regard to the role of the Bolsheviks, but concerning the forces that had plotted to overthrow the tsar and replace his regime. According to these voices, there had been a Masonic conspiracy to which most bourgeois leaders belonged. This was by no means a new concept; it had strong support among the right-wing émigrés and some advocates among the liberals. However, these disputes preoccupied only a small number of experts – on the crucial issues there was no doubt.

Then, between 1989 and 1991, within less than two years, the Soviet regime collapsed. In that short interval, some daring historians suggested that in certain decisive questions the Mensheviks rather than the Bolsheviks had been right.[22]

Pavel Volobuyev, an even more daring spirit, suggested that Soviet historiography had not made any progress since the early 1970s. He maintained, quoting Lenin, that the victory of Communism in 1917 had by no means been predetermined.[23] In various roundtable meetings arranged by the leading historical journals, speakers denounced dogmatism (always evoking the authority of Lenin) and demanded that historiography join the mainstream of *perestroika*. Some members of the older generation bitterly complained about deviations from Marxism-Leninism. They were shocked that individuals such as Bukharin and Trotsky should be mentioned in historical literature without the ritual condemnations. These and similar exercises in historical face-lifting were welcomed by some Western specialists as "dramatic," "exciting," "stunning," and "bold." However, by 1991 the discussions had gone well beyond what Lenin really meant with his April 1917 theses. Some of the specialized journals had been closed down; others, including *Kommunist*, had been renamed.[24] Professionals specializing in the history of 1917 had to look for gainful employment in other fields.

History has been written and rewritten since time immemorial, but never, except perhaps after a lost war, has there been such a sudden and radical reversal. Having been the most wonderful experience and achievement in the history of mankind, the Russian Revolution became for many Russians the greatest disaster that had ever befallen the Russian people, the source of all evil up to the present day. Those who had been instrumental in overthrowing the tsarist regime were bitterly denounced by the Russian right for having opened the gate to the onslaught of foreign hordes, while a great many traditional heroes of Russian history were reinstated. Milyukov and Kerensky, central figures in the provisional government of 1917, were not among them, nor were the other liberal, centrist, and socialist ministers and their parties. They had all been part of a giant Masonic conspiracy aimed at destroying the Russian nation, its political and military power, and its economic and cultural values.

The register of sins of the Bolsheviks was even larger. They had engaged in a holocaust, killing all the best sons and daughters of the fatherland or forcing them to emigrate and, destroying the church and its servants, the Russian middle class, the peasantry, the Cossacks, and Russian culture.[25] Under the Bolshevik yoke, Russia had been ruled by aliens, those who hated the Russian idea and the Russian people. Many of them had been Jews. Dozens of articles and several books analyzed the composition of the leadership of the Communist party—the Politburo, the Central Committee, the Council of Ministers, the senior staff of the Ministries of Foreign Affairs and Foreign Trade, and the senior commanders of the Red Army and the Cheka (the predecessor of the KGB). They reached the conclusion that the overwhelming majority had been of Jewish origin, including Lenin, who had been half-Jew, half-Kalmyk.[26]

Those who were not of Jewish origin had Jewish wives, including Bukharin, Rykov, Voroshilov, Molotov, and allegedly even Stalin. However, by 1991 the pendulum was swinging back; the reason was not so much the realization among right-wingers that they had been exaggerating wildly or the fact that the revelations were highly repetitious.

The reasons for second thoughts about the onslaught against the revolution of 1917 and Bolshevism in general were both ideological and pragmatic. While the right detested Lenin and Trotsky, their attitude toward Stalin was more positive. Under him, after all, the Soviet Union had become a global power, there had been a resurgence of Russian nationalism, and the "aliens" and "cosmopolitans" had been purged. Since Stalin was so bitterly attacked by the liberals, he could, obviously, not be all bad. But how could Stalin be embraced if those who had paved the way for him were said to be monsters?

More important yet, the Russian right soon realized that by taking an uncompromisingly hostile stand against Bolshevism, it was isolating itself from Communist elements, which it needed in the struggle against liberals and reformers. The neo-Stalinists, for their part, were willing to make certain concessions. As they saw it, the October Revolution was not the work of any single party, but the culmination of a powerful popular movement. True, various "crooks and adventurers from the [Jewish] Bund and *Poalei Zion*" had joined it. However, the outcome of the revolution was not shaped by a Jewish–Masonic plot; it was determined by the character of the Russian people.[27] And since the main commandment was now to save the fatherland, the red and the white (or brown, as others said) movements had to reconcile their differences. Such appeals were echoed by conservative ideologists like Mikhail Antonow, who denounced sterile anti-Communism, suggesting that Russia's history ought to be regarded in its entirety—including both the Red and White armies and Nikolai II and Stolypin, as well as Lenin and Stalin. These ideas had been voiced as far back as the 1920s by certain groups of the White emigration who had looked for a reconciliation with Stalinism.

While the right tried to come to terms in this way with the revolution, which had given birth to the system that had lasted for seventy years, a strange silence fell on the professional historians. They could not revoke all they had written before 1989. Even the more enlightened Marxists among them had considered 1917 a liberating act and Lenin a great and good leader. They could not suddenly argue that the revolution had been a mistake, let alone a disaster, and thus they preferred not to put themselves on record. They were helped by the lack of newsprint, which made the publication of nonfiction–non-best-selling literature–next to impossible after 1990. And even if there had been enough paper, it is more than doubtful whether there would have been any public interest in what yesterday's official historians were saying. Overnight they had been turned into annalists of a prohibited political party. The historical journals featured the memoirs of figures who had been taboo in the past, ranging from Trotsky and Kerensky to General Denikin, or invited contributions from Western writers specializing in Soviet history, such as Sheila Fitzpatrick, Alexander Rabinowitsch, Dietrich Weyrau, Robert Tucker, and Martin Malia. Only gradually and hesitatingly did a discussion about the true correlation of forces and the mood of the masses in 1917 get under way. Papers on subjects such as "Illusions and pragmatism in the movement of the masses" were read in conferences analyzing the October Revolution for the first time in seventy years without embellishment. Erstwhile Marxist historians reached the conclusion that while there had been more illusions among the intelligentsia than among the working class (let alone the peasants) in 1917, radical illusions prevailed only among déclassé elements.[28] This was a far cry from what Western social historians had been telling their readers since the 1970s.

III

The question of leadership in the February Revolution has been discussed at great length. My own conclusion, expressed in 1967, that "the overthrow of Tsarism is not really a bone of contention," was somewhat premature, because disputes have broadened the argument in various directions.

There was the thesis (of which mention has already been made) that Freemasons collectively played an important role in the revolution. Others argued that it was not the politically conscious engineering workers who took to the streets in the decisive days in Petrograd, but the "politically backward" women textile workers.[29]

Such minutiae can be discussed endlessly. There was a real danger that specialists would go on quarreling about less and less. It did not matter greatly whether certain members of the provisional government were Masons or not—or whether the Bolsheviks had 3,000 members in Petrograd at the time of the revolution. As their leaders were in exile or under arrest, the revolution was still spontaneous and leaderless. The military, political, and economic situation deteriorated so much during the fall and winter of 1916/1917 that the tsar had become utterly isolated and totally divorced from reality. Only the slightest push was needed to remove him from the scene. Everyone had turned against the ruler, who had committed every possible mistake, including taking over the supreme military command and leaving domestic affairs to his wife and Alexander Protopopov, her only confidant. His own family was consulting as to how to replace him, and even the extreme right demanded a change. Talented military commanders such as Brusilov said that if they had to choose between the monarch and Russia, the choice was clear. When the president of the Duma sent the tsar a cable after the disturbances had already begun in Petrograd, Nikolai commented, "Some nonsense from the fat Rodzianko—I am not going to reply." In such a situation, the pertinent question is surely not why a revolt broke out and who was leading it, but why it had not occurred earlier.

A prolongation of these debates seems pointless. At most it can be asked whether the course of events would have been radically different if there had been a determined, successful coup at an earlier date. Alexander Guchkov, one of the leaders of the center, had observed well before February that after the revolution, power would fall into the hands of those who seized it. What if a popular general, one of the less discredited members of the royal family, or a forceful and ambitious politician had seized power? Would there have been sufficient support to sustain the new government?

Russian society was in a state of turmoil. None of the various political parties had more than a narrow social base. These and other factors have been adduced to explain why a constitutional regime was bound to fail,[30] but the Bolsheviks were also weak. Their attempts to mobilize the masses were by no means at first overwhelmingly successful, and the question of alternatives remains a perfectly legitimate one.

The history of the first act of the revolution could not be written before the curtain finally went down on the whole drama. This stage was reached only seventy-five years after the event. Even now it may not be the final curtain, for the horrible consequences of Communist rule may have made the transition to a freer system exceedingly difficult and a temporary throwback to the old system possible. But sufficient time has now passed to enable us to see the October Revolution of 1917 in a wider perspective. Seldom, if ever, has an event had such fateful and negative consequences.

What could have been done to forestall the victory of a cause that was to lead the country to such grim consequences? Some historians have reasoned that the Bolsheviks won because of their "organizational weapon" and their ability to manipulate the masses. According to the Leninist concept of a political party, they were better organized than the rest. This is true but still does not explain the failure of the provisional government, which at one time had most of the cards in its hands.

The Bolsheviks saw the situation more clearly than the others on two issues, one of which was absolutely crucial as far as the outcome of the struggle for power was concerned. This was the issue of peace; after three years of war, the country was tired and no longer in a position to continue the war. The attempt to do so was fatal and caused the downfall of the provisional government.[31] All the members of the government and the parties backing them bear the responsibility for this decisive blunder. Above all, it was the fault of Milyukov, the foreign minister. This outstanding student of history and politics, once an inveterate critic of Slavophilism, had turned, for reasons not entirely clear, Russian imperialist, impervious to the weakness of the country and the army. In retrospect, leaders of the left realized that they had been too timid and irresolute in the face of Western pressures to continue the Russian war effort.[32] By the time they understood, it was of course too late.

Instead of launching a new offensive, they could have engaged in a slow strategic retreat or, if necessary, an armistice. The Allies would have been unhappy, but the result of the war would not have been different. For America had already entered the war, and by late summer 1917 Germany was in no position to engage in a major offensive on the eastern front. Jonathan Frankel has correctly observed that a parliamentary regime surviving into 1918 presumably would have prevented the civil war, and by the end of the war Russia would have found itself among the victorious powers: "Under those totally changed circumstances, a parliamentary regime in Russia would surely have had a fighting chance of indefinite survival."[33] If one replaces the word "parliamentary" with the word "nontsarist" or "non-Bolshevik," the prospects appear in retrospect even more likely.

The other major issue, land and rural rebellion, was of greater importance for the outcome of the civil war than the October Revolution. Lenin launched his famous slogan "The land to the peasants" at the second conference of the Soviets after the revolution. By that time, almost 90 percent of the arable land was in the hands of the peasants in any case, and the only question was whether they would be permitted to keep it.

IV

Under *perestroika*, Soviet and Russian history had to be extensively rewritten, even though some of the old-timers argued that large stretches of

Russian history– "from the mamoths to Peter the Great" –had been fairly treated and there was no need to cover this period all over again. Others agreed with regard to the mammoths, but not the period thereafter. But as Gorbachev's *perestroika* petered out, interest in the Soviet period of Russian history faded. Instead of the unending stream of party publications, there were now books and booklets on religion and the "occult sciences," with a sprinkling of ever-popular historical romances.

It was an unprecedented situation. Even Germany and Italy after World War II provided few clues for the interpretation of Russian politics. For Nazi Germany had lasted a mere twelve years, and very little contemporary history had been written under Hitler. Sociology had been virtually abolished by the Nazis, and historians did not deal with the period after 1918 –only journalists did, and not frequently. There was not much literature about Nazi doctrine except the basic writings by Hitler and Rosenberg and some commentaries. National Socialism and fascism were "vitalist" movements and, unlike Marxism-Leninism, had few intellectual pretensions. It is inconceivable to imagine Hitler as the author of a book on empiriocriticism or Goebbels writing on linguistics and party history.

Nazism and Italian fascism focused on the future rather than the past. Thus after 1945 it was sufficient to shelve the writings of Hitler, Rosenberg, and Goebbels; to delete anti-Jewish and antidemocratic references in the books published after 1933; and to tone down the ultranationalist tenor of some publications in order to pass muster in the new democratic order. There had been Nazi philosophers and Nazi economists, but no specific Nazi doctrine and party line in these fields. Thus these disciplines did not face major difficulties of transition in the years after 1945.

The situation in the Soviet Union was radically different, inasmuch as the party line was infinitely more detailed and binding. Society and even daily life had been much more ideologized. A period of more or less enforced silence was not only inevitable, but probably welcome. It enabled Russian historians to ponder how to face from then on the past of the country. For the right, the dilemma was less difficult–patriotic nineteenth-century historians such as Karamzin, Solovyov, and Kliuchevsky were republished. But this did not solve the problem of how to face the century that had passed since.

The position of Western students of Soviet history was not enviable after the collapse of the Soviet Union. We shall refer in the present context only to those specializing in the early days of the Soviet regime, the revolutions of 1917, and the civil war. In the 1960s and 1970s, an important change had taken place in Western historiography that became known as the revisionist trend.[34] There had been earlier writers on the Soviet Union, including Sir Bernard Pares in his dotage, Frederic Schuman, E. H. Carr, Isaac Deutscher, Barrington Moore, Harold Berman, Rudolf Schlesinger, Theodor von Laue, and Alec Nove, who were far from hostile to the Soviet Union in their writings. Some were apologists for Lenin and Stalin; others argued that sufficient credit had not been given to Soviet achievements. The influence of these writers was considerable.[35] But it was only in the 1970s that, with the rise of a new generation, a whole school of historians emerged whose views toward the Soviet Union were far more sympathetic than those of their predecessors. Some of them were Marxists; others were not. All of them sincerely believed that their basic approach was more detached and objective than that of the earlier "Cold War" writers.[36]

This rewriting of the history of the revolutions of 1917 took place, broadly speaking, between 1970 and 1985; it was accompanied by a rise in esteem for Lenin and, to a lesser extent, the other Bolshevik leaders of the early days. At the same time, considerable respect was paid to the work of Soviet historians. While extenuating circumstances can perhaps be found for the Soviet experts, who had to stick closely to the party line, it is more difficult to fathom what induced Western historians to praise mainline Soviet historiography of their own free will.[37]

The "discoveries" of the revisionist school included the thesis that the October Revolution had been proletarian in character. As David Mandel put it: "It was, among other things, a soldier's mutiny, a peasant rebellion, a movement of national minorities. But it was also–and especially–a worker's revolution." And as S. A. Smith added, "[T]his working class movement was permeated by a commitment to direct democracy."[38] Or, in the words of Rabinowitch, the October Revolution was a popular, democratic movement "in which the Bolshevik party as a whole expressed the fundamental interest of the masses."[39] This emphasis on the allegedly democratic character of Red October raises further questions, however: If the uprising was so democratic, how can we explain the fact that it gave rise to one of the harshest dictatorships in the history of mankind? The usual answer provided by the revisionists is that the civil war and foreign intervention brought about the collapse of Soviet democracy.[40] But this response ignores the basic nondemocratic thrust of Bolshevik thought, the emphasis on a dictatorship by the party leadership, which can be found in Lenin's works virtually from the beginning. So convinced was Mandel of the truth and pertinacity of his thesis that he found it inconceivable and outlandish that another recent historian of 1917 had dismissed the proletarian character argument as belonging to the realm of "revolutionary mythology."[41] Only a few years later, yet another historian went into minute detail over the same ground (the Petrograd workers in 1914 to 1917) in what is so far the most exhaustive study of the subject. But he found precious little to justify the "proletarian" thesis. The workers were politically weak and disunited; there was no mature, hereditary, urbanized proletariat that was allegedly captured by the Bolsheviks on the eve of the war. Their demands concerned mainly wages and conditions of work. Their politicization was exaggerated; there was no massive support for the Bolsheviks. In fact, all the socialist parties were weak in 1917.[42]

Even if the findings of the revisionist historians were wholly correct, however, they would have proved very little in retrospect. The emphasis on the "proletarian" character of the revolution made sense only on the basis of the Marxist assumption that the working class, being the most progressive of all social classes, must have been a priori right. But as the subsequent course of events was to show, the revolution was not the blessing the orthodox Marxists had believed, even from a proletarian point of view. Hence the heated debates on the class character of the revolution—whether it was a coup d' état or there was mass support for it—are irrelevant in the final analysis. Whoever was responsible for it, whoever had supported the seizure of power, had been a partner to a fateful decision that was to involve Russia in a major civil war, a totalitarian dictatorship, and, in the end, not victory but ruin.

All this, it might be argued, could not have been known at the time and should not be held against the Bolsheviks. But it was known to Bertrand Russell and Rosa Luxemburg and others who were not right-wing counterrevolutionaries, and there is no way, in the end, to escape historical responsibility.

A Western historian of Russia observed in 1990 that the most stimulating recent developments in the historiography of the Russian Revolution were the emergence of studies of institutions, social groups, and the non-metropolitan regions.[43] This kind of history had the advantages of not repeating previous research and of providing potential work for many people for many years to come, for there were thousands of towns and villages to be covered from Minsk to Vladivostok. But to what purpose? It was, after all, in Petrograd and Moscow that the action—the decisive battles—took place. The study of institutions may be of considerable intrinsic interest, but as far as the crucial issues of the revolutions were concerned, it did not enrich our knowledge: social groups did not essentially change between February and October 1917.[44] On balance, the impact of these approaches was in retrospect harmful, because by shifting the emphasis from the center to the periphery, and from political leaders and parties to social groups, the essential issues were neglected or dropped altogether.

Stressing that Russian and Soviet realities were much richer and more complex than earlier students had believed and that much more sophisticated approaches were needed to understand them, the proponents of revisionist historiography produced no significant new insights that survived the downfall of the Soviet Union.

The "behavioral revolution" in the field of Soviet studies took various forms; it concerned the behavior of bureaucracies as well as the dictates of group interests, and there was always the admonition to engage in comparative studies. As intellectual fashions changed in the social sciences, so did the nature of the nostrums that were recommended to deepen our understanding. The most influential school was probably that which put the emphasis on modernization. It suggested that the Soviet Union should be regarded as a developing country following a specifically Russian way of modernization. It was argued that West and East faced the same long-term problems, such as industrialization, urbanization, the spread of education, and the participation of individuals and groups in the political process.[45] This argument supported the assumption that it was legitimate to transfer concepts and theories based on Western historical experience to developments in Russia, and the conclusion that the two seemingly very different social systems were growing more similar as time went by.

True, not all accepted the idea of "convergence," but even many of those who did not believed that it was indefensible to blame the Soviet order for the absence of political freedom. Given the traditional political backwardness of Russia, it seemed that such an approach was ethnocentric. Even those who took a more critical view of the absence of political freedom in the Soviet Union believed that the system could be reformed and that the reforms were imminent. They saw in *perestroika* and *glasnost* the advent of their expectations.

Seen in this perspective, the Russian Revolution of 1917 had been a success—perhaps not a full success, and certainly not a success by high Western standards of human rights. But since the Soviet Union had other tremendous achievements to its credit, it seemed indefensible to concentrate on its shortcomings and to ignore its many triumphs—such as social security, the absence of unemployment, the spread of education and health services, participation of the masses, and general political stability. The positive appraisal of the October Revolution, which prevailed in Western Sovietology in the 1970s, can be understood against the background of the changing image of the Soviet Union, now viewed as a strong power that had made great strides and was destined to endure. The earlier skeptical and largely negative assessment seemed more and more mockingly out of place. A leading proponent of the revisionist school summarized the outdated and unbalanced Cold War version in 1984: "In October 1917 the Bolsheviks, a small, unrepresentative and already an embryonically totalitarian party, usurped power and thus betrayed the Russian revolution. From this moment on, Soviet history was determined by the totalitarian political dynamics of the Communist party."[46]

This was a somewhat exaggerated account (the critics of Communism were not all cut from one cloth), but it was a fairly symptomatic assessment. At long last, a positive approach was prevailing in the West. As Edward Acton put it, shortcomings of the shallow, superficial liberal version had been exposed by the revisionists,

> who had traced the process which led to mass radicalization and underscored the autonomous and rational nature of the intervention by workers, soldiers and peasants. They had demonstrated the decisive impact of that intervention upon the fate of the Provisional Government and of the moderate socialists. It had brought out the strength of the Bolshevik party derived from its relatively decentralized, tolerant and ideologically heterogeneous make-up and from its readings to defy as well as to follow Lenin. They had highlighted the plebeian composition of the party, the mass popularity it enjoyed in October 1917, and the extent to which support for the party arose from its identification with the cause of Soviet power.[47]

In 1988, in what was probably the last work of its kind to be published, Soviet historians noted with satisfaction the important, positive changes that had taken place over the past two decades in Western historiography concerning the year 1917. The leading role of the Russian working class was now finally recognized. The Bolshevik Revolution was no longer considered an accident of history, nor was it claimed that it had merely been a coup carried out by a group of conspirators.[48] Western revisionists received high marks from Soviet historians for their objectivity, even though in some respects they were not going as yet far enough.

But time was running out. Soon afterward, the institutes dealing with party history were liquidated, as were the publishing houses and professional journals. In the West, positive views on 1917 could still be encountered, but inside Russia it became difficult to find anyone who had a good word for the October Revolution and its consequences. The new consensus was much closer to the views of the old right-wing émigrés—Solzhenitsyn and Govorukhin and his *The Russia We Lost*. The revolution had been a total disaster and Lenin, a criminal.

The revisionists, who firmly believed they had destroyed the "liberal" — that is, critical—version of the October Revolution, suddenly were confronted with far more extreme views, which in the past they had simply ignored because they seemed not worthy of serious intellectual debate. So far, the revisionists have not attempted to come to terms with the eclipse and disappearance of the Soviet Union. They could argue that the eventual breakdown of the system does not necessarily invalidate the promising beginnings and their arguments concerning 1917. In this case, they would have to show what, in their view, went wrong with the revolution—under Lenin, Stalin, or Stalin's successors. Or they could argue that those Russians now condemning the revolution of 1917 in toto are overreacting, motivated by the dramatic events of 1987 to 1991. This could be true, but it could apply equally to the revisionist school, which would hardly have come into existence but for the fact that the Soviet Union had become a superpower by the 1970s, its rulers seemed firmly in the saddle, and its achievements were grossly exaggerated. By and large, the revisionists are fighting a rear-guard action. In the meantime, the pendulum is swinging back to the view common to most eyewitnesses of the revolution: that after the spring of 1917, conditions in the Russian empire were increasingly chaotic and that power was in the streets to be picked up by any groups of people determined and self-confident enough to do so. The confusion and lack of resolution on the part of others led to Lenin's famous line, "There is such a party!" The rest is Russian history.

V

Even in the 1970s and early 1980s, the myth of Red October did not have the field entirely to itself. There had always been dissenters in the academic world, unwilling to share the view that the Bolshevik Revolution had been a great liberating turning point in the history of Russia and mankind.[49] Not surprisingly, *glasnost* and the downfall of the Soviet empire gave birth to a new literature of reinterpretation amounting to a scathing condemnation of the revisionist gospel. That these works were bitterly resented by those against whom they were directed goes without saying and needs no special explanation. They were rejected by the aggrieved parties as unscholarly and hopelessly antiquated because of they ignored the social history literature of the earlier decades and the social science approaches in general. Among the works that raised much ire were Richard Pipes's two volumes on the Russian Revolution and Martin Malia's articles and recent book.[50] Closely reasoned books, they took the view that the October Revolution had been a monumental failure and that the main question to be asked was how such a deeply flawed regime had succeeded in maintaining itself in power for so long and hoodwinking so many well-meaning people in the process.

These reappraisals of the post-Communist era agreed on the outcome of the Soviet experiment and did not accept that the revolution had been inevitable. But they did not agree on the causes of the disaster. Malia put virtually the entire blame on the idea of socialism, which had been the source of all evil. It had not been "Mother Russia" (meaning Russian backwardness) that had spoiled socialism, as many radicals thought, but vice versa. At long last, the awful truth had to be faced that Russia had become totalitarian because it was socialist, socialism being the ideal formula for totalitarianism. Pipes, on the contrary, expressed the view that while Communism had been based on an erroneous doctrine, it was also true that Bolshevik practices had been indigenous. For nowhere in the West had Marxism led to the totalitarian excesses of Leninism-Stalinism. In brief, the authoritarian strains in Marxism had gained ascendancy in Russia because they fitted the country's patrimonial heritage.

Such outspoken indictments were anathema to historians who argued that their assignment was not to judge, but to understand and explain. But such advocacy of Olympic detachment usually hides special pleading by those afraid of the historical verdict.

The idea that "detached" and "scholarly" are synonyms for "equidistance" is common among those wishing to put Nazism as well as Stalinism in "proper historical perspective." But indifference vis-à-vis human suffering on a massive scale and monstrous crimes is neither a virtue nor in the tradition of scholarship, and it makes a mockery of the search for historical truth.

But it is also true that major pitfalls face those who reconsider events such as the October Revolution under the immediate impression of its disastrous end: an earthquake may sharpen the senses, but it is not necessarily the ideal condition for quiet reflection. There is the temptation to assume that, like Lucifer, Communism has fallen, never to hope again. But this, as even the immediate aftermath of the Communist debacle has shown, is by no means certain. The old order had many supporters, and in one guise or another, as left-wing or right-wing populism, the attempt is being made to restore it or at least to salvage some of its major components. Judgment made under the immediate impact of such momentous events may easily err toward the side of exaggeration.

Malia's emphasis on the role of equality is one example.[51] Excessive egalitarianism was certainly not the most pronounced feature of Soviet ideology and even less of Communist reality. Pipes, however, not content with pointing to the many indubitable similarities between Communism and fascism, goes on arguing that the Soviet experience provided inspiration and guidance for Hitler.[52] This comes perilously close to the arguments of the German nationalist school of history (Ernst Nolte and his disciples), which has argued for a long time that the Nazis got the idea of concentration camps (and ultimately mass murder) from the Soviet gulag. While Hitler and Mussolini were impressed by Stalin's ruthlessness, they had no interest in Soviet domestic affairs, they discovered the uses of nationalism well before Stalin, and they had no need of Communist inspiration and made no effort whatsoever to learn from Soviet experience.

The register of the failures and crimes of the Soviet regime is enormous, even without adding to the indictment charges that cannot be substantiated. And yet, with all these caveats, there can be no reasonable doubt about three basic conclusions with regard to the results of the October Revolution: that it was a failure in light of developments since 1917 in other, comparable countries; that it was an even greater failure in terms of what its leaders wanted to achieve; and that it has made a gradual, peaceful transition to a better future very difficult indeed.

3

The Fall of the Soviet Union

The fall of the Soviet empire will preoccupy students of history for a long time to come. There is no unanimity even now with regard to the collapse of Rome and other empires, and the fate of the Soviet Union is bound to be a subject of similar controversy. It will be interpreted and reinterpreted in the future in the light of changing events. There will be orthodox and revisionist views as well as post-revisionist schools, dependent to a large extent on the fate of Russia and the other successor states in the decades to come. The breakdown of 1991 could lead to the re-emergence of a great power on the ruins of the old. Equally, the process of disintegration could continue, leading to a long period of tension and perhaps internecine warfare. There are various possibilities in between these extremes.

The study of the fall of empires has intrigued historians since time immemorial. Each case has been different but there have also been certain common features or at least similarities. Certain collapses have been more of a mystery than others. There are dozens of explanations for the decline of Rome, ranging from moral degeneration and intellectual crisis (as many ancient historians thought), to racial dilution and demographic problems,[1] economic decline and the disarray of the monetary system, to lead poisoning from the water supply of the eternal city. While Gibbon argued that Christianity sapped the morale of the empire so that in the end the civilian population showed inertia in the face of the barbarian invasions, other historians pointed to the high death rate, the presence of too many idle people, the inflation of government officials, and overcentralization.[2]

But for each argument, counterarguments have been adduced. The economic recession was not really too severe. There had been continuous warfare for almost two centuries on the German and Persian borders. If some prophets had predicted the imminent fall of Rome, others, such as

Claudian and Ammian, had maintained right to the fall that there would never be an end to the power of Rome and that "as long as there are men, Rome will be victorious."[3]

The limitation of all these interpretations (and even of all of them taken together) is that they explain perhaps the weaknesses of Rome but not necessarily its fall. Everything that has been offered as explanation—the downward trend in population, the deleterious effects of slavery, the coercion by the state to keep the armies content, the dead hand of the bureaucracy, and the decay of the middle classes—applied equally to Byzantium, the eastern Roman Empire, which continued to exist for another thousand years. The fall of Rome was explained with reference to the "orientalization of classical man"; this was a fortiori true with regard to Byzantium. It may have caused an intellectual crisis, but not every intellectual crisis brings about the disappearance of an empire. Or was it perhaps because the eastern part of the empire was strategically less vulnerable? Hardly so, Rome was sacked by Alaric in 410, but Constantinople was besieged in 626 by the Avars, again in 717 to 718 by Muslim armies, and yet continued to exist for many centuries. The eastern empire faced chaos and civil war at frequent intervals; it waged wars against Vandals and Ostrogoths, against Persians and Seldjuk Turks, against Venice and Sicily. It was under constant pressure for eight hundred years from Islamic forces. But it did not fall until much later.[4]

In trying to explain the decline of the Spanish and Dutch empires, emphasis has been put on demographic decline, the collapse of industry, and a prevailing mentality of conservatism that caused the spirit of enterprise gradually to fade. There were obvious differences in each case. The fact that the demand for herring decreased played a role of some importance in Holland, with its dependence of foreign trade, but not, of course, in Spain, and "hidalgism" (the social role of the lower aristocracy) was a specific Spanish feature with no equivalent in the Netherlands. In both empires, as an eighteenth-century observer noted, "their power no longer corresponded with their inclinations."[5]

But why did their power correspond at one time and cease to do so at a later stage? Was it because the belief in a feeling of mission gradually disappeared? To find answers, one would have to investigate why empires have come into being in the first place. Stronger states have dominated weaker neighbors since time immemorial, but this is not tantamount to systematic expansion—that is, imperialism. How important were economic factors such as the need of and search for raw materials and expanding markets? How important in modern history was aggressive nationalism and militarism, the belief in a global mission, and the aspiration to glory and big power status? These and other questions have been studied with the unstartling result that what was true in one case does not necessarily apply in another. Under the impact of Marxism, there has been a tendency to overrate the role of economic motives, which were important in some cases, unimportant in others.

The absence of a consensus on these issues has been noted. A recent historian of Russian imperial expansion in the nineteenth century, for example, regards expansion as the manifestation of economic and political weakness rather than strength – the wish to compensate in Central Asia for defeat in Europe in the Crimean War. But the concept of "psychological compensation" is rejected by a military historian who puts the stress on the Russian "strategic imperative," as interpreted by the generals at the time and by such thinkers as Rostislav Fadeyev.[6] Every conquest had to be safeguarded by further conquests.

However, not all imperial breakdowns have been complicated and unfathomable. There are no major differences of opinion with regard to the causes of the fall of the Ottoman Empire and of Austro-Hungary: the rising tide of nationalism, the weakening of the political and administrative center created a situation in which the empire could no longer function – imperial power was no longer sufficient to maintain its hold beyond the center. Perhaps either of these empires could have transformed itself by far-reaching political reform into a commonwealth of nations. But this is not certain, and in any case such a commonwealth, as the British example has shown, would have been largely meaningless. Appearances would have been kept – it would have been a more elegant way of deimperialization, but the final result would have been the same.

II

Where should an investigation of the Soviet breakdown start? There is much to be said for the thesis of the Russian right that but for the reforms of Gorbachev, the apostate, the collapse would not have occurred; at least the old framework could have been preserved for another five or ten years, perhaps even longer. And no one can say for certain what would ultimately have happened in this case. Historically, even old and weakened empires broke down only after years of costly war and eventual defeat. It could also be argued that but for the failure of the antireform coup in August 1991, the breakdown might not have occurred. One of the main reasons for the coup was to prevent the signing of a new union treaty that was to put the relationship between the various republics on a new footing.

Even among diehard Communists, few tend to deny that there was indeed a crisis well before Gorbachev, that the economy did not function well, that Soviet society was affected by various serious evils, that the cultural life of the country was impoverished, and that, generally speaking, Communism faced insurmountable difficulties adjusting itself to a changing world.[7] This school of thought uses terms such as *zastoi* (stagnation) and *tormozhenie* (literally, braking) and puts the main emphasis on negative economic trends, extreme bureaucratization, and insufficient de-Stalinization. It stresses economic factors and regards nationalist tension as relatively subordinate, assuming that if everyone had lived well, people would not have been preoccupied with national self-determination. National consciousness had grown stronger rather than weaker under Communism (as Andropov conceded), but the growth of nationalist tension and assertiveness was explained mainly with reference to such factors as economic and social underdevelopment in the Central Asian republics, and the fact that the share of industrial workers in the Communist parties of the Baltic republics was declining. Even if true, however, these circumstances were of no great significance with regard to the unfolding national crisis.

Orthodox Marxist-Leninists have put most of the blame on the shortcomings of the leadership of the 1960s and 1970s, who did not recognize in time the threats facing the country. This is true only in part. Looking for the deeper roots of stagnation, one cannot ignore the system created under Stalin, which, for all one knows, was not capable of radical yet peaceful change. An investigation of Stalinism leads inevitably back to Leninism, despite the protestations of those who consider Stalinism its illegitimate offspring. Once a tyranny of a new type had been established firmly, changing political institutions and the economy, sooner or later there would be a violent reaction, resulting not only in the liquidation of the "distortions" of Leninism and Stalinism, but in the collapse of the house built by the Bolsheviks. But why should an investigation of the causes of the collapse of 1991 stop with 1917? The Bolsheviks, after all, inherited an empire, the roots of which were far less solid than it appeared at the time.

In contrast to the growth of the colonial empires, Russian and Soviet imperial expansion affected contiguous territories. There was no Russian overseas empire with the exception, for a short time, of Alaska. Writing in 1906, Dmitri Ivanovich Mendeleev, the great Russian chemist, predicted that the population of the empire would grow to almost 600 million, virtually all of them Russians or assimilated Russians. Had his projection been even remotely right, the empire would not have fallen apart in 1991.

Russia's westward expansion came to a halt after 1815. Russia eventually gave up Poland (Rousseau had predicted that it would be "too heavy a meal to digest"), Finland, and, for a while, the Baltic countries and Bessarabia. The expansion to the east, which gathered momentum in the nineteenth century, was to some extent official tsarist policy, but there was no system and overall blueprint behind it. It came at the initiative of military commanders such as General Mikhail Dmitreyevich Skobelev (Gorchakov was later to remark, "I cannot do anything against the ambitions of the generals"). It was fomented by ideologues such as Dostoyevsky, who preached that Russian advance into Asia would bring about a regeneration of the national spirit and "give Moscow a civilisatory mission which it could never have in Europe."[8] In 1917 this mission received a completely new ideological underpinning.

It is easy in retrospect to draw up a register of sins of commission and omission of tsarist and Communist policy vis-à-vis the peoples of Central Asia. Although these groups continued to lag behind in their development, it cannot seriously be maintained that this was a case of colonial exploitation. Rather it was a case of the colonies economically exploiting the metropolis. And it should also be borne in mind that for many years Soviet nationality policy in these parts was thought to be a success, even by the staunchest critics of Soviet Communism. Hans Kohn's early book about Soviet nationality policy published in the 1920s is a case in point. Solomon Schwartz, the leading Menshevik expert, wrote soon after the end of World War II that the Soviet Union was "one of the few countries with a very heterogenous national composition which is close to a success-ful solution of the National Question."[9] Walter Kolarz, a noted student of the subject and a very hostile critic, wrote about the same time, "the [Soviet] federal system, despite its shortcomings, can teach a considerable lesson to the small countries of Central and Eastern Europe."[10] Even in the 1960s, articles and books were widely published in the West discussing Soviet Central Asia as a "model for third world development."[11]

Such optimism was exaggerated even at the time, but it seemed then much less outlandish than now. Soviet power, with all its repressive policies and its social and economic mistakes, aimed at the development of these regions. The experiment failed; it was probably bound to fail in any case. Whether this could have been foreseen is a different issue altogether. As late as 1984, Mary McAuley upbraided fellow Sovietologists for being too eager to see in Soviet multiethnic society a threat to the Soviet state. This view, she thought, was based on dubious and unproven assumptions. As she saw it, the administrative arrangements, cadre policy, and eco-nomic policy had in general worked against a nationalist response.[12] But, in fact, very few of her colleagues had made such claims, and none had predicted the end of empire.

The issue of nationalist tensions as one of the main factors in the downfall of the empire will preoccupy us later on. It is easier to enumerate the issues that did *not* apparently play a central role. Soviet dissent in demonstrations in Red Square after the invasion of Czechoslovakia in 1968 (and sporadically even before) was courageous and admirable. But it affected altogether a few hundred people. The literature of dissent reached thousands, perhaps tens of thousands, but the great majority of the people were not even aware of it. True, the exodus of leading musicians (to give but one example) was an embarrassment, and it had repercussions among the intelligentsia. But did it decisively undermine the self-confidence of the *nomenklatura*? There is no evidence that it did. Courageous dissent perhaps shamed some even in the party leadership into sneaking admira-tion, and it perhaps caused some to reconsider certain fundamental beliefs, but there are no certainties in this respect. If some of the more intelli-gent members of the middle echelons of the party bureaucracy gradually reached the conclusion that reform was urgently needed, the inspiration did not come from the dissidents.

What did Soviet citizens really believe in the 1960s and 1970s? It is difficult to answer this question with any certainty. Gibbon, in his chapter on Julian, the apostate, writes that "in every age the absence of genuine inspiration is supplied by the strong illusions of enthusiasm and the mimic arts of imposture."[13]

The same was certainly true in the Soviet Union at the time, but it was far more manifest among those in key positions than in society in general. Workers and peasants had little to lose, and there was much less dissimulation among them. There is evidence, for instance, that Stalin's death was not mourned among manual workers.[14] The "liberal" and "revisionist" views among the Soviet intelligentsia in the Khrushchev era were manifested in many ways, not least in party-inspired novels warning intellectuals against dangerous deviations.[15]

In most contemporary revolutionary movements, the young generation and the working class have played a significant role, but this was not the case in Russia. After the 1930s, successive young generations in Russia were remarkably unpolitical. The system encouraged them to stay out of politics, and on the whole it was successful in its endeavor. It was less successful in propagating conformism among the young; there was contempt for the official youth organizations and party doctrine. There was increasing enthusiasm for rock culture, and there was alcoholism and the beginning of a drug scene, but no articulate opposition to the regime. When Communism faced its great crisis in the early 1990s, it found no support among the young generation, but the challenge against the system was not spearheaded by the young—it was an affair of the middle aged, the *shestidesyatniki*, the men and women of the 1960s. Young people came to the White House in August 1991, but it was a small minority.

What has been said about the young applies by and large to the working class. There was widespread dissatisfaction, but little open protest. It should be conceded that less was (and is) known about the mood of the industrial workers than about any other group in Soviet society. Apart from a few rare exceptions (Novocherkask in 1962), there is no evidence of open labor unrest turning into political action. Of course, there was no happiness among the workers, and Western theories concerning a "social contract" between ruler and ruled were not really appropriate—it was not a contract but a *diktat*. Unlike the young people, workers could not opt out and ignore the system. They had to clock in at their workplaces more or less on time and go through certain motions: "They pretend to pay us, we pretend to work." This situation affected labor productivity and resulted in the production of shoddy goods. It made for a climate of sullenness, apathy, social polarization between "them" and "us", indifference, and even despair. But it did not pave the way for a revolutionary upsurge.

Soviet peasants could do even less to show their unhappiness. Their living conditions, in particular in the non–Black Earth region, were miserable. Peasants voted with their feet; whoever could, moved out of the villages, leaving behind the less enterprising and weaker elements. Between 1981 and 1988 alone there was an unplanned exodus of almost 5 million peasants. Hundreds of billions of rubles were invested in agriculture, but the returns were lamentable. And even the modest figures given for yearly harvests were largely misleading, because a substantial part of the produce was lost or spoiled on the way to the consumer—more than 20 percent in the case of the grain harvest, one-third of vegetables, and 40 percent of the potato crop. (These were the official figures given in 1989 and 1990.)

All this made for despair in the countryside but not for active resistance. In modern times peasants have seldom revolted, and the Soviet peasants were no exception. The performance of Soviet agriculture was additional proof that the system worked badly, and it helped to undermine belief in the efficacy of the regime. But there were few acute shortages of staple foods—grain could be bought abroad—and the misery of life in the villages did not translate into a factor of political urgency. The early 1970s were bad years, as was the period between 1978 and 1982. Grain production in 1978 was 237 million tons but dropped to 179 million the year after, severely affecting the whole economy. After that there was some improvement.

III

A discussion of the state of affairs in the Soviet countryside has a bearing on the economic situation in general, inasmuch as it hastened the demise of the empire. Not much could be learned from official Soviet declarations in the post-Stalin era, which, by and large, were optimistic if not jubilant in tenor. True, Khrushchev made some critical utterances, but he also announced that by 1980 the Soviet Union would catch up with America and eventually overtake it. According to official announcements, Soviet capital investment equaled American investment in 1970, and the Soviet Union had overtaken in the early seventies the United States in coal and steel output, cement, the number of tractors produced, and essential raw materials and machines. At the beginning of the twelfth five-year plan, Soviet industrial output was allegedly about 80 percent of America's, rising from 30 percent in 1950.[16] But machine tools were antiquated, labor productivity had fallen, and the talk about a scientific-technological revolution was largely eyewash.

During the late Brezhnev period (in November 1978, November 1981, and May 1982), some pronouncements were made on the highest level that the economy did not function well and that the food question was a matter of prime political as well as economic importance.[17] Closer examination showed that the slowdown of the economy had started in the early 1960s.

To what extent were outside observers aware of the problems facing the Soviet economy, and how did they see its future prospects? Even in the early postwar period, George Grossman and Alexander Gerschenkron predicted that the growth attained between 1945 and 1950 could not be sustained and that there would still be high outlays for nonconsumption goods. In 1953, Vasili Leontiev took a much more optimistic view, writing that the Soviet Union had to a large extent caught up with the thirty-to forty-year lag behind the industrial West.[18]

In the 1960s, Alec Nove and Harry Schwartz wrote that the Soviet system could not cope with a mature economy—hence the slowdown of growth. But they still expected substantial progress in the years ahead.[19] Such observations were made virtually every year during the postwar period: the situation was serious but not desperate. Western comments about the Soviet economy became more pessimistic in the late 1970s, but with a few exceptions such as Igor Birman, the émigré economist, they were by no means utterly gloomy. Most observers (including the CIA) thought it unlikely that far-reaching reforms would be attempted: the long-term benefits were uncertain, a high cost had to be paid in the short run, and there would be strong opposition from within Soviet society.[20]

Or as a Western economist of Russian origin put it some years later, there was no economic inevitability about the downfall of the Soviet Union. The performance was poorer than in other developed countries, but the system was still workable, and even capable within limits, of technological innovation.[21] G. Khanin, a leading Russian economist and one of the most critical, takes a more skeptical view, noting the steady decline of growth rates over twenty years; but he too points to the fact that national income grew under Andropov and the years after (1983–1988) by 11 percent; it was not just a matter of the fundamental inefficiency of the command economy."[22] As Khanin sees it, the crisis was aggravated by other long-term noneconomic factors: the degradation of the human factor, the enormous population losses from World War I onward, the destruction of the most prosperous peasants and many of the most qualified members of the intelligentsia—in brief, the practice of negative selection and the reign of self-perpetuating mediocrity.

The general view in the West during most of the 1960s and 1970s was that the Soviet Union had no monopoly on serious economic problems, which seemed by no means incurable. In fact, as one commentary put it: "Troubles abroad may seem worse than troubles at home, and optimistic party leaders may feel that the positive aspects of their domestic situation still warrant confidence in their economic prospects."[23] In some cases one could encounter such optimism as late as 1988. The postwar Soviet record was considered decent by world standards; performance was very good, there was a high degree of personal economic security, and real incomes were continuously rising.[24]

Western comments on Soviet economic performance are by and large of symptomatic interest only, but they were circulated in Moscow, not only among professional collectors of intelligence, but also their consumers. Some Western studies, including some of those we have just quoted, were translated and made accessible to leading Soviet officials, such as members of the Politburo and the Central Committee. Thus the Soviet leadership could base its assessment on relatively optimistic estimates that came not only from their own, but also from foreign experts.

The first dent in this rosy picture came with the publication of Vasilii Selyunin and Grigorii Khanin's famous article "Lukavaya tsifra" (A

Cunning [i.e., deceptive] figure) in February 1987,[25] in which it was revealed for the first time that the relative decline had started in 1960 at the latest. Their work claimed to be based on official figures. If so, those with access to unofficial figures must have known even more about the real situation all along. Thousands must have had a fairly realistic picture–or could have had if they were interested.[26]

Even if we assume that the dismal state of the economy, especially the decline in productivity and the inability to innovate, was known to all and sundry, what political impact would it have had? While the production of nonconsumer goods was growing to the very end, the provision of goods and services to the population was qualitatively bad and quantitatively insufficient, especially in such vital sectors as housing; and the rate of growth was smaller than in most European countries. (Expenditure on education was relatively high in the Soviet Union in the 1950s and early 1960s but substantially declined thereafter.) When there were acute bottlenecks that necessitated, for instance, the import of grains and other agricultural produce from 1972 on, their costs could be covered by revenue from the export of Soviet oil. While the diet of the Soviet citizen was bad from a nutritional point of view, very few were acutely starving. In brief, even if the full truth had been known, would there have been demonstrations and riots?

Two related issues have figured highly in the debates on Soviet economic decline: the cost of empire and military spending. Although Moscow had exploited Eastern Europe in the early postwar years, later on the empire became a losing proposition from a strictly economic point of view. The imperial costs included not just Eastern Europe but Cuba, Vietnam, Afghanistan, and various Third World countries that received assistance and subsidies. Altogether, according to some estimates, the cost amounted to $44 billion in 1980.[27] Costs declined substantially after 1980 as the Soviet Union sharply cut subsidies to Eastern Europe.

However, the Soviet empire had not been established for reasons of financial profit, and the maintenance of an empire provided benefits as well as costs. While these imperial ventures were a drain on a shortage economy, there was no serious open opposition to maintaining the empire, apart from some grumbling about ungrateful Third World countries that did not repay their debts. It can be taken for granted that when Russia first entered Afghanistan in 1979, no one had an inkling that this would result in a protracted and costly war. But even in the early 1980s, when the economic situation had further deteriorated and the war costs were, according to some estimates, $5 billion, there were no protests except from dissidents such as Sakharov. From the documents of the 1988 Politburo meetings concerning the decision to bring the war to an end, it is now known that the economic burden played no decisive part.[28]

That the defense sector always received huge priority is, of course, well known. There was a vast amount of literature available to the public on the size of Soviet military spending and much more that was classified. Acrimonious debates continued for two decades among Western experts as to whether the Soviet defense burden was 6 percent, 10, 15, or 20 percent or even more. Estimates partly depended on whether calculations were made in dollars or rubles, and, of course, on how large the total GNP was thought to be. The size of the GNP was in many respects a decisive issue, not just with regard to establishing the extent of per capita defense spending. It was crucial because a defense outlay of, for example, 20 percent of a small (and stagnating) GNP left little room for further expansion.

With a few exceptions, Western experts grossly overrated the Soviet GNP, and thus underrated per capita arms spending and thus the defense burden for the population. The share of defense in the economy was considerably higher, perhaps 25 to 30 percent rather than 6 to 15 percent, as generally assumed earlier on. Throughout Soviet history, similar disregard of cost had been part and parcel of the system. The population had been indoctrinated to believe that a rapacious and aggressive enemy made it necessary for the Soviet Union to engage in costly defense to preserve the achievements of the regime. This state-of-siege mentality was widespread and deeply rooted. How could the party dictatorship and the police apparatus be justified without an omnipresent enemy? In the 1980s the Soviet leadership did not pursue the détente policy, which would have eased the defense burden. Instead, a new arms race began at a time when defense procurement costs were spiraling not only in the West, but also in the Soviet bloc.[29]

The arms race certainly caused great harm to the Soviet economy, but was it the decisive factor in the breakdown of the Soviet empire? Critics of defense were few and far between, whereas the armed forces had a very strong constituency, comprising above all the defense industry, which employed many millions. Soviet leaders could not fail to remember that the last Soviet leader who had tried to introduce substantial cuts in defense spending (Khrushchev) was removed from power primarily for this reason. Lastly, there was the matter of secrecy; while everyone knew that the Soviet Union spent a great deal of money and resources on the military, secrecy and the prevailing confusion (not all deliberate) made it virtually impossible to reach a reasonably accurate estimate of the extent of the burden. If the CIA, with its sophisticated models and elaborate means of collecting information, could declare in 1976 that Soviet defense costs were no more than 12 to 14 percent of the GNP (15 to 17 percent after an upward adjustment in the 1980s), how could one expect Soviet dissidents to know the full truth? (Sakharov, however, came up with the much more pessimistic estimate of 40 percent.) All an informed Soviet citizen could know for certain was that the economy was not in good shape and that its performance was deteriorating, but there could be no certainties with regard to the reasons. In the absence of reliable facts and figures, there could not be an informed debate inside the Soviet Union.

IV

One of the major weaknesses of the Soviet system, more decisive perhaps in the long run than economic failure, was the dismal state of the quality of life. Yet for a long time little attention was paid to these problems outside the Soviet Union; and until the rise of *glasnost* protest against pollution with all its evil consequences played a "very minor role" in the Soviet Union compared with the impact of the environmental movements in the West and Japan.[30] The two exceptions were the movement to save Lake Baikal, which began in 1963, and the resistance against rerouting the major Siberian rivers. In these two instances, private protest had some impact, because it was supported by powerful official interests, as in the case of Lake Baikal, and the Siberian (Russian) regional bosses in the case of the rerouting of the rivers.

The ecological disaster that took place in the Soviet Union affected nature and health and thus, directly or indirectly, every Soviet citizen. In theory, the disaster should not have happened because of the constantly trumpeted advantages of Communist planned economy over chaotic capitalism. Every Soviet republic had stringent laws regulating the environment. Yet in actual fact there was near total neglect. The air and water were ruined by pollution, forests suffocated, the soil was poisoned, and natural resources were depleted, because everything was subordinated to maximizing output in industry and agriculture, irrespective of the consequences. "Everyone knew the reason why everything was so bad, and everyone knew that they couldn't do anything about it."[31] It was only in 1986 with the Chernobyl catastrophe that the magnitude of the disaster could be openly discussed, partly because of the extent of the damage and partly because of the new policy of *glasnost*.

Not only were plants and animals disappearing. Environmental pollution–the combination of high concentrations of harmful substances in the air, pesticides, and poisoned water–had a severe effect on the state of health of the Soviet population. In the late 1960s, infant mortality began to rise, life expectancy had declined from sixty-six years in 1965 to sixty-four (in the countryside even more than in the cities), and infections and chronic disease became more and more widespread.[32] At the same time Soviet medicine found itself incapable of dealing with the results of adverse living and working conditions. Underpaid and overworked physicians (except for leading specialists) were usually not familiar with the advance of modern medicine. Modern technology was available only for the *nomenklatura* hospitals, and there were acute shortages of drugs.

The decline of the quality of life expressed itself in the rise of alcoholism and crime. Alcoholism had been a plague throughout Russian history, except for the short period during World War I when the production of spirits was banned. Its effects on health, labor productivity, and family life are well known. During the postwar period, abolition was occasionally suggested only to be rejected. Accurate statistics do not exist, but partial studies claim that chronic alcoholism rose among working class males from 3.5 percent in 1925 to 37 percent in the late 1970s. There could be no doubt about the general trend.[33]

Work in certain areas of the union came to a virtual standstill on payday—or when spirits were locally delivered. Drunken orgies in the countryside were on more than one occasion described in contemporary Soviet writing, particularly by the village writers, most powerfully in Valentin Rasputin's novel *Pozhar*, (*The Fire*) which appeared at the dawn of *glasnost*.

As for crime, the party program of 1961 had announced that crime and its causes were about to be stamped out. In official speeches and articles, it was proclaimed that there was a steady decline in crime, yet the figures pointed to a different trend. Between 1973 and 1983 crime almost doubled; crimes of violence increased by 58 percent, theft doubled, and cases of corruption trebled.[34] There was a further increase in 1984, a record year during which 2 million crimes were reported. Again, the figures were incomplete because far from all transgressions were reported, but the trend was unmistakable.

Politically, more important than petty theft was crime in high places, especially *kumovstvo* (nepotism) or, in party language, "the violation of Leninist norms in the selection of cadres." The problem in the 1970s was no longer the frequent occurrence of this phenomenon. It had become the norm rather than the exception in many parts of the Soviet Union, particularly in Central Asia, but also elsewhere in the union, from Moldova in the west to the eastern regions of Rostov and Krasnodar, and of course Moscow. From time to time, an unfortunate victim (such as a deputy minister) would be selected as a scapegoat and sentenced to the "highest measure of punishment."[35] But the real culprits were, of course, Brezhnev and the cronies he appointed to key positions, including Kunayev, first secretary in Kazakhstan, and Shchelokov, minister of internal affairs, as well as Churbanov, Brezhnev's son-in-law.

Those who had leading positions in the party, the state apparatus, and the economy became multimillionaires. Their families and clans profited likewise. There were legendary figures such as the Fergana district secretary who built racetracks for his private use, or Adylev of Uzbekistan, a friend of party first secretary Rashidov, who established a feudal kingdom, complete with its own prison. The building of palaces and the staking out of hunting reserves were quite common. Embezzlement and corruption became the norm. Anything could be obtained for money—a place in a leading university or a profitable job in the administration.

There was no possibility of legal redress. The underpaid police and judiciary were as corrupt as the rest of society, and in any case, they had no freedom of action. It was unthinkable that they would pass sentence not to the liking of their political bosses. Not everyone succumbed to corruption. Aliev, the all-powerful boss of Azerbaijan was challenged by the attorney general of the republic. In the end, the attorney general had to flee, hiding in Moscow from Aliev's vengeance. Andropov, head of the KGB and eventually the party first secretary, was powerless; his attempts to restore order and discipline and to root out the worst excesses of corruption were proved ineffectual in 1983.[36]

It is difficult, however, to think of regimes and societies in the annals of mankind that dissolved mainly as the result of corruption, no matter how widespread. Of course, the degree of corruption has varied considerably from country to country; standards that were normal in one have been unacceptable in others. In some societies corruption has been the norm rather than the exception and has acted as a social stabilizer, making existence possible in conditions that would have been intolerable otherwise. If there was a problem in the Soviet Union, it was not so much corruption per se as the enormous disparity between the professions of honesty and social justice and the real state of affairs. Third World regimes have not had such pretensions.

To what extent were Soviet citizens familiar with the state of affairs in their homeland prior to *glasnost*? Everyone knew, of course, about his (or her) immediate neighborhood, but could there have been perhaps illusions that elsewhere the situation was different and better? Hardly so. Although Soviet newspapers, radio, and television painted a rosy picture of a society of giant achievements and constant progress and improvement, foreign radio stations had many avid listeners. In 1950 only about 2 percent of Soviet citizens had short-wave radio sets, but about 50 percent had access by 1980 to the broadcasts of Radio Liberty, the BBC, and other foreign stations. The impact of these was considerable, and their role in the downfall in the regime remains to be investigated.

Soviet literature and to a lesser extent the cinema also rendered a far from rosy picture. True, certain subjects such as nepotism and other forms of high-level corruption, were taboo in even the most realistic novels. Lower officials could be depicted as villains, but they were invariably punished in the end of the novel or the play. A novel, to be sure, could not convey a message of near total despondency; this became possible only with the dawn of *glasnost* examples are (Viktor Astafiev's *Sad Detective*, Vasilii Belov's *Everything Is Still Ahead*, and Valentin Rasputin's *Pozhar*). But new themes appeared in the 1960s as the mood turned from optimism to pessimism. This was particularly obvious among the village writers, and it was equally pronounced among those writing about northern Russia (Fyodor Abramov), the eastern regions of European Russia (Belov), Siberia (Rasputin and Astafiev), and Central Asia (Zhingiz Aitmatov). In the beginning there had been a tendency to glorify life in the countryside, or at least the village tradition. Human goodness, respect for the elderly, and diligence all originated in the village, according to the early novels of Rasputin, Belov, and Vladimir Soloukhin. Ten years later, Rasputin's *Pozhar* was a picture, dark on dark, of the moral decay of the villagers. About the dismal state of city life Russians could read in the stories of Makanin and in Yuri Trifonov's last novels. Working-class life found few writers, but those who wrote about it with inside knowledge dealt at great length with the effects of alcoholism, shortages, and crowded housing. Vitaly Syomin, the author of *Seven in One House* (1968), is a typical example. The most famous "alcoholic novel," Erofeyev's *Moskva-Petushki*, was circulated only in clandestine publications (*samizdat*) at the time. Vasily Shukshin, the most gifted of this cohort, wrote movingly about criminals and ex-criminals trying unsuccessfully to rehabilitate themselves, in *Kalina Krasnaya (Red Berry)*, which also became a film. The emptiness of life drove even those who had succeeded in terms of material achievements to drink–and suicide such as in Alexander Vampilov, *Duck Hunting*, 1970.

Party politics in the narrow sense quite apart, there was a striking decline in faith in science and technology. There were frequent references to the destruction of traditional life and the growing imbalances in the relationship between man and nature.[37] There were hints of a coming ecological disaster and a growing sense of impending doom. Another related trend in Soviet literature, almost constantly attacked by the authorities, was "Remarquism," named after the author of the famous World War I novel *All Quiet on the Western Front*. This work expressed an inchoate pacifism–the belief that war was wrong per se–that it was no longer a feasible posture in the nuclear age. These trends were countered by accusations against the politically incorrect as early as 1961, buttressed by continuing Soviet anti-Western propaganda and the constant emphasis on military preparedness, both physical and "spiritual."

These few examples have been singled out more or less at random. Most of Russian literature up to the 1950s was permeated with the pathos of reconstruction, and not just because this was the official party line. In the 1970s, it was difficult to find any writers of significance willing to produce even "optimistic tragedies," despite the countless appeals in official journals for more optimism. The belief in progress had clearly been displaced. It was no longer a question of certain "negative features" of Soviet society. There was a widespread feeling that life had become worse in most respects, that there was spiritual emptiness, crass materialism, growing coldness, and indifference–a far cry indeed from the building of "our new world," which "The *International*" and the songs of the Komsomol had once celebrated.

All those reading Russian literature in the 1960s and 1970s (and many millions did) could not fail to detect that the general mood had changed. Those who did not read were familiar with the songs of the leading bards of the period–Vysotsky, Galich, and Okudzhava–which contained the same message. The cinema was always under stricter control, but there too the waning belief in progress manifested itself all too clearly, as in the film version of Rasputin's *Farewell to Matryona*, the story of the island village that was to give way to progress in the form of a power plant.

Lastly, an issue that could not be openly discussed in the Soviet Union, but of which everyone was aware: poverty. There are poor people in every country, but about Soviet society it could be said with greater justification than about any other developed country: "For ye have the poor always with you," in the words of the New Testament. About a third of the population, perhaps even more, lived below the poverty line according to the minimum budgets and family baskets of Soviet social scientists. The poor included old age pensioners, single women, many peasants, and low-paid occupational groups such as teachers and junior clerical workers.[38]

The issue of poverty was both a social and a political problem, because only in the Soviet Union (and the other Communist countries) was it claimed that the country was growing richer and happier all the time. As the 1940s receded into the past, the explanations for the hardships of the war and immediate postwar period failed to carry conviction. Forty years after 1945, no one believed anymore that the ravages of war were to blame for the shortcomings of the 1980s. Other countries too, had suffered in the war, and their standards of living had risen immeasurably since.

To survey the Soviet standard of living and the quality of life in the 1970s and 1980s is to chart a sea of troubles. But, with regard to the crisis of the 1980s and the collapse of the empire, how relevant was the widespread dismay generated by economic grievances and social complaints? To say that the system was not working well is a gross understatement, but it continued somehow to operate even during the early 1980s. There was enough bread, and virtually everyone had a television set. There was a second economy that provided some of the goods and services the state could not give. Housing conditions in the big cities were dismal, but many had a little dacha or at least a primitive shack somewhere in a forest or near a river; they hunted, went to collect berries and mushrooms, and had a little allotment for growing vegetables. True, the very poorest sections of the population had no such resources and were totally defenseless. Old age pensioners and peasants did not count—there was no danger that there would be an explosion among these groups. There were no demonstrations even after the most dramatic of all ecological disasters, that at Chernobyl. It was taken as if it were an act of God; it seemed as pointless to protest against it as to demonstrate against an earthquake. The so-called unwritten social contract, frequently invoked by some Western observers, could not be seen with the naked eye. In any case, the *nomenklatura* was still well provided for, and a sizable part of the population below that level also received small special allocations that made life a little more tolerable. It is impossible to estimate how many were thus provided for, but together with their families they counted several million.

In such a system, there could be no effective protest from below. The Russian people were (much suffering) *mnogostradalnyi*—they had always suffered. They probably no longer believed in the official indoctrination that told them they were well off and there was steady improvement. This loss of faith did not necessarily lead to political action, however. It only made political mobilization of the masses more difficult in the face of long-term demoralization and widespread alcoholism, which also blunted mass protest.

Although the regime had lost its dynamism and could no longer generate enthusiasm, it was not wholly discredited. Corruption and graft, now rampant, had always existed in Russia–and even more in Central Asia.[39] But this did not lead to a tidal wave of moral indignation; Brezh--nev's "live-and-let-live" policy had many supporters. There was no irresistible groundswell, no sentiment that "We cannot go on living like this", and no growing demand for economic and social–let alone political–reform. On the contrary, as events under Gorbachev were to show, the prospect of reform aroused suspicion and fear. It was widely believed that while the system did not work well, it was perhaps the only one suitable to Russian conditions. No democratic party was willing to go on the barricades to fight for political reform.

The few opposing voices in the wilderness had been almost wholly silenced by 1985; some were in camps or exile and others had emigrated or defected. Those exiled included, to give but one example, a substantial number of the leading Soviet musical performers. Second raters soon took their places, however; for a twentieth-century dictatorship, the exodus of leading writers (as in the case of East Germany) or musicians was not a mortal threat.

Among the intelligentsia pessimism was growing. It found expression in demands to save the Siberian lakes, rivers, and forests, and in heart-to-heart conversations around the kitchen table in Moscow apartments, as well as bitter jokes among all echelons of the party and state apparatus, who were the most informed about conditions. They listened to foreign radio stations, and some of them had visited abroad and shared their impressions with family and friends. But pessimism did not inspire revolutionary ferment. Most believed the system was so strong that it would never essentially change. Others, more optimistic, thought that change was perhaps possible over a long period–decades, or more likely, generations.

V

Had the limits of Soviet power not been shown in the 1970s and 1980s? There were serious setbacks: The East European empire was a shambles. Romania and Yugoslavia more or less did what they wanted. The Polish situation was highly unstable; but for the imposition of a military dictatorship the regime would have collapsed. Hungary had pursued a slow course of reform that was followed with misgivings in Moscow. The East Germans trumpeted their conviction that they knew much better than the Soviets how to build Communism. Russia was unpopular in Eastern Europe, and every Russian knew it. There was the suspicion that sooner or later Moscow would again have to intervene as in Hungary and Czechoslovakia to restore order–but how long would order last?

The war in Afghanistan did not go well; how was it possible that a small and backward country could resist the military might of the most powerful nation in the world? Back in the 1950s and early 1960s, it was believed that key Third World countries would gradually move toward "socialism," or at least become countries of "socialist orientation." But Nasser, Nkrumah, and Sukarno had disappeared from the scene, and their successors showed no interest in proselytizing for Communism. Third World countries were only too willing to accept Soviet economic assistance and above all arms, but political gains were not impressive. Egypt had ordered Soviet personnel out of the country, and there were similar cases of ingratitude in other parts of the world.

Inside Russia the help given to Asia and Africa was unpopular, as were the nationals of these countries who came to the Soviet Union. Nevertheless, no one but a few dissidents argued that the Soviet empire had overreached itself. The war in Afghanistan was certainly not popular, but the official propaganda, claiming that Soviet borders had to be defended against world imperialism in Kabul and Herat, still found many believers. The costs of the war were considered tolerable; 15,000 soldiers were killed over a period of ten years, fewer than the number killed in one hour in the battle of Kursk in 1943. The financial burden was a major irritant but not crushing.

Generally speaking, the cost of empire, including trade subsidies and economic and military aid, was not overwhelming. Although the burden had risen sharply between 1970 and 1980, when it reached about $44 billion, it declined to $28 billion in 1983 – 4 percent of the Soviet ruble GNP and 1.6 percent of the dollar GNP.[40] The benefits of empire were military bases and the import of certain goods and raw materials otherwise obtainable only for hard currency. (The hard-currency income of the Soviet Union sharply declined in the 1980s as the result of the fall in the price of oil.) Above all, the existence of the empire provided something that could not be quantified in monetary terms – the feeling that the Soviet Union, once a backward country, had become a superpower. This power was a source of pride and demonstrated that the future belonged to Moscow, whereas capitalist imperialism was inexorably doomed.

This is not to underestimate the various external crises facing the Soviet Union, but Soviet leaders were persuaded that the West was facing infinitely graver difficulties. Even a staunch anti-Communist such as Solzhenitsyn was firmly convinced that the final defeat of the West was only a question of time. The United States was suffering from the political consequences of the Vietnam War, neutralism was rampant in Europe, and resistance to NATO and its strategy was rising. In some European countries such as Italy there was even a chance in the 1970s that Communism (albeit its Euro-Communism variant) would come to power. The decade after 1973 was bad for the Western economies. The great postwar prosperity, it seemed, had come to an end: perhaps the great depression of the capitalist system was at long last at hand.

We do not know as yet what Soviet ambassadors and KGB residents stationed in the West reported to their bosses, but there is every reason to assume that their dispatches did not cause sleepless nights to the occupants of the Kremlin: the West appeared to be in disarray. If the assessment of the situation in the West changed, if it was realized that the West was not about to collapse, the shift came only gradually. As it happened, the improvement of the situation in the West coincided with growing signs of weakness in the Soviet Union. The Soviet eclipse had been caused, at least in part, by the armament race, which, as argued earlier, could have been prevented by a more conciliatory policy. By needlessly provoking the West, the Soviet Union triggered a competition it could not win.

A few Western economists have maintained that Soviet rates of investment peaked at 32 to 33 percent at the very same time–the late 1980s–that military spending peaked.[41] But this argument ignores the fact that most of the investment went to heavy industry, to the "military-industrial complex" rather than the military alone. Thus the investment rate per se is not very meaningful in the context of our argument.

Looking back on the history of the Cold War and its results, the views of Valentin Falin are of considerable interest. Falin was for many years Soviet ambassador to Germany and later head of the Department of Foreign Relations of the Central Committee of the CPSU. In an interview with the German weekly *Die Zeit*, he was asked whether he thought that Reagan had been right (from the Western standpoint) when he forced the Soviet Union to arm itself to death, Falin replied that it was not really Reagan who had started this policy; it had been general U.S. policy since 1945. The interviewer asked whether this meant that this had been the correct policy to follow and that "all of us who favored détente had been mistaken?" Falin replied: "Détente would never have resulted in the tearing down of the Iron Curtain."[42] Other leading Soviet officials, as will be shown further on, shared this opinion.

Such views are not acceptable to some of the old school (such as Georgii Arbatov) and also not to some Western commentators of the revisionist persuasion. Perhaps events were more complicated than Falin saw them in retrospect. No Western leader expected at the time that the Soviet Union would collapse as the result of an arms race. The arms race was regarded in Western capitals as a highly undesirable necessity rather than a deliberate strategy that would have dramatic results. And it is also true that the arms race was only one of the causes of the great Soviet crisis and eventual downfall–and for all one knows not the most important single factor. But the burden of proof is now on the revisionists, who will have to think of new arguments to replace the old one: that the arms race was from the Western point of view an unmitigated disaster that would in no way affect Soviet policy–except perhaps in an undesirable way.

According to the evidence now known, Western "toughness" in foreign policy in the 1970s and 1980s did play a role in the Soviet breakdown. Seen in retrospect, Sakharov's message to the West (in connection with the U.S. deployment of the MX missile) saying that an arms race could prevent nuclear war, shocking as it appeared to many in the West at the time, was perhaps not that farfetched. The Soviet leadership found it increasingly difficult and ultimately impossible to shift more of its limited resources to the military.[43] Internal forces were, in all probability, more decisive in bringing about the demise of the Soviet Union, but foreign political pressures also played a role.

VI

In 1924, a short time after Lenin's death, Grigorii Zinoviev, one of Lenin's closest aides, declared that the national question had been solved, and all that was needed in the future was giving attention to details.[44] This remained the official party line; almost fifty years later Brezhnev announced, "We have fully solved the national question."[45] When the storm broke in the late 1980s Politburo member Alexander Yakovlev conceded that it "did happen rather suddenly."[46]

There had been warning signs, such as protests of various kinds, well before, especially in Georgia and Abkhazia. A slow but steady exodus of ethnic Russians from Central Asia began about 1970. The Russian exodus from the Caucasian republics had been under way since the late 1950s. At the same time, the proportion of non-Russians in the Communist parties of the republics declined, above all in Central Asia and the Baltic. In 1973 Roy Medvedev, the semi-licensed dissident, wrote about the exacerbation of tensions among nationalities, but when Andropov became secretary general, he claimed in a speech that national consciousness among Russians and non-Russians was growing in the same measure as economic and cultural progress. (He did concede that national differences would continue to exist much longer than class differences.) In many instances Communist leaders in the republics put great emphasis on local concerns, even when these collided with the interests of other republics or the center. The native intelligentsia was in the forefront of cultural nationalism with its interest in language, literature, and film. There was a modest religious revival, and on the popular level old customs persisted or were revived, particularly in Central Asia.

Both central and local authorities tried to foster assimilation. The integration of non-Russian soldiers in the army proved to be difficult and there were fewer mixed marriages than earlier on, except among Slavs. There was a palpable decline in the publication of books and periodicals in non-Russian languages; for instance, 80 percent of all books published in Uzbekistan were in Russian. But this policy provoked a sharp reaction in favor of native languages, most strikingly perhaps in Georgia and the Baltic countries. While some of the smaller nationalities were assimilated, the larger ones became more assertive during the 1960s and 1970s. One aspect of the situation could not be discussed in public, namely demographic trends. The birthrate in the Central Asian republics was far higher than in the Slavic republics, and according to various predictions the

Soviet Union would be one-quarter (or even one-third) Muslim by the year 2000.[47] Furthermore, since the late 1970s the Tartars had repeatedly demanded to return to the Crimea, and many Jews applied for emigration.

Still there was no acute crisis endangering the very existence of the empire. The nationality problems were perceived by the leaders in the Kremlin as mainly economic – conflicts about the division of resources and of labor, problems that could be fixed with a minimum of good will. The issue of historical memory as one of the mainsprings of nationalism was almost entirely ignored.

How important was historical memory as a factor in politics in contradistinction to culture? In contrast to other empires, the Soviet Union beginning with *Korenisatsia* (nativization) in the 1930s had produced a local indigenous leadership that could be trusted, because it had a vested interest in the existing system. In fact, according to many party leaders (including Andropov) nativization had perhaps gone too far. The non-Russian republics were traditionally represented in all the party and state organs, including the very highest.

Traditionally, there had not been very much anti-Russian opposition throughout the history of the Russian empire, except in the case of the Poles, who had left the empire in 1917. Custine, the famous French visitor, had written early in the nineteenth century that Russia was "a prison of the peoples" – and Lenin among others had repeated it after him. But as imperial prisons go, Russia was one of the more comfortable ones. Most of the Russian empire had come into being not so much by military conquest as by migration and settlement (in Siberia and Northern Turkestan), or by diplomatic treaty, as in the case of the Ukraine and Georgia (the treaty between Irakli II of Kakhetia and Catherine II in 1783). Armenia had opted for Russia as a protector against Turkey. It has been argued that the Union of Pereyaslav (1654) was concluded behind the back of the Ukrainian people. But there was no significant Ukrainian resistance until nearly three centuries thereafter. There were differences between Russians and Ukrainians, and a well-informed British visitor wrote that the differences between the two were greater than those between the English and the Scottish.[48] But the town population, including the middle class and intellectuals, were largely assimilated. If there was a historical enemy, it was Poland, not Russia.

The tsarist establishment was quite effectively integrating the elite of the territories it had acquired. There were generals and prime ministers of Georgian and Armenian extraction. Baltic Germans had leading positions in government, the diplomatic service, and the upper reaches of the administration. The Russian government wanted social, economic, and political uniformity, but "it did not aim at eradicating or destroying nations and nationalities."[49] There were exceptions – Russian policy toward Jews in the nineteenth century, sporadic bursts of Russification, and suspicion and enmity toward Poland. By and large, however, the Russian empire was free from deep racial prejudice. The Russian aristocracy was in the majority non-Russian in origin, and there was a great deal of mixing on the lower levels of society.

Nationalist strife existed prior to the revolution of 1917, but not much in comparison with other empires; and it manifested itself as much in the struggle of the nationalities against each other (for example, Sunnis against Shiites in Turkestan) as in hostile acts against Russia. The revolution of 1905 brought an upsurge in nationalist revival and political organization in the non-Russian regions in the empire, but it was modest in scope. In brief, with the exception of Poland and Finland, separatism was not on the historical agenda.

In 1917 the Bolsheviks inherited a multiethnic empire, and in contrast to their tsarist predecessors they were willing to admit this much. In practice, Russians and non-Russians alike (Stalin, the Georgian, was an outstanding example) were strict centralists like the Jacobins before them: it was clearly a blessing for the smaller or less developed republics to have made the transition to "socialism" in conjunction with the older Russian brother. Paternalism was combined with a policy of economic and social development, and, quite frequently, positive discrimination. The regime fostered insensitivity to local beliefs and customs, made grievous mistakes in economic policy (above all, in Central Asia), and, of course, imposed as much political repression as in Russia proper. The Balts and the western Ukrainians were incorporated against their will in 1939 and 1940. By and large, however, it cannot be argued that the non-Russian territories were treated much worse than the Russian Republic itself. There were incipient tensions: As Russian nationalism was fostered from the late 1930s on, how could similar trends be suppressed in the long run among the non-Russians?

But the Soviet Union in the 1970s and 1980s was still not a seething cauldron about to boil over, a country on the eve of a major explosion held together only by KGB terror. No one thought at the time that the union would fall apart in the near future. Non-Russian nationalists were fighting for greater autonomy, not total separation, which seemed unattainable – perhaps not even desirable. Divisive trends threatened in a long – term perspective, but there seemed to be no immediate prospect of a total breakdown.

And yet, it was precisely this issue that proved to be the Achilles' heel of the Soviet Union. As the Moscow leadership loosened the reins, separatist processes were triggered in the non-Russian republics over which they had little control. Even at this stage, however, the total disintegration of the union was not a foregone conclusion; there were other possibilities, federative and confederative solutions. What brought about the total breakdown in such a short time remains to be studied in detail.

VII

Perhaps there was, as some observers have argued, not one big crisis but several small crises feeding on one another and aggravating the general

situation. Perhaps there was (to use a fashionable term) a negatively syner-
gistic crisis. (Kant is said to have observed that some physicians think they
are doing a great deal for the patient if they give a name to his disease.) This
view is shared by Alexander Dallin, who has argued that it was the
interaction between various negative trends that was critical for the survival of the regime. Had the control structure not loosened up, much of the
articulation of grievances could not have occurred.[50] This observation is
certainly correct as far as it goes, but then no great crisis in history can be
traced to a single cause. Military defeats were usually accompanied by
economic setbacks or shortages, and few cases are reported of a mood of joy
and exuberance at a time of economic disaster. That for a long time
negative trends were observed in many areas of Soviet life is beyond
dispute.[51] But the same is true for many societies in many ages. Was there a
feeling of despair and doom in the air in the Soviet Union in the 1980s, of
having reached the end of the line and of finding no solutions within
reach? It is a long way from disillusionment to the conviction that the
apocalypse is at hand.

As one reviews the various components of the unfolding Soviet crisis of
the late 1980s, it appears quite clearly that some were far more important
than others. While the economy was working badly, the country could
probably have muddled through for years, without an acute political crisis.
The quality of life in the Soviet Union was bad and deteriorating, but there
was no public outcry against conditions perceived as intolerable. Setbacks
in the foreign political field were bothersome but not fatal: Moscow could
have cut its losses in Afghanistan without the empire unraveling. Eastern
Europe was not in a state of revolt; there was still the fear that the Soviet
army would put down any serious challenge without much difficulty. The
dissidents were few and isolated—their message did not reach the masses.

In brief, the Soviet regime in 1987 seemed infinitely stronger than
tsarist Russia in 1916 or the Ottoman Empire in early 1918 after years of
defeats and huge losses. If so, was the Soviet regime perhaps much weaker
than perceived by foes and supporters alike? This is not very likely,
because the levers of power were firmly in the hands of the rulers—the
KGB, the army, and the various sections of the party. These organs of
political and social control obeyed orders; no single case of insubordina-
tion is recorded—apart perhaps from the abortive escape of a submarine in
the Baltic. Nationalist dissent was growing in various parts of the union,
but it was not yet massive and had not reached an acute stage. The security organs would have put down local separatist agitation and activities
quickly and effectively had they been given orders. An attempt at coordinated action against the center by non-Russian nationalities was unlikely
as long as an effective dictatorship remained at the center.

All this makes the sudden collapse difficult to explain even in retrospect. Why did the huge edifice collapse without even having been seriously challenged? Obviously, there must have been a crisis, but it was not of
the kind that can be quantified, such as economic targets not reached or

casualties incurred in war. It was a crisis of self-confidence, or to use the term so often used in Russia, a "spiritual crisis." Russia in the 1980s could be compared to an athlete who was muscular and well trained but not strong in heart. The origins of the crisis date back to the early days of the regime. At the bottom of it was the growing discrepancy between promise and performance. No amount of propaganda could in the long run bridge this abyss: the sacrifices that had gone into the "Soviet experiment" had been enormous, and the results were poor. The fact that Russia had become a superpower, in some military respects perhaps the strongest power on earth, helped to fortify the position of the regime, but only up to a point: If Russia was so strong, why was life so miserable?

The origins of the acute crisis of self-confidence date back, as has been argued earlier on, to the late 1960s, and by the 1970s the crisis was noticed by astute Western observers.[52] John Bushnell, an American student of Soviet affairs who spent several years in Moscow, had reached the conclusion that the Soviet middle class became increasingly optimistic about the performance of the Soviet system and its own prospects in the 1960s, but in the 1970s this gave way to pessimism. In his view, the crucial determinant was the changing perception of Soviet economic performance – that is, by consumer grievances. However, elsewhere the author notes that optimism had persisted in the 1960s despite economic difficulties. Therefore, one ought to look beyond real economic performance to explain the changes in the mood. On the whole, the standard of living rose, but expectations had risen even more. Soviet citizens were learning more about living conditions abroad; if there was hardly any tourism to Western Europe, hundreds of thousands went to East Germany, Czechoslovakia, and Bulgaria. Hence it followed that "it is extremely unlikely that the present extreme pessimism can be entirely explained by factors internal to the Soviet system."[53]

Pessimism affected above all the Soviet middle class, but the mood pervaded, to a greater or lesser extent, all classes, including the middle and even high echelons of the party. During the 1970s and early 1980s, as the leadership grew older and even less enterprising, the feeling of drift and stagnation became more pronounced, and the belief in the need for reform even more common. Differences in the assessment of the situation between Yury Andropov and some leading dissenters were not enormous. The decisive difference was that Andropov opposed even modest political reform because it would, in his view, have been tantamount to opening Pandora's box. Among the party leadership, just below the level of the gerontocrats, open discussion about the dismal state of affairs was quite common.

Most Western observers, including the experts among them, overrated the depth of ideological belief inside the Soviet Union. Quite possibly, there were more believers in Marxism in Western academic institutions than in the whole of the Soviet Union. Even among staunch supporters of the regime, Communist doctrine as a source of belief had been replaced by patriotism, or the assumption that the present state of affairs, even if unsatisfactory, was preferable to others they could envisage. Or they were motivated by self-interest. For there were millions who had a vested interest in the survival of a regime, which had bestowed on them social status, power (even if only the power of a minor bureaucrat), and material privileges, which they would not have had otherwise. Very few Soviet citizens believed in all of Soviet ideology; even fewer rejected all of it. Propaganda was all-pervasive, and isolation from the rest of the world was still quite effective. The prevailing attitude was not anti-Communism but indifference—even as the crisis deepened.

The growing pessimistic mood must have been a cause of concern to the rulers, if they were aware of it. But pessimistic moods, however prolonged and intense, do not by necessity lead to fundamental political change. There have been such periods in the history of all nations, in Russian history perhaps more often and longer lasting than elsewhere. It has been said that the Russian intelligentsia was nearly always pessimistic. French society, during the last quarter of the nineteenth century was deeply pessimistic. A legion of Cassandras published books in which they predicted the imminent demise of the French state.[54] Yet during the first decade of the twentieth century the mood changed quite suddenly, even though the "objective reasons" that had been adduced to explain French decline had not changed.

The presence of a pessimistic mood is of great symptomatic interest, but moods tend to change as the result of generational change and for other reasons. The importance of the growth of nationalist dissent has been stressed earlier on, but this too, refers more to some republics than to others. The Soviet regime never succeeded in stamping out Baltic nationalism (and anti-Sovietism and opposition to all things Russian). The same is true with regard to the western Ukraine and Moldavia.[55] To a certain extent, it might have been true with regard to the Caucasus, but anti-Russianism was less rampant there, and the concept of a federative solution based on choice rather than coercion was by no means unrealistic. It is far more difficult to explain the defection of the Ukraine, the most important republic after Russia. In 1991 Ukrainians voted overwhelmingly in favor of full statehood and separation, but less than a year earlier, some 70 percent of them had given their vote for the maintenance of the union in elections that were reasonably free. Since it is unlikely that Ukrainian nationalism grew such deep roots in such a short time, the reasons must be looked for on a different level. There was the belief that statehood opened up opportunities (and careers)—economic, political, and social—that had not existed before. Membership in a club such as the Soviet Union (or the Russian empire) had involved certain benefits, and in any case membership was mandatory. Once the club fell on evil times and membership became optional, belonging to the club was no longer prestigious or advantageous. At a time when full sovereignty became fashionable, no one wanted to be left out, and this led to total disintegration.

Deeply felt national (often anti-Russian) or religious convictions did play a certain role in some parts of the former Soviet Union, but in the case of Ukraine and Byelorussia they were almost certainly not the decisive factor, always with the exception of Ukraine's far west. Decisive in the final analysis was the belief by Gorbachev and some like-minded advisers that political reform was possible while maintaining more or less the old Soviet framework. It was, as one of them later put it a "romantic belief."[56]

What had induced Gorbachev and his supporters to become ardent believers in reform and also to assume that it would be possible to control this process? Long after he had been ousted from power, Gorbachev was asked by an interviewer whether he had become a reformer after meeting Western leaders and realizing that they had no intention of attacking the Soviet Union. Gorbachev replied that much earlier, when he had been district party secretary in Stavropol, he had familiarized himself with the writings of Western political thinkers and commentators.[57] He was referring to certain Western studies on the Soviet Union and other subjects translated into Russian in editions of 200 to 400 copies, "for official use only," and made available to members of the Central Committee and a few other leading figures.[58] It would be flattering to think that Western political books critical of the Communist system played a role comparable to the impact of the literature of the enlightenment or German philosophy in earlier periods of Russian intellectual history, but such a comparison would be grossly exaggerated. What could Gorbachev and his comrades learn from Western authors that they did not know from their own observations? Although Brezhnev and Gromyko were cut off from the realities of Soviet life, the younger leaders, having risen recently from the ranks, were less out of touch.

For two generations, historians have speculated whether the Bolshevik revolution of 1917 was inevitable or whether there could have been another outcome.[59] It is the old debate between believers in contingency and accident, on the one hand, and those seeing inevitability, on the other. Most of those living through the last years of tsarist rule thought that given a period of quiet economic and political development, the country would be safe. They included liberals such as Chaim Zhidlovsky and Ivan Petrunkevich and conservatives such as Stolypin. Estimates as to the time needed varied between ten years and one or two generations. In fact, the Bolsheviks, including Lenin, right up to March 1917, were far from optimistic with regard to the likelihood of a successful revolution.

Shall we witness another revisionist debate in the years to come on the causes of the downfall of the empire? The events of 1991 were not a revolution but a case of disintegration. There was no political party challenging the regime, only a group of overoptimistic reformers. But the regime was its own worst enemy. It was moving nowhere. Unlike the last decade of tsarism, the 1980s produced no economic development–only stagnation and decline. Some change had become imperative. But was change possible?

Both historical trends and the action of individuals played a role in the downfall of the Soviet empire. The role of accident was as great in the birth of the Soviet system (the presence of Lenin) as in its demise (the presence of Gorbachev). The Soviet system was, to put it mildly, not very effective in making good its promises, and for this reason, it was doomed in the long run. But how long is the long run? It could still have survived for years, perhaps for many years. Could it have gradually transformed itself in some unfathomable ways? One hesitates to dismiss the possibility altogether; it seems unlikely but it may not have been impossible. The Communist party was destroyed in 1991, Martin Malia writes, and a superpower dismembered, socialism renounced in favor of the restoration of capitalism, and the most enduring fantasy of the twentieth century, the pseudoreligion cum pseudoscience of Marxism-Leninism, simply evaporated: "Nor could any of these things have occurred as a gradual process". Marxism-Leninism, to be sure, no longer exists, but the destruction of the Communist party was less than complete. The present social and economic system in Russia (let alone the Ukraine and White Russia) can hardly be defined as the restoration of capitalism. And events in China seem to indicate that a gradual process is taking place even though it cannot be said how far it will go and its ultimate prospects cannot be predicted.[60]

Seen in this light the breakdown of the Communist order and the Soviet empire at a specific time (1991) was possible only because of certain historical accidents. Although most observers in West and East failed even to consider the possibility of a debacle, they can claim, to a certain extent, mitigating circumstances; for accidents are, of course, unpredictable. They should have realized however (which they did not) that the continued existence of this enormous enterprise depended to a considerable extent not on historical inevitability, not even on the probable outcome of "objective trends," but on accidents.[61]

Mention has been made of Pandora, the beautiful woman of Greek mythology who had all the gifts of the gods. She had been created by Zeus to punish mankind. She went down to earth and married Epimetheus, who had been warned by his brother Prometheus, more clever and devious than he, that he was never, under any circumstances to accept a gift from the gods. Epimetheus forgot the warning, Pandora opened the lid of the box, and out fluttered the host of calamities—misery in countless forms filled the air and the sea.

The analogy is, of course, far from complete. What if the tension inside the box had become so great as to make an explosion inevitable sooner or later? What if Pandora had quickly closed the lid, realizing the havoc she had wrought? (The mythological Pandora did in fact shut the box, but at the wrong time, letting out all the evil and leaving inside one good thing that lay hidden at the very bottom—hope.)

Why look for "superficial" explanations for the collapse, some argue, if the very experiment was doomed from the very beginning because it was based on false premises? This refers to the belief that it was both desirable and possible to change human nature and institutions radically through the imposition of new patterns by force and that this would result in a more humane society, in a new world of freedom, justice, and the pursuit of happiness. This belief did indeed exist, and it had disastrous consequences. But it does not explain why a retreat from a false and untenable position did not take place earlier. If in a totalitarian regime the ruled could not do much to resist, there was still the chance that the rulers would moderate their aims and policies. Such a retreat would have been painful, but it does not follow that it would have been impossible and that a disaster of such magnitude was foreordained.

Far-fetched conclusions should not be drawn from the collapse with regard to the intellectual parentage of Communism. It makes little sense to blame the poor, ineffectual Second International for Lenin and Stalin as Malia has done, nor should one put the responsibility on the Enlightenment (Richard Pipes), with its idea that "man was merely a material product, devoid of either soul or innate ideas." This was the belief of La Mettrie but not of Locke and Hume or Kant and the French *philosophes*. Nietzsche has been made responsible for Eichmann and (with a little more justice) Mazzini for Mussolini.

But such exercises hardly add to our understanding of either fascism or Communism. Marxism was, of course, somehow in the tradition of the Enlightenment. By the time this tradition reached Lenin and Stalin, the kinship was so tenuous as to be virtually meaningless except on the level of slogans. Voltaire as the intellectual godfather of Stalin does not make sense. Lenin's and Stalin's belief that man is not born to be free (at least not yet) had more in common with the philosophers of the counter-Enlightenment, such as Le Maistre, than the apostles of freedom. In addition, the Soviet experience has not shown that all planned social and economic change is a priori bad and bound to lead to catastrophe. If it were true that what cannot be comprehended cannot be controlled,[62] much of modern medicine would have to go out of business; it knows that certain drugs are effective without necessarily knowing why.

In the real world, as distinct from the level of abstraction, there is a large gray zone of phenomena neither fully understood nor wholly mysterious, and it is with these that politicians and the rest of mankind have to deal. There was a saying in Roman legal doctrine that extreme cases make for bad legislation. The Soviet experience certainly was an extreme case, and it provides many insights and lessons. But it is still dangerous ground for sweeping generalization about the human condition in general.

4

Totalitarianism

Was the Soviet Union just another dictatorship or a tyranny of a new and special kind? For a long time politicians and the media have used the term "totalitarianism" indiscriminately, and no issue has been more contentious among political scientists, some of whom developed a violent aversion against the totalitarian label both with regard to Communism and also in connection with Germany. The demise of the Soviet Union is shedding some new light on the issues involved.

Why should a semantical dispute generate such emotions? When Carolus Linnaeus developed his principles for defining genera and species of organisms, when Dimitri Mendeleyev developed the periodic classification of elements, perhaps some colleagues doubted, but there were no violent protests.[1] Classification schemes in the natural sciences ("biosystematics" or "taxonomy" in the biological sciences) rest on other criteria, however, and serve other purposes than the search for common features in the social sciences and history. Historians and political scientists could not aspire to discover true scientific laws; there are no DNA sequences at their disposal. It was precisely for this reason, given so much uncertainty, that the disputes were so prolonged and bitter. Historians and social scientists wanted to be more than mere chroniclers of events; they were looking for causes, patterns, and probabilities to make some sense of past events. This "quest for theory" gave rise to fruitful debate, but it also led to many unnecessary and sterile exchanges recalling medieval scholastic disputations. Looking back on several decades of interpreting the fascist and Communist regimes, it often appears that these interpretations shed less light on the mainsprings and the character of the systems they investigate than on the zeitgeist of the 1960s and the 1970s and the views and the motives of the interpreters.

Unlike some other contemporary controversies, the debate over totalitarianism has not been a purely academic enterprise. In part it is about words, categories, and definitions, but mainly it concerns political realities, and it is (or was) of considerable practical importance.[2] Behind the seemingly semantic hairsplitting were some key issues facing Western policy, in particular with regard to the Soviet bloc, but also, to some extent, the Third World.

It is widely believed that totalitarianism as a concept was invented in the 1940s and 1950s by Western cold warriors trying to prove that there was no choice between Hitler and Stalin. But in fact the term (first as an adjective, later as a noun) goes back to the early 1920s, when it was first used by Italian antifascists (G. Amendola) and later picked up by Mussolini, who wrote a famous article on the subject. While the Italians "invented" totalitarianism as a theoretical concept, their practical contribution was quite modest; of all the great dictatorships of our time, Italian fascism was the least totalitarian.

The concept was taken up and elaborated by social scientists, mostly émigrés from Nazi Germany. It was also used on many occasions by left-wing writers like Victor Serge and by Marxist theorists like Trotsky, Otto Bauer, and Rudolf Hilferding.

The term "totalitarianism" appeared in English first in 1928, the year after it was first used to describe both the Italian fascist and the Bolshevik regimes.[3]

The Mensheviks in exile used the term in 1933 to characterize the use of force, the étatization of all areas of life, and the destruction of all opposition. Marxists were preoccupied throughout the 1920s and 1930s with defining the character of the Soviet state: Was Bolshevism, despite the political repression, a bearer of progress, a revolutionary force that had constructed the essential elements of a socialist order, as Otto Bauer and Fyodor Dan thought? The term "welfare dictatorship" also first appeared in this context, the assumption being that once "socialism" had been built, freedom and democracy would somehow follow. In these debates the contribution of Rudolf Hilferding was of great importance. An Austrian Social Democrat, he was considered the greatest Marxist alive; Lenin's writings on economics were to a considerable extent derived from Hilferding. After grappling with the issue for years, Hilferding reached the conclusion that one had to cut the Gordian knot of Marxist scholasticism to reach a realistic appraisal of the Soviet Union. In a famous article, published in 1940 a few weeks before the fall of France (and frequently reprinted since) he wrote:

> [T]he controversy as to whether the economic system of the Soviet Union is "capitalist" or "socialist" seems to me rather pointless. It is neither. It represents a totalitarian state economy, i.e., a system to which the economies of Germany and Italy are drawing closer and closer.[4]

Some writers of the left argued that while dictatorships and tyrannies were as old as the hills, there was a qualitative difference between previous despotisms and the dictatorships that emerged after World War I. To put the difference negatively, old-fashioned, traditional dictatorship had not used propaganda and other means of social control (including terror) to anything like the same extent as did the modern ones. They had not tried to mobilize the masses. Ideology played a far smaller role in their self-perception. There was no monopolistic state party; and while in a "traditional" dictatorship the legal order was always affected to some degree, it was never disregarded as completely as it was in a totalitarian regime.

Finally, if one wished to be crude about it, one could argue that any regime that attracted 99 percent of the votes in an election was by definition totalitarian. An old-fashioned dictatorship would have been unlikely to feel the need to gain such pseudo-legitimacy, but if it had so desired, it would have been unable to induce virtually everyone to vote, bringing about such a result by fraud or pressure. This definition of totalitarianism may be regarded as simplistic. But it is probably as good as, if not better than, the more complicated ones that developed in more recent decades.

Two works that appeared soon after World War II helped to popularize the idea of totalitarianism—Hannah Arendt's *The Origins of Totalitarianism* (1951) and, more influential, Carl Friedrich's and Zbigniew Brzezinski's *Totalitarian Dictatorship and Autocracy* (1957).[5] Both drew attention to the correspondence between Nazi Germany and Communist Russia. Arendt stated that they were two "essentially identical" systems; and Friedrich and Brzezinski claimed that they were "basically alike." Arendt's book was a success mainly among literary figures but also the public at large, in view of its literary merits and the boldness and innovative character of her ideas. Historians and political scientists found much to criticize both in her facts and her impressionistic and arbitrary approach. In any case, a few years later Arendt dissociated herself from some of her ideas and came to believe that the age of totalitarianism had ended with the Budapest uprising in 1956.

Friedrich and Brzezinski proceeded more systematically and on the basis of greater knowledge of both the Third Reich and Soviet history. Friedrich propounded six typical features for totalitarian systems: a "totalist ideology," a single state party usually led by one man, a fully developed secret police, and three kinds of monopoly covering mass communications, operational weapons, and a centrally planned economy. This model was subsequently modified and refined by various authors.[6]

Juan Linz has stressed three characteristics. The first feature is a monistic center of power. The second is an exclusive, autonomous, and more or less intellectually elaborate ideology. This ideology goes beyond a particular program or definition of the boundaries of legitimate political action to provide some ultimate meaning, sense of historical purpose, and interpretation of social reality. The third is the mobilization for citizen participation in political and collective social tasks channeled through a single party and many monopolistic secondary groups. Passive obedience and apathy, characteristic of many authoritarian regimes, are considered undesirable by the rulers.[7]

Early totalitarianism models were not wholly validated by the subsequent course of events: in particular the claims that totalitarianism was an end in itself, that a totalitarian system was bound to become more totalitarian (and monolithic) all the time, and that an omnipotent leader was a precondition for totalitarian rule. Friedrich and Brzezinski modified their views, conceding ten years after the first edition of their book that Hitler and Stalin represented not the norm but the extreme instances of totalitarianism, and that too much significance had been attributed to certain personal (and therefore transient) features of their regimes that were not necessarily intrinsic elements of totalitarian rule.

Much of the work done in the West in the 1950s and 1960s on Nazi Germany and Soviet affairs was influenced by the totalitarian model. In retrospect this was explained with reference to the Cold War and the resulting tendency to equate Nazism and Communism. However, those specializing in Soviet affairs were perfectly aware of the negative features of the Communist system without constant reference to the Nazi regime. If wide use was made of the totalitarian model, it was mainly because it seemed to correspond closely to reality: Who could deny in good conscience that important features were common to fascist and Communist rule? One could argue that the differences were quantitative rather than qualitative (more terror, more propaganda, and so on); but then, paraphrasing Marx, it could be answered that at a certain stage quantity became a new quality.

It could also be claimed that the totalitarian model tended to neglect economic and social factors, concentrating instead on doctrine, personalities, and various such factors. In other words, it focused on outside features, ignoring the "essence" of these regimes, which was quite different: Nazi Germany and fascist Italy were capitalist, whereas the Soviet Union was not. Seen in this light, it could be argued (as the Communists did for a long time) that the United States and Nazi Germany were birds of a feather, for there were similarities between Roosevelt's New Deal and Hitler's economic policy. It was a manifestly absurd thesis based on the mistaken assumption that the organization of the economy was all important. What made fascism unique was not its command economy, but ideology, propaganda, terror, and aggression. Ignoring the obvious was bound to lead to a lopsided assessment of a whole period in history.

The totalitarian model was seriously challenged in the late 1960s, for a variety of reasons. The political and intellectual climate had greatly changed. University campuses were in an uproar, large sections of the intelligentsia were up in arms because of Vietnam, and there was a concomitant revival of Marxism and other radical doctrines.

Thus more and more voices claimed that the totalitarianism concept wrongly concentrated on techniques, ignoring the fundamental differences between Communism and fascism. How could one compare the humanist goals of Marxism-Leninism such as freedom and social justice with barbaric Nazism? The Soviet regime, furthermore, had considerable economic and social achievements to its credit. The fact that performance still fell short of the claims made for the regime might be accounted for by transient distortions that would disappear in the course of time. Fascism, in contrast, was intrinsically evil, immune to change for the better either through evolution or reform. If useful at all in understanding dictatorial regimes, the totalitarianism concept might be applied to Nazism but not to Communism.[8]

The indignation about equating fascism and Communism was largely misplaced, because few serious students of totalitarianism had ever done this, and if so, for a short time only. All they had claimed was that there were important features common to the two societies, such as a single state party. The analogies could not possibly be dismissed, however; at most it could be argued that the common features were extraneous and accidental. Or one could claim that there had been basic changes in the Communist world between 1953 and 1970: Stalinism had been replaced by something more difficult to analyze and define.[9] The mass purges had ceased, the population of the gulag was greatly reduced, and the worldwide Communist monolith was splitting apart. These and other developments seemed to show that Communist totalitarianism had either passed from this world or had never existed.

And so the burial rites were held. One critic wrote that the so-called totalitarian state had been neither total nor a state. The author of the entry "totalitarianism" in the second edition of the *Encyclopedia of Social Sciences* predicted that just as there had been no such article in the first edition, there would be none in the third.

There was no doubt that changes had taken place. To what extent did they affect the features that had been singled out in the early 1950s as "typically totalitarian"? The ideology had not changed, the state party still had a monopoly of political power, the KGB was still operating without fear of competition, and the economy was still centrally planned and directed. Some dissidents had appeared on the scene. In Stalin's day they would have been shot; now they were merely detained in camps or sent abroad.

Although the totalitarianism concept was to be buried, Communist regimes continued to exist. According to the critics they were "authoritarian." Unfortunately "authoritarian" is a term that can mean a great many different things. A political regime completely devoid of authority is unthinkable, at least for any length of time. Every dictatorship or semi-dictatorship is a priori authoritarian, be it a monarchy (Saudi Arabia, Jordan under Hussein, Morocco under Hassan) or such disparate regimes as those of Pakistan, Vietnam, Indonesia, not to mention, at one time or another, most African, Latin American, and Middle Eastern countries. Even the German government under Adenauer, even Israel under Ben Gurion, certainly France under de Gaulle were to some extent authoritarian. Of what use was a category that could be applied to such disparate states? Having said that the Soviet Union or East Germany were authoritarian, what new light was shed on the specific character of these systems?

If the totalitarian model was dismissed as inapplicable in view of the differences between Nazi Germany and the Soviet Union, what was the point of replacing it with a label that was quite useless?

Aware of this dilemma, scholars over the years introduced new terms to define Communist regimes, ranging from the obvious to the irrelevant or even ludicrous: "neo-feudalism," "mobilization regime," "post-mobilization stage," "welfare state authoritarianism," "failed totalitarianism," "post-totalitarianism," "institutional pluralism," and "limited pluralism."

Others have pointed to the concept of modernization, but this too has been of little assistance; for the term "totalitarianism" refers to the structure of power in a society, whereas "modernization" involves an altogether different set of social processes. Yet another approach–the comparison with Western bureaucratic politics, interest groups, and the running of Western corporations–proved similarly unenlightening when it came to understanding the specific character of Communist societies. The Politburo did not operate like the board of directors of General Motors or IBM.

Whatever the shortcomings of the new theories, the totalitarian model was declared not only political incorrect, it was said to be entirely obsolete not only in the United States but also in Germany, where the debate on this topic had raged for many years, mainly in the context of the interpretation of Nazism. Many younger academics refused to take it seriously because it had been "decisively refuted." Some reported that it was in a state of deep crisis or even agony, others thought that the concept had already died a natural death.[10]

However, by the early 1980s even the more enthusiastic advocates of the various "pluralist" models of Communist society had to admit that the announcement of the demise of the rival concept had been premature. Stephen Cohen of Princeton observed with some regret that the main impact of the critics of the totalitarian concept had been felt in the 1970s, but that it had not succeeded in putting an end to the totalitarianism thesis.

The reason was quite simple and had to do with political reality. The antitotalitarian school would easily have carried the day if de-Stalinization in the Soviet Union had brought about a radical and complete break with the past. If there had been unmistakable signs of the growth of democratic institutions, even the staunchest believers in the concept of totalitarianism would have been unable to keep it alive much longer. But the facts dictated otherwise. After a promising start, de-Stalinization was later halted and even reversed. Soviet political institutions did not fundamentally change– the regime was still an absolute dictatorship, at least until the advent of *perestroika* and *glasnost*. But if the critics of the totalitarianism concept thought that the downfall of Communism in the Soviet Union and Eastern Europe would serve belatedly as justification of their views, they were sadly mistaken. Nowhere was the term "totalitarian" used more often than in Moscow; nowhere were the various concepts of "pluralism," "participation," and "authoritarianism" dismissed with more scorn than in the former Soviet Union.[12]

Looking back after the demise of the Soviet Union, the flaws of the theorizing in the 1950s seemed quite obvious. Nevertheless, two leading political sociologists, reviewing the progress of Sovietology from the outside, wrote in 1992 that "although much maligned by Sovietologists in the 1970s and 1980s [totalitarianism] has proven to be the most fruitful of the paradigms." And another respected writer noted that, in retrospect, totalitarianism had been dismissed prematurely and for the wrong reason, that its successor concepts had been wrongly conceived as models, and that a virtual model mania had developed "to a point of harming our understanding."[13]

II

With the disappearance of most (but not all) Communist regimes, the debate over totalitarianism lost much of its political and emotional edge, but it has by no means been concluded. If the same term cannot be used for a variety of regimes at different stages of development, perhaps there was not one totalitarianism but a whole spectrum of totalitarianisms. Leading students of the subject have devoted much thought to this question, but there is no unanimity among them. The German scholar Karl Dietrich Bracher, a leading authority on Nazism, with all due reservations sees no reason to discontinue using the term both for Nazism and Communism. His four criteria are an official and exclusive ideology; a centralized and hierarchically organized mass movement; control of the mass media for the purpose of information; and control of the economy and social relations.[14]

Even more important are two basic points that Bracher has emphasized time and again and that have caused offense in some circles. Totalitarianism, he said, is not a typical and exclusive product of the interwar period that came to an end in 1945. On the contrary, recent technologies offer modern dictatorship even greater possibilities for the mobilization and indoctrination of the masses and the imposition of strict controls over society. Second, the fundamental dividing line in recent history is not between left and right, and not between capitalism and socialism (despite the differences between them), but between dictatorship, despotism, and freedom.[15]

Such statements are bound to annoy experts for whom the main ideological issue of our time is not political freedom but economic organization. For them a dictatorship may still be progressive, whereas a democracy, so long as it is "capitalist," is still prefascist or potentially fascist. And since all democracies that have ever existed, except perhaps in Iceland or early modern Switzerland, have been either capitalist or based on a mixed economy, they all are regarded as suspect.

Bracher saw a dividing line between totalitarianism and authoritarianism as did Juan Linz, who pointed out that an authoritarian regime could tolerate limited political pluralism, whereas totalitarian rule could not. In an authoritarian regime, ideology was not a central issue–a general perspective usually sufficed. Nor did an authoritarian regime need mass political participation directed from above.[16] Franco's Spain was not total-itarian. There was no central ideology and no political mass party, only an old-fashioned if altogether unattractive military dictatorship. For this reason, after Franco's death the transition to a democratic regime pro-ceeded without great difficulty. By contrast, until 1991 no totalitarian regime had ever transformed itself peacefully in a democratic direction; this had happened only following total military defeat.

The categories developed by Bracher and Linz may be imperfect, but they are the best and most realistic available. They are not a magic wand, for both have pointed to a degree of uncertainty, a gray zone with regard to the specific character of these regimes and the direction they may take in future. The totalitarianism concept described certain common features of fascist and Communist states, but it could not explain how these states had come in-to existence, nor could it predict under what circumstances they would end.

Bracher and Linz were influenced in their work on the totalitarian state above all by the fascist experience. For Richard Löwenthal, a leading political theorist of the period after World War II, it was the impact of developments in the Communist world that was central. Löwenthal be-lieved toward the end of his life (he died in 1988) that the Soviet Union and the other European countries had moved beyond totalitarianism toward something he called "post-totalitarian authoritarianism," or "authori-tarian bureaucratic oligarchy": "Those countries had moved not from tyranny to freedom, but from massive terror to a rule of meanness, ensuing stability at the risk of stagnation."[17]

Löwenthal's relative optimism in the early 1980s was criticized by other experts, who argued that while there had been thaws in the Soviet Union and China, the totalitarian iceberg had not melted. Could it be taken for granted that the experience of Stalin and Mao had immunized these regimes forever against the grosser forms of despotism? Or could it be that they were fated for a long time to come to alternate between cycles of relative relaxation and strong oppression, with the single-party dictator-ship and the old structures and institutions still intact?

Pierre Hassner, another seminal thinker of the 1970s and 1980s, also recognized that far-reaching changes had taken place in the Soviet bloc, but they had not yet gone beyond the point of no return. The new regime was not authoritarian in the traditional sense but represented a form of totalitarianism in decline. Post-totalitarian authoritarianism was total-itarianism that had lost some of its dynamism and its capacity to control a society that had become more complex and/or more resistant. There were fewer purges and less mass terror and perhaps a greater degree of real-politik in foreign affairs, though in this last respect the difference from Stalinism was not that great. (Would Stalin have intervened in Afghan-istan?) The changes had not produced a significantly more liberal regime and not even a massive strengthening of interest groups, unless one re-garded the interpenetration of party, KGB, army, and the state's com-manding position in the economy a form of pluralism.

My own view at the time was that, while the totalitarianism concept was in need of modification, the attempts to substitute the authoritarian label were useless. Perhaps one should have stressed that the totalitarianism of the 1980s was mature, advanced, perhaps even rational in contrast to the frenzied or–to borrow Max Weber's term–"sultanic" regimes of an earlier period: paranoid in Stalin's case, hyperaggressive in Hitler's. Those preferring a label other than totalitarian were obliged to point out that they were referring not to old-style autocratic regimes like absolute monarchies or military dictatorships, but to regimes operating through a full control system run by a leadership of a political party using high-technology means of repression and indoctrination.[18]

After Gorbachev's rise to power, the reform age was ushered in, and within a period of approximately three years Communism collapsed in the Soviet Union and elsewhere in Eastern Europe. What Russians and other East Europeans had to say about the character of the old system was in stark contrast to the theories concerning pluralism, participatory and welfare authoritarianism, which had been voiced in the West. The old system had been a disaster, Westerners were told in Moscow; the idea that it could reform itself, become more liberal, return to a more democratic Bukharin-style Marxism-Leninism was not only far-fetched, it was utterly fantastic.

The main differences between the proponents of the authoritarian model and their critics had been the relative optimism of the former concerning the future of the Soviet Union, its achievements in various fields, and its capacity to reform itself. The events of 1989 to 1992 came as a fatal blow from which the authoritarianism concept could not be rescued, but the advocates of the totalitarianism model were almost equally surprised. They had, by and large, overrated the strength of the regime; most thought that despite all failures it would survive for a long time. Some claimed at one and the same time that the Soviet system was very strong (militarily) and very weak in many other respects, a proposition that could not be maintained for any length of time, for a weak regime could not remain a military superpower indefinitely. There had been no historical precedent, however, for the collapse of a totalitarian regime except as the result of total defeat in war.

The advocates of totalitarian models did not maintain that the Communist system was unchangeable. To the best of my knowledge no Western political scientist ever said, as Winston Smith did in Orwell's *1984*, that the proletarians would never revolt in a million years: "There is no way in which the party can be overthrown." They said there would be change in the more distant future in circumstances that could not be foreseen. But at the same time some were too ready to believe in irreversibility–following the proclamation by Soviet leaders of the Brezhnev Doctrine, and other achievements by the Soviet system that (it was said) would never be given up. One should not have taken such boasts at face value after the breakdown of Communism in Poland in the later 1970s, when a pro-Soviet system was kept in power by the army against the wish of the great majority of the population. But the situation in Poland was very different from the state of affairs in the Soviet Union, and thus most of those who favored the totalitarianism model did not consider the possibility of a breakdown in the near future. The strength of the Soviet armed forces was unbroken; the KGB, the Communist party, and its many subsidiary organizations were still in place and operating normally. In these conditions such a possibility seemed very distant indeed.

In its most extreme form, the belief in the "eternal character" of Soviet totalitarianism was represented by the exiled Soviet logician Alexander Zinoviev, who claimed that the Stalinist regime had been an organic growth and that it was the most suitable for *Homo sovieticus*. When it appeared in the late 1980s that most Soviet people did not share this gloomy outlook, far from welcoming this development, Zinoviev expressed considerable anger and became one of the main advocates of a return to Stalinism.

In contrast, Richard Löwenthal argued that totalitarianism of the Communist type could not create and preserve its unique character without a profoundly utopian faith. But this faith was bound to flounder as it conflicted with and eventually succumbed to the necessity for economic modernization. The loss of utopian faith had ended recurrent attempts at ever "new revolutions from above; it spelled the end of totalitarianism. Seen in this perspective, the present Communist regimes [in 1983] were post-totalitarian, single party regimes. A return to their totalitarian origin was excluded; that particular secular religion is dead, at least in those countries that have tried it out."[19]

This was as realistic an assessment as any made at the time, even though the specific weight of "utopian faith" was perhaps a little exaggerated. Utopian faith had been typical all along only with regard to a relatively small part of the elite. On the other hand, there is no reason to believe that Molotov and Kaganovitch ever lost their faith, nor Khrushchev or even the leadership of the next generation. Brezhnev, Suslov, and Andropov must have had doubts about the doctrine they proclaimed, but it is still unlikely that they ceased to be believers. Even Gorbachev and his contemporaries in the leadership thought that the shortcomings of the regime, even if substantial and deep, could be remedied and that, by and large, the socialist system was still superior to all others.

Where then did the loss of faith occur? In the lower echelons of the leadership, among the Soviet intelligentsia. But how important had the utopian faith been in their mentality all along? To what extent had they been true believers? This is part of the wider syndrome of optimism turning into pessimism, and it remains to be studied in considerably more detail.

The issue of nationalistic antagonisms was underrated by the advocates of the totalitarian model and ignored likewise by the proponents of pluralism. True, the experts pointed to strong separatist centrifugal trends, mainly in Central Asia, that would have far-reaching consequences for the survival of the Soviet Union and at the very least cause grave demographic and ultimately political problems.[20] But virtually no one expected that it would also affect the Caucasus and the Ukraine.

The strongest argument against the totalitarianism paradigm was seldom raised. What was the purpose of classification? (The question applied, a fortiori, to the pluralistic schools trying to replace it.) The basic task, after all, was not to find ingenious formulas covering a variety of political systems but to reach a deeper understanding of their essential character and the direction in which they were likely to develop. Unless a theory or a concept served this purpose, it was merely an abstract exercise that could never be quite successful, because reality was always more complex than any formula. This problem, the question of the purpose of classification, had also arisen in the life sciences. It was even more palpable in the social sciences.

What important new impulses have been given to the study of modern dictatorships by these various models?[21] The totalitarianism concept did have an impact in the 1950s; one could quarrel with the resulting studies, but no one could ignore them. It is impossible to think of works of similar importance that were inspired by concepts such as "welfare state authoritarianism." The pluralism concept helped to identify certain interest groups in the Communist system and to describe how they were functioning, but the existence of such groups had never been denied.

The critics of the totalitarianism model have always claimed that such a system in a pure, unalloyed form had never existed—a correct, if trite, observation. There are no pure, unalloyed systems; there has never been perfect capitalism or democracy or liberalism. Outside the confines of literary works such as Orwell's *1984*, there has never been total totalitarianism, only approximations. As there is no perfection in human beings, there is none in political institutions, which are always shaped to a greater or smaller extent by history, geography, and the economic environment, as well as other factors, not to mention the limitations of human nature. Critics of totalitarianism believed that they had administered the coup de grâce to the model they disliked, once they proved that underneath the appearance of order and monolithic rule, there was frequently considerable disorder. But they have proved much less than they thought, as the debates on Nazism in Germany have shown: the fact (to give but one example) that there was corruption even under Hitler and Stalin did not necessarily make Nazism or Stalinism either chaotic or pluralistic.

One American political theorist writing in the 1980s suggested "failed totalitarianism" as an accurate definition of the kind of regime prevailing in the Soviet Union at the time. This concept had at first sight much to recommend it. As far as economic performance was concerned, the system was certainly not a success. The Stalinist terror had ended, the frenzy had ceased, enthusiasm faded—"ideological zeal is a sign only of conformity and not of conviction."[22] Seen in this perspective, the Soviet system had indeed been totalitarian for a brief moment—under Stalin—but subsequently reverted to the authoritarian norm.

If there is some truth in these observations, there is also much that cannot be squared with the historical facts. Although the Soviet Union proved to be inefficient in the economic field, its rulers built up a powerful army and made their country a political superpower. If the frenzy of the 1930s had vanished, the reason was that great breakthroughs (such as the collectivization of agriculture and the first five-year plans) were no longer needed. Furthermore, it had appeared that the regime could be maintained with much less violence than had been the case under Stalin. To this extent, the regime had succeeded rather than failed. Whatever the reason, the totalitarian elements in Soviet rule had receded even if they had not vanished. And did not the sudden and nonviolent collapse of the Soviet regime show that it had been less totalitarian than some had thought?

There is no clear-cut answer: if the Soviet regime had been merely authoritarian, the transition to a democratic system should have been as smooth as, for instance, in Spain or in Portugal. The fact that the transition proves to be so difficult tends to show that it had been subjected to rule of a very different kind, that the social and political changes that had taken place had been deeper and more radical.[23]

A suggestion made in this context by Francis Fukuyama deserves attention: perhaps there existed even before Gorbachev something akin to a proto-civil society that laid the groundwork for Gorbachev's reforms?[24] Fukuyama refers to the fact that while churches and unions had no influence, there was a certain diffusion of power inside the party on a regional basis and that the lower reaches of the party had a substantial degree of bargaining leverage against the center. To this extent there was indeed decentralization, and one could also point to the emergence of organized crime as further proof. These important developments were dismissed by some leading Sovietologists, mainly because of the sweeping claims made by certain colleagues, who argued that democracy had taken root in the Soviet Union. To a degree the "post-totalitarian" concept had much to recommend it—things were clearly not what they used to be. These trends, however, only help us to understand why the Soviet Union disintegrated so quickly and completely in 1991 to 1992. They weakened the center but did not strengthen democracy in Russia to any marked degree. If there had been a significant proto-civil society in the days of Gorbachev and Yeltsin, the political and economic reform movement would have been considerably more successful.

There are weighty reasons not to prolong the taxonomic debates on the Soviet Union, and they are mainly pragmatic in character. Unless the interpretations open new vistas, renew the impulse to study this regime, and provide better insights into its character, the purpose of these exercises is no longer obvious. Conceptional typologies have been of little help to political scientists in predicting future trends in the Soviet Union.

Those who referred to totalitarianism in the 1950s and 1960s were less ambitious in their claims than purveyors of models of a later age. With perhaps a few exceptions, they thought of their findings as of interest and significance to the effort to understand an essentially new phenomenon, but they did not think they had discovered a key for deciphering a superior truth. Seen in retrospect, the "model mania" of the 1970s caused some harm and little good; the totalitarianism concept was given up too early. "As we revisit the successor concepts of totalitarianism," Giovanni Sartori wrote in 1993, the thrust of their message is that the history-shaking implosions of 1989 to 1991 could not happen and had no reason for happening, for *perestroika* had, in fact, already happened.[25]

III

As the totalitarianism debate among students of the Soviet Union and communist affairs has come more or less full circle, the controversies about National Socialism have run a somewhat similar course. This debate began in the 1960s, partly under the impact of a resurgence of Marxism on university campuses, but also as the result of a resurgence of German nationalism.[26] There were historians whose anti-Nazi credentials were above suspicion who claimed that the earlier interpretations of Nazism had been moralistic and unscholarly, that they had focused far too much on individual leaders and on ideology, and that the time had come to put Nazism into proper historical perspective. To "historicize" Nazism meant not to regard it as a wholly unique phenomenon but to put it into a wider historical context. In some respects the ensuing debate is different from the discussions on the Soviet Union. It concerned, for instance, the question whether the rise of Nazism was the result of specifically German circumstances ("the pre-modern" character of German society)[27] or the question who (if anyone) had given the order to carry out the mass murder of Jews.

In other respects the bones of contention among German historians were quite similar (or even identical) with those argued by the students of Communism. For this reason the debate is of considerable interest—not with regard to any sensational new insights that emerged, for the light generated was in inverse ratio to the heat engendered. It has shown how much dissent there could be as the result of quarrels over a system that no longer existed and that in principle all those engaged in the debate emphatically rejected. Perhaps there will be at some future date a second round of the debate on Communism. This is likely to happen once those who had personal, firsthand experience of the Communist regime have disappeared. Distance in time certainly favors revisions in history.

Nazi policy, some German scholars claimed, far from being mono-lithic and centralized, was frequently incoherent. Nor is it true that all power was concentrated in Hitler's hands; the old social structures continued to exist and to be active under the surface.[28] According to the revisionists, Nazi ideology too was much less important than had commonly been thought: Nazi policy developed as the result of an interaction between doctrine and improvization, the latter being triggered by all kinds of objective pressures and factors over which the Nazis had little or no control.

In short, if according to Nazi mythology everything in the country was done in a purposeful way, the machine ran smoothly, Hitler's power was unlimited, and there were no serious conflicts among the Nazi leaders, according to the revisionists, Hitler's power was quite limited, and his underlings maintained their private empires virtually up to the end. Some revisionists went so far as to describe the political structure of the Third Reich as "polycratic chaos"; others used less extreme formulations. But the general trend of the critique was unmistakable: like Stalin, Hitler was a mere "authoritarian."

The history of the Holocaust also came in for radical reinterpretation. It was not denied that millions of Jews were actually killed, but it was argued that there was no straight line leading from Nazi ideology to the Holocaust (the so-called "linear thesis"). There was no coordination and planned Nazi policy toward the Jews, and the mass murder was not an aim that Hitler had set a priori. Rather, it was claimed, the Holocaust was a *Flucht nach vorn*, an endeavor to find a way out of a blind alley into which the Nazi leaders had maneuvered themselves. These leaders did not plan the Final Solution but stumbled into it because so many Jews had already been taken away. The others also had to be deported; and since there was no place to resettle them, they had to be exterminated. And so one thing led to another, in considerable part by mere accident, with the resulting cumulative radicalization of policy during the war that Hitler had neither foreseen nor planned.

If the traditionalists, to give one example, pointed to a well-known Hitler speech in the Reichstag in January 1939, in which Hitler announced that in the case of a world war the Jews in Europe would be exterminated, the revisionists shrugged it off: it was a mere manner of speaking. Why should one take seriously the theatrical thunder and the bragging of politicians?

The controversy between "intentionalists" (those stressing the impact of Nazi ideology on Nazi policies) and "functionalists" (or revisionists) has been part of a wider debate over the character of Nazi rule. Some of the points the revisionists made were irrefutable. There were indeed inner inconsistencies in Nazi Germany, and rivalries and accidents did play a role. But human beings are not robots; institutions are never perfect, and there is always some overlapping and infighting. Whether to call this "chaos" is a moot point; it is probably the natural state of affairs in every society. If it was chaos, it did not stop the Nazis from building up the strongest military power in Europe, conquering most of Europe, and exterminating European Jewry. It is perfectly true that, as the revisionists claimed, it was physically impossible for one man, even the most efficient and hard-working leader, to control every aspect of life in a big country. Decisions concerning the school curriculum in Uzbekistan were not made by Stalin personally, nor did Hitler, who had no interest in economics in the first place, set the norms of production for the Upper Silesian coal industry. Although Nazi mythology, like Communist mythology, described the leader as omnipotent and omniscient, that was even less true in Germany than in the Soviet Union, if only because Hitler had a mere six years from the seizure of power to the outbreak of war to establish his control mechanisms—insufficient time for a major endeavor of this kind. Once war broke out, everything was subordinated to the military effort, and tinkering with political and social institutions was discouraged.

Nevertheless, it is crucial for the understanding of totalitarian regimes to recognize that while not all decisions were actually made in and by the center, no truly important decision was made without the knowledge, let alone against the wish, of the leader. It is equally important to realize that while not all decisions were made by the supreme leader, all could have been made by him. Private empires and divergent interests existed in the Third Reich. But without the good will of the leader, without access to him, satraps lost their power base from one day to the next. There is no justification for calling a society pluralistic simply because some of the satraps try to stab each other in the back.

"Functionalist" historians claimed that "intentionalists" have taken Hitler's speeches, *Mein Kampf*, and Nazi editorials at face value. They argue that Nazi ideology was in actual fact never that important—and, in any case, the Nazi empire like all others was subject to "routinization," the iron law according to which revolutions lose their impetus through the passing of time, human nature, and the need to make concessions for various reasons. (Similar views, it will be recalled, were made by writers in the Soviet field.) Yet the law applied only to a very small extent in Nazi Germany, precisely because Nazi rule did not last long, and in any case the trend was toward radicalization rather than moderation. What would have happened if the Nazi regime had lasted fifty or a hundred years is another question altogether. The law of routinization disregards the basic feature of totalitarian rule, in particular the fact that unprecedented power is concentrated in a few hands.

Functionalism did put excessive emphasis on "objective" social factors. It largely ignored ideology, and though unintentionally, it trivialized the crimes of the dictators. If, as the revisionists see it, certain social aspects of life are of paramount importance, there seems little choice between life in a dictatorship and in a democracy. In both situations, people are born, go to school, work, and eventually die. In this view, Hitler (like Stalin) turns into a mere figurehead, a modern Hamlet unable to make up his mind and only half aware of what is going on around him. So many other historical culprits, individuals as well as "structures" such as bureaucracies, have been discovered by the functionalists in their searches that any competent lawyer acting for Hitler and Nazism in the courts of history could without great difficulty plead for a verdict of diminished responsibility by reason of extenuating circumstances. According to this view, Hitler (like Stalin) was in the last resort, a weak dictator.

This kind of interpretation makes a travesty of what really occurred. Why should political scientists and historians who had no wish to act as apologists for Nazism have embraced an approach that was at best irrelevant to understanding the Nazi phenomenon, at worst patently absurd? Was it the wish to dissociate themselves from the previous generation of scholars and to say something novel and different? Was it the fact that as Nazi studies became more and more involved in details, they got lost in the byways of history, ignored the main issues, and became preoccupied with the exception rather than the rule? Was it the impact of a hypertrophied social history or the fear of writing "moralist history"? Was it the fact that the older interpretation was inconvenient to a new generation of scholars and writers anxious to absolve the German past of its unique character and to see Nazism as just another, albeit repulsive, variant of a general modern disease? To what extent was it connected with their critique of liberal democracy and modern capitalism? The German revisionists reacted violently when they were criticized for belittling Nazi crimes and Nazi responsibility and, generally speaking, the profoundly evil character of the regime.

As they saw it, they set out to understand the mainsprings of Nazism and the way it functioned better than their predecessors, without moral indignation and prejudice. But they still ended up with conclusions that were historically wrong and politically embarrassing, because it put them in close proximity to those who made no secret of their wish to prove that there had been nothing particularly evil about Nazism and that Hitler's Jewish policy (for instance), while regrettable in its crudity and excesses, had been something like a preventive war.

The impulses for revisionism in the field of Nazi studies did by no means emanate only from the left; some of its most notable exponents came from the right.[29] Some of them tend to believe that World War II was not unleashed by Hitler but "broke out"; Hitler, as they see it, did not want it. They condemn the Auschwitz law of 1985 (according to which victims of Nazi terror must not be defamed with impunity), arguing that such an approach creates taboos as far as the unprejudiced study of history is concerned. Above all, they dislike moral condemnation of Nazism on the grounds that such a stance is incompatible with a truly scientific, detached, and academic approach.

No historical school or concept is perfect; all are subject to modification and eventually lose their usefulness. "Functionalism," however, seems to have gone astray more profoundly than others. Why this happened remains to be studied in detail and is of no direct concern in the present context. It may be a question more difficult to answer than the search for the motivation of the revisionists in the Soviet field, in which political motivation was more manifest.

There was a certain amount of cross-fertilization between the Russian and German schools of revisionism; as Stephen Cohen put it: "Uncharitably, we might contrast the post-revisionist situation in Sovietology to that in Nazi studies, where a totalitarianism school also once prevailed. A major scholar in that field told us: 'Each new detailed study of the realities of life in Nazi Germany shows us how inadequate the concept of totalitarianism is.' "[30]

But the debate over Nazism did not provide much comfort to revisionists in the Soviet field. There was an anti-totalitarianism trend in recent German historiography, mainly in the wake of the resurgence of Marxism in the late 1960s and the emphasis put at the time on social history at the expense of other disciplines. But to a large degree the battle against the concept of totalitarianism was a battle against windmills, because the thesis that only Hitler's personality mattered, that everything in the Third Reich was totally coordinated, purposeful, and worked like clockwork, had long ago been discarded; in fact, it had never been official orthodoxy.

But intellectual fashions change; as Soviet revisionists became defensive or fell silent at the end of the 1980s, German revisionism also lost its impetus. In a scholarly journal in Germany every few years, massive review articles on specific topics are featured. In 1975 the review article on totalitarianism noted that the concept was on its last legs, in a "state of agony." Ten years later, the review article was entitled "Renaissance of the Totalitarian Concept?".[31]

IV

The totalitarian controversy reached the Soviet Union only as *glasnost* unfolded. Orwell's *Animal Farm* and *1984* had been circulated in samizdat, and a few experts had access to the foreign books and journals in which the Western debate had taken place. One can only speculate what they thought when reading Herbert Marcuse's strictures against the use of the term "totalitarianism," in which he argued that there was not much choice between the restrictive and dictatorial features of the Soviet Union and those of the United States.[32]

Soviet authorities did not like the term. Even apart from the fact that it was used by foreign critics to point out common features between Nazism, fascism, and Bolshevism, "totalitarianism," as the Soviet authorities saw it, was an unnecessary term characterizing fascist dictatorship. Since fascism could grow only in capitalist societies, all Communist regimes were by definition immune to it. The term was only seldom used in the Soviet Union. Some works of reference briefly mentioned it; others did not refer to it at all. Fascism was no legitimate subject of study in the Soviet Union and totalitarianism even less so.

As a Russian political philosopher wrote under *glasnost*: "In our country totalitarianism was used only for propagandistic purposes to characterize fascist and pro-fascist regimes in the West."[33] It was always accompanied by adjectives such as "aggressive," "terrorist," "imperialist," and the like. According to the second edition of the *Great Soviet Encyclopedia*, a totalitarian state was simply a subspecies of a bourgeois state, an openly terrorist dictatorship of the most reactionary and imperialist elements. The third edition of the same encyclopedia was a little more detailed;[34] it quoted Hobbes and Hegel and said that it was a trend in bourgeois political thought that justified étatism and authoritarianism–adding further confusion. Even the *Soviet Encyclopedical Dictionary* of 1986 merely noted that the totalitarianism concept was used by bourgeois-liberal ideologists to criticize fascist dictatorship, mainly as a tool of anti-Communist propaganda to vilify the socialist regimes by identifying them with the totalitarian regimes and juxtaposing them to the "free, democratic" societies.[35]

Change came with the publication of novels like Vasili Grossman's *Life and Fate* and the essays of Klyamkin, Tsypko, and others, as well as collections of articles in 1988 and 1989 in which leading Soviet writers tried to come to terms with the Stalin phenomenon.[36] By that time, almost everyone in Russia–even conservatives and old Communists such as Yegor Ligachev–used the term, sometimes perhaps too sweepingly. Those who did not, really meant "totalitarianism," when for some reason they used another term.[37]

The Russian political philosophers, too, became interested in the topic the moment it became possible to discuss it freely.[38] By that time the revisionist wave had run its course in the West and was mainly of historical interest to the Russians. Even among the Russian Marxists there was disbelief when they read, after many years, the writings of Isaac Deutscher or Herbert Marcuse, or the strange theories of an American professor who had described Stalin as a moderate and the prisoner of a bellicose Politburo.[39]

The younger Russian political philosophers, unlike the Western Communists, had no compunction about calling a spade a spade. They had grown up under the regime, and they knew– "not from hearsay" (to use the Russian phrase) – that the old Soviet Union had never been a welfare state nor a participatory democracy. Even the Marxists agreed that the moment Russian social democracy opted for Leninism, it engaged in the construction of a political organization that was to concentrate all power in its hands, making the tragedy more or less inescapable.[40] Could it be argued that Lenin and his comrades were perhaps unaware in 1917 of the consequences? But if the American founding fathers had been aware of the danger of excessive concentration of power 150 years before Lenin, this could hardly be called an extenuating circumstance.

In fact, Russian historians tend to believe that the Stalinist system was more totalitarian than the Nazi regime, an idea that had previously been suggested by British sociologist Stanislaw Andreski.[41] Soviet authors broadly speaking followed the lead given by their Western colleagues as defined in their writings of the 1960s and 1970s: totalitarianism was a phenomenon of the twentieth century and of mass society. Totalitarianism was not the same as authoritarianism or bureaucratic power. Other terms developed by Russian experts to describe the political-social system, such as *Ideokratia* and *KratoKratiia* ("bureaucratic authoritarianism" and "administrative command system of a repressive type"),[42] were not of much use either.

According to Russian authors writing under *glasnost*, Western critics of the totalitarianism concept (of the "consultative authoritarianism" pattern) found it more and more difficult to produce persuasive alternative models in view of the developments inside the Soviet Union when hopes of de-Stalinization faded after Khrushchev. Russian historians noted the striking parallels between Nazi and Soviet totalitarianism, which, as one of them put it, can be seen with the naked eye.[43] In fact, they believe that a comparison between Nazism and Soviet Communism could be very productive, as well as the problem of the gradual "totalitarization" of Soviet society. Whereas German *Gleichschaltung* (imposition of the new order) took place within a period of six months, this process continued for more than seven years in the Soviet Union.

If there are differences of opinion among Russian political philosophers about totalitarianism, they concern other issues. Obviously, there were important differences between Stalinism and the post-Stalin regime. Seen in retrospect, was the regime after 1953 "totalitarianism in decline," or was it merely an extreme form of dictatorship that no longer engaged in mass terror and had given up the attempt to control all aspects of life— whether because this was no longer necessary or because the regime had mellowed?[44] If there is freedom to continue the debate, it will go on for a long time, simply because the tyranny lasted longer in Russia than elsewhere and had such tragic consequences.[45]

5

Sovietology: An Epitaph (I)

Could the collapse of the Soviet empire have been foreseen by the experts? If it came as a near total surprise, what were the reasons? The record of the experts, which will be analyzed for a long time to come, offers an excellent case study as far as success and failure in political assessment are concerned.

It would be unfair to claim that no one saw the coming of the disaster. A famous essay by a young Soviet dissident published years earlier was entitled "Will the Soviet Union Survive Until 1984?" Books by French *litterateurs* addressed the same question.

Andrei Amalrik, writing in 1969, originally wanted to take 1980 as the date of the Soviet downfall, this being a round number, but was persuaded by a friend to change it to the Orwellian 1984. He said that his essay was based not on scholarly research but only on observation and reflection: "From an academic point of view, it may appear to be only empty chatter. But for Western students of the Soviet Union, at any rate, this discussion should have the same interest that a fish would have for an ichthyologist if it suddenly began to talk." Amalrik was mistaken in some of his assumptions, notably a coming military collision with China, and the fatal event occurred seven years after the date indicated by him. But he got the main issue right: "If however, one views the present 'liberalization' as the growing decrepitude of the regime rather than its regeneration, then the logical result will be its death, which will be followed by anarchy."

Amalrik's essay was welcomed as a piece of brilliant literature in the West, as another link in the chain of Russian apocalyptic writing. Virtually no one tended to take it at face value as a piece of political prediction, which, though based on "only" observation and reflection, proved to be astonishingly accurate.

Nor was much attention paid to the extremely negative reports by several Russian émigrés on the economic situation. As a distinguished American expert put it: "All countries have usually been immersed in their own seas of troubles and yet managed to muddle through. Will the Soviet Union be an exception?[1]

Negative trends in Soviet politics, society, and economy were of course noted; references to the "coming spring" in Moscow disappeared; and the term "decline" appeared with increased frequency. One astute observer noted that "the New Soviet Man" had turned pessimist."[2] The author of this essay had spent four years in Moscow as an exchange student and translator, a position that provided a unique vantage point of observation. An economist writing in 1982 titled his book *The USSR in Crisis: The Failure of an Economic System.*[3] But there were many others–diplomats, journalists, and above all academic experts–who returned from prolonged stays in the Soviet Union without subscribing to such conclusions.

What had caused the growth of pessimism? Was it limited to the Soviet middle class, or was it equally shared by the working class and peasants? To what extent was the leadership aware of the trend? Was the reason mainly economic, stemming from the 1975 crop failure, acute consumer good shortages, or general disappointment with economic performance and the standard of living? Or was it a mixture of economic and political causes, the feeling of political drift and stagnation, the realization that the aged leadership had neither new ideas nor fresh initiatives to offer? The war in Afghanistan did not go well, and there was lack of progress in the Third World. Those who detected the new wave of pessimism also noted that the discontent was not for the time being political in nature, and that, in any case, public opinion was not the most important factor in Soviet politics. But the popular mood was certainly one factor in the general equation and the longer the discontent lasted, the more important it was likely to become. Likewise, it was only a question of time until "unpolitical discontent" would turn political.

Another interesting case of political prescience was the book of a French student of historical demography, Emmanuel Todd, who was finishing his dissertation, *La Chute finale.*[4] Todd argued that the Soviet Union was likely to collapse in the near future. Soviet economic statistics were wrong and unreliable except for those that could be independently verified (such as figures for foreign trade). The general picture that emerged from other sources was that of an underdeveloped country, less modern than Spain, which had entered a period of inescapable and final stagnation. The claims that Soviet real income had risen eightfold since before the revolution were ridiculous. The prevailing centralization and the low productivity made a recovery most unlikely. Widespread corruption and the advanced age of the leadership also made reform difficult. The upsurge of non-Russian nationalism (separatism) and the fact that so many citizens had been killed in the process of building Communism further complicated matters. While the Soviet leaders were acting rationally from their point of view, they were prisoners of the system and would most likely leave reform until too late. The Communist state would not disappear but gradually rot.

Todd did not take Communist ideology very seriously,[5] and he thought that, generally speaking, Soviet power was much weaker than believed in the West. The West had no interest in seeing anarchy prevail in a country replete with thermonuclear weapons, for the consequences could be dramatic. But nor was it in a position to save the Soviet Union from collapse. Todd's study was based on various mistaken assumptions, for instance with regard to the role of the KGB and the relationship between the USSR and the satellites (which he thought more stable than the Soviet Union). His knowledge of specialized Sovietological literature seems to have been sketchy, and he apparently did not know Russian. It is all the more astonishing therefore that he spotted the central trends far more accurately than most Western experts, who believed at the time that Soviet power was far greater than it really was.

The consensus among most Western experts on the Soviet economy was that Soviet growth up to the late 1960s had been impressive (more than 5 percent per year) and that up to the mid-1970s GNP had increased faster in the Soviet Union than in the United States—reaching about 55 to 60 percent of the U.S. level in 1975. After that date, there were diminishing returns on inputs to agriculture, rates of investment declined, and so did productivity. But as the experts seemed to agree,

> slower growth has characterized all economies recently and the USSR has no monopoly on serious economic problems. Current low percentage growth rates, moreover, are generating absolute increments that match earlier increments and that yield impressive additions to national power. At a time when many countries, West and East, are troubled by inflation, unemployment, high energy costs, trade imbalances or government deficits, the economic problems of the USSR (however unique their underlying causes) cannot seem so unfamiliar or so incurable.[6]

This was written in 1981. In 1987 the consensus had become more somber; Soviet performance (it was now said) had been poor since 1975 and was getting worse. Industrial output was frequently of low quality, and the lag in technology was threatening the superpower status of the Soviet Union. But the estimates were still based on the assumption that Soviet GNP was about half that of the United States, and that the Soviet defense burden about 15 percent of GNP.[7] There still was much emphasis on the strength of the Soviet economy.

The Sovietological fraternity had discussed since 1983 whether Soviet growth ceased after 1978 and 1979. But the old inflated figures about Soviet economic performance were still generally used. As late as 1991/1992 the *World Factbook* of the CIA estimated that the GNP of the Soviet Union (prior to the breakup) was $2,660 billion, or $9,130 per capita; but the

World Bank Atlas of 1992 gave a figure of $479 billion for Russia and $121 billion for the Ukraine. *The World in 1993*, published by the *Economist* in 1992, quoted even lower figures: $137 billion for Russia and $9.7 billion for the Ukraine ($929 per capita in Russia, $188 in the Ukraine). If these figures were accurate, the Russian gross domestic product would have been about as big as South Africa's, the Ukrainian not larger than Kenya's.[8] If correct, these figures would indicate that the Russian and Ukrainian economies had shrunk to less than 10 percent of what they had been the year before, which is, of course, unthinkable. From 50 percent of America's GNP, they would have suddenly declined to something like 5 percent, showing that the U.S. government (like most others) had enormously overrated Soviet economic performance and that the statisticians, in the intelligence community as in academe, were in a state of disarray.

According to a study published as late as 1988 by a well-known Western economist specializing in the Soviet Union, Soviet citizens enjoyed "massive economic security": "An egalitarian wage system, combined with subsidized prices for most necessities, fills out the USSR's institutionalized cushion of economic security which is unmatched in capitalist countries."[9] Seen in this perspective, there was no good reason to expect major political discontent, for a population enjoying such unprecedented benefits would be more than foolish to revolt against a system that had brought them "such a high degree of personal economic security." A balanced picture was needed: "To believe that the Soviet economy is incapable of an adequate response to President Ronald Reagan's Strategic Defense Initiative—is self-delusion. . . ."

What political conclusions were drawn from this analysis of a pre-crisis situation: Was it a crisis of leadership or the system? Would the Soviet Union muddle through without major reform? Again, the consensus was that the Soviet Union was *not* on the verge of economic bankruptcy and political disintegration:

> Everyone knows the prediction of some Westerners about the "coming revolution in Russia," the "imminent revolt of the nationalities and the Soviet internal" empire and the spread of dissidence which "will engulf the Soviet intelligentsia.". . . Those scenarios are possible but most unlikely. What has been built through generations with much blood, sacrifice, ruthlessness, cunning and conviction, will not simply disintegrate or radically change because of critical problems. In the coming succession the Soviet Union may face a leadership crisis and an economic crisis, but it does not now and in all probability will not in the next decade face a systemic crisis that endangers its existence.[10]

The writer was by no means a wild optimist; on the contrary, he noted in passing that his views might be criticized by some of his peers as unduly pessimistic.[11]

A few years later, it appeared that the "most unlikely scenario" had been the one nearest to the truth, however unlikely and even absurd it appeared at the time. Everything the author had said seemed reasonable: there was every reason to assume that what had been built up over generations would not easily disintegrate. And it can be argued even with the benefit of hindsight that the disintegration came to a considerable extent as the result of an accident. If at the time of Chernenko's death some Politburo members had not voted for Gorbachev, or if a year or two later the general secretary had been overthrown by Ligachev or some other conservative, events in the Soviet Union would have taken a different turn. The traditional leadership might have muddled through for another five or ten years; they might have engaged in a controlled economic reform program unmatched by any substantial political reform. In this case there would have been no *glasnost* or *perestroika*, and the Soviet Union would not have disintegrated; the crisis would have been postponed by a number of years.

However, even if the leadership had not lost its nerve, the situation would still have deteriorated. Discontent would have grown, the ineffectuality and unpopularity of the regime would have manifested itself in various ways. In brief, it should have been clear that the roots of the system were much more shallow than most outside experts believed. The cardinal error of many Sovietologists was not their failure to predict the arrival of Gorbachev, his policy, and its consequences; the emergence of Gorbachev was a historical accident that could not possibly have been predicted. What they failed to see was that the process of decay had proceeded much further than generally assumed, that the self-confidence of the leading stratum had largely been undermined, and that as a result the existence of the regime depended on mere accidents.

These miscalculations were, of course, not an exclusive American domain. Expectations with regard to the future of the Soviet Union were more or less the same in other countries: great difficulties above all in the economic field were perceived, but no systemic crisis jeopardizing the very existence of the regime was thought at all likely. Bonn certainly did not foresee dramatic developments in East Germany. The consensus in West Germany in 1988 was that the Honecker regime was firmly in the saddle. In this respect, there was no significant difference between the experts and the media, between the Social Democrats, the Liberals, and the ruling Christian Democratic Union. Should they have known better? While the Soviet Union was still somewhat of a mystery in the eyes of many Westerners, there was nothing mysterious about East Germany as far as the Federal Republic of Germany was concerned. They shared a language and a culture, and there was frequent coming and going between the two German nations. There were few if any secrets—except with regard to the most essential issue, the stability of the Communist regime. As a result, the breakdown came as a total surprise even to professional German observers, including those stationed in East Germany.

The misapprehension among American Sovietologists (and their colleagues in Britain and Germany, less so in France) was compounded by the rise of the anti–Cold War school of thought in the 1970s and 1980s.

Whereas the earlier generation of Soviet experts had been on the whole critical or hostile vis-à-vis Soviet politics, such "cold warrior" attitudes were now rejected as outdated by many newcomers to the field. As they saw it, their predecessors had become wedded to a wholly static, monolithic totalitarian model of Soviet affairs that no longer corresponded with realities. A profile of this new generation was given by one of the new writers:

> They were not collectively smarter than their predecessors, but they had real
> intellectual advantages. They could learn from both the achievements and
> fallacies of original Sovietology. They were freer of cold-war political con-
> straints. And they benefited not only from new Soviet materials but from the
> more self-critical and less culture-bound perspectives in American cultural
> life in the 1960s. Many younger Sovietologists also had an educational
> experience generally denied to the older generation—the opportunity to live
> and study in the Soviet Union.[12]

Whereas the "Cold War experts" tended to regard the October Revolution of 1917 as a coup carried out by a small and unrepresentative party that was already embryonically totalitarian and that prevailed in the struggle for power owing to ideological orthodoxy, ruthless tactics, disciplined leadership, and centralized bureaucratic organization, the new generation took a radically different and much more favorable view of the events of 1917 and thereafter.[13]

As they saw it, the Bolsheviks could not have won if their policy had not corresponded with objective needs and had not enjoyed genuine mass support and thus legitimacy. Tied into an ideological straightjacket, the Cold War experts had systematically derided or ignored the great achievements of the Soviets, whereas the "revisionists," as they came to be called, introduced a far more objective and therefore realistic approach.

Perhaps the most impressive description of the change of guard in the field of Soviet studies was given by Moshe Lewin. Western perceptions of the Soviet Union, he wrote in 1987, had been seriously hampered by a cognitive schema that prevented practitioners from seeing the world in a realistic way. But through the 1960s a considerable number of Western scholars finally abandoned this ideologically biased tool and serious scholarly efforts were undertaken, enriching our understanding.[14]

The introduction of social and societal factors into our reasoning, Lewin argued, at last allowed us to see Soviet history and state institutions as much more flexible and responsive to social realities than generally perceived. The Soviet Union was much more complex and richer, hiding more than one trick up its sleeve from unsuspecting and ill-advised commentators, Lewin maintained. To restrict our analysis to simplified and quite inadequate ideas was a prescription for constant failure of intellect and politics. It led by necessity to claims that the Soviet government was unstable, that it could not handle succession. There was the "widespread misconception of an inherent weakness stemming from an almost sclerotic institutional creed that cannot but be what it is and is finally destined to go under." The richer, more realistic approach on the other hand was based on the assumption that far from being "finished," Russia was just beginning. In Lewin's opinion, "one of the most remarkable stories of our time is now unfolding."

The timing of these predictions, alas, could not have been more unfortunate. While the revisionists complained about bias, blunders, and the politicization of old style Sovietology, they were in fact also advocating the politicization of the field—only in a different direction. For instance, they advocated a "return to Bukharin's" orientation, that is to say, an enlightened, pristine Leninism, a Soviet system shorn of excessive violence and harsh repression. They were often motivated by a highly critical attitude toward U.S. foreign policy and American society in general. Others were genuinely intrigued by the new "scientific" approaches, which promised to put the study of Soviet affairs on a secure, objective basis far in advance of the subjective, instinctive, prejudiced ("folkloristic") approach of the early Sovietologists.

> Four decades ago the interpretation of Soviet policies was largely the preserve of old Mensheviks, former Trotskyites, former Communists or at least fellow travellers—people steeped in Marxism-Leninism who had over many years closely followed the development of Soviet and world Communism. They had acquired an intuitive understanding which helped them grasp the essentials of development inside the Soviet Union, of Stalin's motives and those of his disciples, and to guess how they were likely to react. These older experts obviously had axes to grind, and they were often heavily biased. But their prejudices, far from being an impediment, actually sharpened their perceptions. . . . The new Sovietologists no longer had that instinctive empathy. . . . As academic scholars who had never been active in politics, moreover, they lacked a sense of power, and their interest in ideology was also limited. In fact, their heavy preoccupation with methodology sometimes left them only limited time to follow events in the real world.[15]

It has been one of the fundamental beliefs of intelligence theory and practice that bias and the politicization of analysis are cardinal sins and the most frequent causes of assessment failures. This assumption had seemed to me doubtful and I had mentioned, on another occasion, Edmund Burke, whose negative, prejudiced attitude toward the French Revolution nevertheless had helped him to predict its future course of development. Other things being equal, bias and politicization are reprehensible, but the decisive criterion is success or failure in assessment. If, for instance, the bias-free analyst argued that the Soviet Union and the other Communist regimes did not significantly help terrorist groups, and if the (political) bosses decided otherwise; if, as it subsequently appeared, the prejudiced political bosses were closer to the truth than the detached analysts, this provides yet another example that absence of bias is no guarantee of success.[16]

The collision between "Cold War" Sovietologists and their "revisionist" opponents was indeed in large part ideological in character. If the revisionists argued, for instance, that the Soviet Union was a participatory democracy of a new kind or that it was a welfare state or a pluralistic society, these were as much ideological assumptions as President Reagan's famous "evil empire" speech. What mattered in the last resort is that one school came closer to Soviet realities than the other.

Various theoretical models were advocated by the "revisionists" to replace outmoded totalitarianism. One included political modernization, the more or less inevitable trend toward pluralism, economic and political decentralization, and the ever-rising demand not only for consumer goods, but for spiritual values as well. But modernization was of little help in explaining Brezhnev's regime and of no assistance in predicting Soviet political behavior. Another model put the emphasis on the written and unwritten rules of bureaucratic politics. Seen in this light, the Soviet Union was a giant bureaucracy subject to the laws governing all bureaucracies, including our own: fundamental divisions were all-important, institutional interests played a great role, performance and affiliation to a group were more decisive than ideology, and legal procedure became significant.

Whatever the merits of these models in explaining events in other parts of the world, the most likely result in the case of the Soviet Union was the belief that West and East were converging, a hypothesis that could not survive a closer look. Other Sovietologists developed an interest in a comparative approach or in cognitive psychology (the issue of perception and misperception), or in various quantitative techniques. There was probably no harm in trying these and other hypotheses. But they should have been discarded as soon as it appeared (and it should not have taken long) that far from being of assistance in explaining the course of events in the Soviet Union, they were leading nowhere. As applied to the Soviet–American conflict, cognitive psychology showed (as did the bureaucratic politics model) that Russians and Americans, despite their different mentalities, were closer than generally believed; their common interests outweighed divisions. Indeed, but for the fact that the hardliners on both sides constituted an "objective alliance" validating one anothers' expectations (invariably of the worst case type), they would have been even closer.

This mixture of the obvious and the nonsensical showed no understanding of how a Communist dictatorship worked and no appreciation of Communist ideology (or of nationalism), and it did in no way alert its practitioners to the coming of a great systemic crisis.

The story of "revisionism" and of Sovietology in general since World War II remains to be written.[17] But there can be no serious dispute that revisionism was a failure and that the failure of Sovietology "perhaps the greatest case study of the behavioral age, is also the failure of the social studies per se."[18]

Martin Malia has taken issue with various revisionist assertions: the view of October 1917 as the logical working out of Russia's social processes;

the idealization of the New Economic Policy (NEP); the "cultural revolution" concept; the interpretation of Sovietism as "developmental authoritarianism," "developmental bureaucracy," and "institutional pluralism" –
up to the thesis that the Communist regime produced the resources for
transforming itself into a democracy in an evolutionary way. The positive
evaluation of "mature Sovietism" had become something like the new
orthodoxy by the 1970s; seldom, if ever, in intellectual history has a school
of thought been proved so dramatically wrong by subsequent events. What
mattered in the final analysis was not the condemnation of revisionism by
Western critics such as Malia, but the fact that Western revisionism–in
history, economics, and other fields–was disproved by events inside the
former Soviet Union. The negative version of 1917 and subsequent Soviet
history derided by Stephen Cohen as biased and simplistic in 1983 met with
virtually unanimous acceptance inside the Soviet Union less than ten years
later. Totalitarianism became probably the most frequently used term in
Russian political discourse, even though Western revisionists had proved
to their own satisfaction that there never had been such a thing, or that, at
the very least, it had ceased to exist long ago. The denial of the great terror
of the 1933s, or at any rate its downplaying by some Western Sovietologists,
became a thesis difficult to maintain after 1987 – more difficult in Russia
than in the West.

The mistaken Western assessments of the achievement of the Soviet
economy became a cause of wonderment in the Russian capital. The
various social science models attracted little, if any, interest because, for
Soviet citizens who had lived through the postwar period, these models
obviously had no bearing on their own experience, on what really happened in their country.

But there is the danger of forgetting that the breakdown of the Soviet
empire in 1990 and 1991 is not the end of history but merely the end of an
historical chapter. The Communist regimes in Eastern Europe may be
replaced eventually by aggressively nationalist and undemocratic forces;
as a result, future observers may take a more benign view of the Gor-
bachevs, Jaruzelskis, and Kadars. This should not provide much comfort
to the revisionists, for if such regimes should emerge, it will be in large part
the historical fault of their Communist predecessors.

Those who rejected revisionism were also not free from errors in their
assessments. Some believed that the Soviet system was not only unchanging
but also unchangeable–except as the result of a violent cataclysm. The
contest between the two systems was likely to go on for decades, if not for
centuries, and they were by no means certain with regard to its outcome.
Lastly, when *perestroika* and *glasnost* came, some of the conservative analysts
were slow to realize how important and far-reaching the changes were.
Above all, they underrated the momentum that they generated and their
likely ultimate consequences.[19] Some predicted as early as 1987 the most
horrible catastrophes and bloodshed within a year. Others had long tended
to overrate the depth of the commitment in Russia to Marxism-Leninism.[20]

In his postmortem on Sovietology, Martin Malia noted the total and final collapse of socialism. But socialism elsewhere had led to the European welfare state and maintained parliamentary democracy. On the other hand, the emergence of a Western-style economic and political system in the former Soviet Union and most other East European countries seems unlikely for some considerable time to come.[21]

II

With the critique of Western Sovietology by Igor Shafarevich, a noted mathematician and ideologist of the Russian right, we pass from the realm of legitimate controversy to the absurd. According to Shafarevich, the Western intelligentsia refrained from ever finding fault with the Soviet regime and Stalinism until about 1953. To substantiate his startling thesis, he calls on Albert Einstein, Sidney and Beatrice Webb, Lion Feuchtwanger's book *Moscow 1937*, the British fellow traveler Dudley Collard, Vice President Henry Wallace, and Isaac Deutscher's biography of Stalin.[22] Shafarevich says that only with Stalin's last campaign against the doctors shortly before his death did a change take place in the attitude of the Western intelligentsia. But the real turning point in the attitude of Sovietology came only later, after Stalin's death and after Khrushchev's revelations, at the very time when millions were released from the camps. In brief, Western attitudes became critical when the actual situation in the Soviet Union improved. The reason was certainly not ignorance; as Solzhenitsyn told Shafarevich, he had discovered that, long before his *Gulag Archipelago*, there had been dozens of books denouncing Stalin, including some brilliant ones in the West, but they had been wholly ignored and hardly anyone knew about them.

Fantasies of this kind are largely rooted in Russian isolation and consequent ignorance. Russian critics were cut off for decades from the mainstream of Western intellectual thinking. If Western observers often did not know about, or failed to understand, the true state of affairs in the Soviet Union, Russian writers, on the whole, knew even less about Western views on their country–a situation that, under the circumstances, is not surprising. What causes concern is the eagerness to persist in error, the unwillingness to check facts now that it is possible to do so. While the West had its Webbs, Feuchtwangers, and Romain Rollands, there was substantial literature written by people with real knowledge and understanding, written at a time when Solzhenitsyn and Shafarevich were still ardent believers in the system under which they had grown up.[23]

III

The story of revisionist Sovietology is of relevance to the student of international politics as both a specific and a general case study. On the specific level, political thinking on the Soviet Union was deeply influenced. CIA economists reached the conclusion that the Soviet GNP was 55 to 60 percent of that of the United States and that East German per capita income was almost as high as Britain's and one-third higher than Spain's or Israel's.[24] These calculations were based on work done in collaboration with (and under the influence of) academic experts. SOVA, the CIA office of Soviet Analysis, was never far behind academic fashions. (The directorate of operations, it would appear, was less influenced.) There were in government few, if any, believers in the more radical forms of revisionism. But revisionism per se was so much of the zeitgeist that even middle-of-the-roaders were influenced by it and occasional (or frequent) kudos in that direction became the rule rather than the exception.

Leading figures of this school of thought were invited for consultations, lectures, and special projects in the 1970s, whereas there was not the same regard for the "cold warrior" types. Nevertheless, the "scientific" approach did not help in the forecasts concerning truly important issues, such as nationalities conflicts. The general assumption was that while certain tensions continued to exist, by and large the nationalities issue had been solved. And since one could not take pictures of nationalism or quantify it, the intelligence community missed out on this crucial issue, although there were a very few knowledgeable individuals (usually too far from the seats of power to have any influence).

It is only fair to add that among some revisionists there was a growing awareness of the problem. Thus Ronald Suny wrote in 1980; "The erosion of Marxist ideology within the Soviet Union has cleared the way for its replacement by patriotism and nationalism."[25] The great majority of commenters, however, were simply not interested in the problem that was eventually to emerge as the most important one leading to the downfall of the Soviet empire.

If there was not sufficient native talent, it would have been only natural to make use of research done in other Western countries, for instance in the field of the nationalities and nationalism; but no one apparently paid attention. When *glasnost* and *perestroika* came, half the government analysts thought the new reform policy would succeed, whereas the other half could not make up their minds and preferred not to take a long-term view in their estimates. Almost the only innovation that came from the intelligence community was the use of the term "Eurasia" for the successor states of the Soviet Union, an unhelpful and even misleading term, which in Russia is frequently used as a slogan by the extreme right with a very specific anti-Western meaning.

Why did many experts fail to see the shape of things to come? There were many reasons, some of which have been mentioned: ideological bias; pseudo-academic, pseudo-scientific aberrations; the belief that true detachment meant political and moral equidistance; cultural parochialism; and mirror imaging. As a result, not a few experts came to see events in the Soviet Union in much too rosy a light, exaggerating the achievements of the regime and its popularity. But it must also be admitted that not all the causes are clear. Perhaps some never will be–in the area of economic analysis, for instance. The experts lacked neither intelligence nor a sense of reality; nor were they blind admirers of Soviet policies. Were they misled, after all, by official Soviet figures–or was it perhaps impossible to penetrate the veil of secrecy? Should they have made greater use of the knowledge of Soviet émigrés, who could have told them that quantitative indicators were of very limited help (and could be positively misleading) in the context of a realistic assessment of Soviet output? These and similar questions will have to be investigated for a long time to come; they are of more than historical interest.

The general lesson that emerges from a postmortem of Sovietology (and of the study of Eastern Europe and Cuba) is the commonsensical, even trite one that it is all-important for a government to identify the issues that are likely to be of significance in the years to come and to have a sufficient number of knowledgeable and experienced specialists minutely following events in their respective fields. It is far more important that these experts be endowed with common sense than that they be wholly free of bias, or have a thorough knowledge of Bayes theorem. It is crucial that experts for Kazakhstan be able to read a Kazakh newspaper and converse with the customers in an Alma Ata bazaar. If they want to keep abreast of the most recent fashions in academe, this could be done in their spare time. In any case, it is a preoccupation best reserved for practitioners of intelligence of some years, standing, who are in a position to decide for themselves, on the basis of their practical experience, whether the theoretical approaches will be of any help in their work.

Some Russian émigrés believed that the errors of Western Sovietology were so enormous that they could be explained only against a background of "foul play"; in other words, agents of influence must have been at work.[26] The belief in agents of influence is as widespread among the Russian right as it is among liberals, but this interpretation is unconvincing. To gain influence among Western academic experts or journalists, the Soviets would have needed the good will not just of a few, but of a substantial number of people in key positions; and success in a venture of such magnitude strains one's imagination. True, a KGB colonel related that his organization engaged in disinformation as well as the recruitment of agents of influence among the experts. But as he interpreted it, an agent of influence was not a person who received a salary; the KGB would have been able to offer only pennies. These were people who were given visas and were received well in Moscow when this was by no means very common.[27] Such attempts to exercise influence, however, were by no means exclusively a Soviet phenomenon. The same dilemma faced academics and journalists in Third World countries (and not only there) perhaps in an even more acute way. If they wanted access to sources of information, they had to engage in some degree of self-censorship. Some critical Western visitors were willing to run this risk; others preferred circumspection. As a result, some disinformation probably crept in, but on balance this was of little importance compared with the misjudgments that were self-administered and sincerely believed.

IV

How do the fortunes of Sovietology compare with the record of Sinology? In the 1950s the consensus was that Chinese Communism was a totalitarian regime.[28] But in the later 1950s and early 1960s, views began to change: Confucianism and Chinese traditions were thought to be more important than Marxism-Leninism, which was considered a foreign importation. And even if Communism appeared to be troublesome in some respects, many mainline American experts came to believe with John Fairbanks, the grand old man of Chinese studies, that while Communism was bad for America, it was good for China, as he candidly put it in his autobiography.[29]

America and China were two different cultures, and it was clearly inadmissible to apply Western yardsticks while assessing Chinese Communism, which, in any case, was a predominantly nationalist movement.

There were several motives for these misjudgments: China was an exotic country that held great fascination for those studying it–stronger than in the case of Russia. The Chinese Communists had had a good press in America since the very early days when they had been considered mere agrarian reformers.[30] And lastly, China was, of course, different in some important respects; in the course of its transplantation to China, Marxism had undergone some mutations and produced strange flowers. The rift between Moscow and Beijing seemed to confirm this thesis.

Social and political science methods played a minor role in Chinese studies compared with Sovietology; the study of the economy was more important. But Chinese statistics were quite unreliable, and in the early days of the Cultural Revolution the Chinese Statistical Office was closed down altogether. Still, there was widespread belief that, as the *New York Times* put it, impressive progress had been made; American Sinology was the best in the world and well on the road to demystifing China altogether.[31] This was in 1966, but soon afterwards the late Mao period dawned, with the cultural revolution and its other antics. The Sinological fraternity was greatly bewildered. With all the allowances that had been made for a specific Chinese road to Communism, they were unprepared for these lunacies. However, some of the younger generation of Sinologists welcomed these developments. A new group, the Committee of Concerned Asian Scholars, denounced brutal U.S. aggression in Vietnam and the "complicity of silence of our profession." Whatever the merits or demerits of the U.S. invasion in Vietnam, it hardly excused the follies of these China watchers, who denied the existence of famine at a time when millions in China were dying of starvation and who justified the terror of the Red

Guards. For them the Cultural Revolution became almost a matter of religious belief. The views of the radical scholars had an indirect albeit limited impact on the U.S. establishment, including the CIA and the White House. With all its antics, Maoism was believed to have brought progress to China; among other things it had solved at long last the food problem.

When the Cultural Revolution came to an end and Maoism was gradually dismantled, when the ravages it had caused became obvious from Chinese sources, the intellectual end of radical scholarship was inevitable.[32]

During the 1980s, Maoism found few supporters among foreign China watchers. On the contrary, it was widely accepted that the Cultural Revolution had been a major disaster. But at the same time a new paradigm emerged, according to which the Chinese regime was "authoritarian and modernizing," no longer committed to Communist ideology.[33] This kind of assessment was, of course, closer to reality than the earlier fantasies, but there still was the irksome issue of human rights. The Tiananmen massacre provoked violent protests even among China watchers of the left, one of whom called the Beijing regime "fascist." Michael Oksenberg, a mainline Sinologist, who had served in the National Security Council, published *Confessions of a China Watcher*. There had been no such confessions by a major figure in the Soviet field. Forgiveness for the policy of repression by the Chinese leaders came from the right rather than the left of the political spectrum.

As the Beijing leadership increasingly turned from the planned economy to the market, it could no longer serve as a lodestar for radical scholars abroad. Western attitudes toward China had vacillated for many decades between admiration and enthusiasm, on the one hand, and criticism and even hostility, on the other. As business circles discovered the potential of the Chinese market, the attitude of radical Sinologists became one of indifference; there were a great many promising markets all over the world. After all the efforts and the suffering, after the proud announcement of the creation of a new kind of man, they had expected more than the emergence of a south Chinese brand of capitalism – however successful.[34]

6

Sovietology: An Epitaph (II)

The repentant sinner is one of the key figures in classical Russian literature from Raskolnikov and Alyosha Karamazov to Nekhlyudov (in Tolstoy's *Resurrection*). In the last quarter of the twentieth century repentant sinners have become rare in Russia. There were some exceedingly brave dissidents in the 1960s and 1970s who saved Russia's honor by resisting injustice and oppression; most of them suffered for the risk they took.

But it would be very difficult to find more than a handful of political figures or intellectuals who, having faithfully served the regime, were willing to admit any serious wrongdoing in later years. There was great reluctance to concede that they had been profoundly mistaken and knowingly or unknowingly served a cruel, repressive dictatorship. One can think of various reasons why the great majority did not become dissenters. At the beginning of their career most of them believed in the official ideology, albeit often with some reservations. In later years, when they gained a better understanding of the kind of society in which they lived, they had families and other commitments. To criticize the party and the government openly would have meant the end of their careers, suffering not only for themselves but their wives and children, and very likely arrest.

The number of heroes is sparsely sown at any time and in all countries. Nevertheless, one would have expected in later years a self-critical note, a mea culpa, even if not as extreme as that of Karamazov. But the time of admission of guilt, individual or collective, seems to have passed, and not only in Russia. Again, one can think of mitigating circumstances; many of the Russian liberals of the 1990s had been closet dissenters, even in Brezhnev's day, while paying lip service to the official ideology. It is also true that the revolution of 1988 to 1991 was largely their work, not that of the younger generation. The conservatives, in contrast, had nothing to be ashamed of and could therefore not be blamed, at least in their own eyes.[1] In fact most nationalists of the 1990s had been staunch party members and served it faithfully to the best of their ability. But great and wonderful is mankind's capacity to suppress unpleasant and embarrassing events in one's own past: The Russian conservatives persuaded themselves that they had always been fervent patriots and devout churchgoers rather than ardent believers in Marxism-Leninism.

Nor did guilt and atonement figure prominently among Western students of the Soviet Union. Their main concern after 1988 was damage control rather than heart searching. True, there was the general admission that no one had seen the coming of the disaster. But if everyone had been wrong, there was no reason to engage in public self-flagellation: to admit mistakes goes against the human grain. In actual fact many practitioners of mainstream Sovietology had something to answer for. Most of them had not gone remotely as far as the Soviets in extolling the virtues of the regime, but unlike the Soviet intellectuals they had not been under pressure to conform. They would not have lost their jobs had they expressed doubts about the Soviet Union as a welfare state or as a developing regime or participatory democracy. True, conservative critics of Communism had also erred in overrating the rootedness of the regime and underrating the possibility of early change. But unlike the revisionists, they had never suffered from delusions concerning Soviet economic and social, – let alone political – achievements. Nor had they thought of the Soviet Union as a democracy of sorts.[2]

How did Sovietologists of the revisionist persuasion react when it appeared that their assessment of the Soviet Union had led them astray? Did they look back in a questioning way to ask where it had gone wrong in the light of what we know and are learning now.[3] Robert Tucker, a biographer of Stalin, put much of the blame on the lack of knowledge of Russian history among his colleagues. The Soviet system, as he saw it, replicated patters in Russian history under the tsars. Had the Sovietological profession not regarded the Soviet system as a fundamental break with Russian history, had it been more receptive to historical thinking, it would have been less inclined to assume that incremental change would be sufficient to deal with the problems of the 1980s.[4] The author could have added that the profession not only lacked a sense of history, but was interested in current Soviet affairs mainly as seen through the prism of changing facts and fashions in political science. It was not much interested in Russia's past and culture, let alone the experience of other countries. Kipling's "What should they know of England who only England know?" applies equally to Russia. But it is not at all obvious that a greater sense of historical continuity would have been of much help in this specific situation. For the acuteness and depth of the "Problems of the 1980s" ("crisis" would have been a more appropriate term) were by no means common knowledge in these circles. In such a case, why delve into Russian history for answers? Tucker claims, inter alia, that Amalrik's capacity in the 1960s to foresee what Russia's future might contain can be explained with reference to his professional specialization as a historian of tsarist Russia.[5] There is, of course, some merit in stressing the cultural-political continuation between the old Russia and the new, which political scientists (having such high hopes for the political effects of modernization) often ignored or dismissed. But Amalrik specialized in the Middle Ages, really the pretsarist period, which does not offer much guidance with regard to Soviet policy in the second half of the twentieth century; there were greater experts in this field who were not inspired in the way Amalrik was. While a knowledge of Russian history is an essential tool (and while many political scientists were not well versed in this field), imagination and an instinctive feeling for the undercurrents in Soviet society were needed to reach such prescient conclusions in the 1960s.

There was no collective admission of error, nor could there have been one, because not all practitioners had erred in equal measure. But how to explain that there were virtually no individual admissions either? There was no confession, primarily, because there was no guilt feeling. There were many ways to rationalize error. These practitioners had been in good company, and who can know for certain whether apparent errors will not be the truth of tomorrow? There is a psychological mechanism that makes human beings prefer pleasure over pain, and admission of error is certainly a painful experience.

II

Critics have cited a dismal failure of political science in general, as well as myopia and excessive optimism with regard to the Soviet Union. But these charges came mainly from outside the profession, or at any case from experts who had not been involved in the methodological discussions of earlier years.[6]

How did mainstream Sovietology react? Generalization is difficult. A definite summing up may be far off, but an interim balance sheet is clearly called for. Major research centers were running "What went wrong?" seminars, but as Peter Rutland noted, expressions of mea culpa at such gatherings were noticeably lacking.[7]

George Breslauer, who had sponsored the concept of "welfare authoritarianism".[8] believed that the "very intemperate polemics" against Sovietology were based on misrepresentation and expressed the fear that the intellectual history of Sovietology would be replaced by the caricatures advanced by today's critics.[9] He was echoed by Thomas Remington, who argued that the strictures on Sovietology were partly based on unrealistic criteria of evaluation, while others were not borne out by an examination of the record of scholarship in the field.[10] According to Breslauer, the last thing Sovietology needed was an acrimonious debate about "who got it right?" But there still remains the question: who got it wrong—basically, consistently, confidently—and why?

As two leading sociologists put it, there is the inherent inability of social science to predict the particular—the predictive successes of sociology and political science on the macro level having been meager.

> What we could have reasonably expected from the social scientists working in the Sovietological field was something more modest than a prediction of the actions of Gorbachev and Yeltsin or their opponents. Rather they should have produced, on the basis of mapping out the broad, gradual social and economic changes, a description of the conditions on the eve of the great transition which would have left open, at least implicitly, the possibility of what actually happened, leaving specific predictions for daring spirits, scholars or outsiders, who were willing to make risky bets. Most Sovietologists, however, assessed the situation in the late 1980s in ways which did not allow for the coming revolutionary changes. What they did was, in fact, no less daring than to expect a revolution. They expected just the opposite of what happened.[11]

In other words, it is one thing not to have predicted in 1988 the impending demise of the Soviet Union (which virtually no one did), another to misjudge the essence of the regime and to stress its stability. The revisionists did not just believe that the Soviet system was a going concern, they were convinced that some form of pluralism had already replaced the old monolithic structures: modernization and socioeconomic progress had transformed the Soviet Union. *Perestroika* was already an established fact. Hence it was no longer necessary to focus on the leadership and on ideology but to do empirical research in certain sections of Soviet society. The revisionists were optimistic with regard to the resilience of the regime, its ability to resolve existing conflicts such as the nationality problem, and failed to see that modernization, far from helping to resolve those tensions, exacerbated them. They thought that the Soviet regime was becoming gradually more rational, and they were optimistic with regard to the success of reforms and the transformability of the Soviet regime.

It is certainly intriguing that the more pessimistic Soviet citizens became in the 1970s and early 1980s, the more optimism prevailed among some people in the West. How can one explain this curious dichotomy? Various explanations come to mind. Revisionists could argue that their assumptions and analysis had been basically correct but that the downfall of the Soviet system had been the result of Gorbachev's miscalculations and inept policies. (But if Gorbachev had illusions with regard to the reformability of the regime, he shared them with the Western revisionists.) This line is also taken by orthodox Leninists in Russia; they failed to see that while Gorbachev's reforms may have been ill-timed or bad, the system could still have been unreformable.

The revisionists asked the wrong questions and opted for the wrong approaches. They were preoccupied with peripheral issues in the Soviet system in which they detected growing similarities with Western societies. They ignored basic factors in the dynamics of Soviet politics. At the same time, there was a strange effort to import all kinds of fashionable concepts from other fields—economics, political sociology, and social psychology—which had little, if any, relevance to the subject at hand. These concepts included developmental theory, modernization, interest group politics, state corporatism, social contract theory, devolution of power, self-stabilizing oligarchy, administered society, and bureaucratic politics. Various rational-technical "ideal types" were bandied about without much attention to the specifics of the Soviet system and its unique and unprecedented character. To paraphrase Mikhail Bakhtin, the theorist of literature, something akin to the carnivalization of Sovietology was taking place.

As late as 1988, a report by a committee drawn from the leading scholarly institutions in the field on "bridging the methods gap" in Soviet foreign policy studies was wholly preoccupied with operational definitions of variables, deductive theory, the interaction of multiple factors, predictive underdetermination, and other issues bothering the theoreticians of international politics. The report reached the conclusion that "both positivism and holism can make valuable contributions to the study of Soviet foreign policy."[12] But time was running out; two years later, a senior member of the fraternity who had been close to the revisionists made it known that he did not think that Soviet studies could learn all that much from political science theory, with its commitment to quantification and its overarching models of political systems that were mostly abstractions.[13]

While the revisionists were only too willing to take up loans from colleagues outside the Soviet field, they showed parochialism once it came to familiarizing themselves with the research on Soviet affairs in other countries such as Britain, France, or Germany. Among Soviet émigrés there was a considerable body of knowledge about the society in which they had lived, but it continued to be ignored. Nor were the political scientists greatly interested in the findings of Soviet experts belonging to other disciplines. In the final analysis they seem to have taken notice only of those who attended their own conferences and seminars and contributed to their professional journals.

And thus it came to pass that ordinary Soviet citizens, total strangers to theory building and conceptualization, were feeling in their bones in what direction their society was moving, whereas many Western scholars, fortified by what they thought to be trustworthy theoretical models, had no such misgivings. In retrospect, they would have spent their time more effectively if they had engaged in reading Soviet novels, or watching Soviet plays or movies, an impressionistic method, but one far more likely to provide important insights concerning the state of Soviet society.[14] These novels and plays, reflected Soviet realities, whereas revisionist scholarship much of the time steered clear of the real world.

III

British writers, Alec Nove and R. H. Davies belong to an older generation and another discipline (economics and economic history). Both published books early on during the *glasnost–perestroika* period, running commentaries on the startling *glasnost* revelations. Their writings reflect the genuine excitement generated by the reform movement (whose prospects they overrated), but it would also appear that they were motivated by the realization that at least some of their own books of an earlier period had now been put into question, especially insofar as they concerned the Stalin period. Nove had never been uncritical of Stalin; unlike some American revisionists, he had not downplayed the human cost of the forcible collectivization of agriculture.[15] Nor had he ever claimed that Stalin and his practices had been altogether inevitable. But he had argued that in all probability Stalinism was bound to happen and that there had been no real alternative. Without Stalin, the Soviet Union would not have become a major industrial power, defeated Nazi Germany in the war, and eventually become a superpower. Thus success, in the final analysis, justified Stalin's practices – at least up to a point. This was the line taken earlier on by Carr and Deutscher; and while Nove was not uncritical of their writings, while he saw clearer than they did the negative aspects of Stalinism, he did not stray too far from their views. The situation drastically changed with *glasnost*, and as the house that Stalin built came crashing down, when requiems for socialism were officiated in Russia, a re-examination of these judgments of yesteryear clearly became necessary.[16]

Davies, an economist teaching in Birmingham, had taken a line close to Carr's, with whom he had collaborated on his history of the Soviet Union. Davies's approach was sympathetic to the Soviet Union without necessarily supporting all of its policies. True, even Carr had to some extent modified his position vis-à-vis Stalin toward the end of his long life. In a short book, *The Soviet Union from Lenin to Stalin*, Carr went so far as to call Stalin "a ruthless despot."[17] One would look in vain for such an emotional comment in Carr's multivolume history of the Soviet Union. Davies certainly did not agree on all issues with the new generation of American revisionists – partly perhaps because they did not recognize the merits of their predecessors (the Glasgow group, including Jacob Miller, Rudolf Schlesinger, and Alec Nove), who had rejected even in the 1950s the totalitarian hypothesis as a "crude oversimplification." Davies also criticized the excesses of American revisionism for dismissing ideology and the personality of Stalin as of little importance and focusing instead on allegedly inexorable economic and social factors. In their writings Stalin had emerged not as a powerful dictator but as a moderator or referee choosing from various policy possibilities.[18] A certain shift in Davies's views under the impact of the Gorbachev era is unmistakable, but for a radical reassessment one looks in vain.

Michael Lewin, a leading social historian, exerted a powerful influence on American revisionism. He had concentrated on agrarian questions and, like Nove and Davies, published a book on the enormous prospects of *perestroika*. Some of his comments have been quoted elsewhere in this study; as time went by, his predictions became more cautious, but there was no re-examination of the optimistic and positive views he had expressed with so much emphasis and consistency in the past.

The same is true of some younger American revisionists such as Sheila Fitzpatrick and J. Arch Getty. The basic tenet in Fitzpatrick's writings prior to 1987 was that there had been great progress and upward social mobility under the Soviet regime (admittedly at a price); that the true lesson of the Russian revolution, as many saw it, was the superiority of a planned economy; and that as the regime had become permanent, it must have satisfied at least some social demands and honored some of its promises.[19] As she saw it, moral judgment on the Soviet system was reprehensible: "The Russian revolution is now part of history, not an aspect of contemporary politics. I have tried to treat it as such."[20]

This approach is similar in many ways to the line taken by the revisionist school in Germany, with its opposition to moral condemnation of Nazism, its call to "historicize" Nazism, and its objection to such crude terms as "heroes" and "villains." With the passage of time, these eras should become the object of quiet and scholarly study. The historical reality of Nazism had been as complex as any other historical reality; the time had come to stop using only black and white and to start painting in shades of gray. These were the words of Ernst Nolte, the best known of Germany's revisionists,[21] but they could have served as the guiding principle for Fitzpatrick, except perhaps that she would have preferred shades of light gray in view of the positive aspects of Stalinism. Writing in 1991, Fitzpatrick showed little enthusiasm for the "root and branch" denunciation of Stalin and the "maximalist" (that is, anti-Stalinist) mood of the Soviet intelligentsia. The concept of totalitarianism had acquired (she reported) an aura of radical chic among the Soviet intelligentsia.[22] Like some other revisionists, she evidently resented being stabbed in the back by Soviet colleagues.

Her feelings were shared by J. Thomas Sanders. "Anti-Sovietism is faddish these days," he wrote in 1992, noting that the profoundly negative evaluation of the Soviet experience was grossly overstated.[23] He seems to have been particularly annoyed by the rejection of the totality of the Soviet experiment by Soviet thinkers such as economist Vasili Selyunin, philosopher Aleksander Tsipko, and film director Stanislev Govorukhin, as well as the publication in Russia of Solzhenitsyn's work and "such examples of Cold War historiography as Robert Conquest's *The Great Terror* and Richard Pipes's *The Russian Revolution*." These warnings against participating in discarding the baby with the bathwater are frequently heard after the fall of modern dictatorships.

Lastly, in 1985, the year Gorbachev came to power, J. Arch Getty published a book entitled *Origins of the Great Purge*, in which he argued that the terror of the 1930s arose mainly out of disagreements at the top over various political, social, and economic issues. He did not argue in so many words that the terror was an optical illusion fabricated by unreliable witnesses, but he came close to it. He conceded that many thousands of innocent people were arrested and executed. Stalin was not exonerated, but his main crime was apparently not to have paid enough attention to what his underlings were doing. Getty called previous scholarship on the terror "sloppy and methodologically bankrupt," claiming that he based his own work on "real sources" – KGB and party files.[24] Getty's revolutionary theses were welcomed by some fellow revisionists, who called it a "landmark" in the writing of Soviet political history, an "exciting and timely book, a new and original explanation".[25] Others considered it a monstrous aberration showing a naïveté bordering on the ridiculous.

Four years later, a fellow revisionist noted that Getty "had become far less-one sided" under the impact of *glasnost*. However, Davies still compared him with Rudolf Schlesinger.[26] Like Fitzpatrick, Getty was not happy about the *glasnost* revelations ("from a scholarly point of view all may not be as rosy as it appears").[27]

According to Getty the critics of Stalin were missing the "plebeian dimension" – class struggle and conflict in Soviet society, which had provided support for Stalin. Thus the debate shifted to a different topic, the measure of social and political support for Stalinism. Getty moderated his original thesis about the purges (now called a "holocaust"!). But there was no admission that the basic approach had been wrong.[28]

The history of all sciences is strewn with false assertions and contentions. If there were bitter controversies in the natural sciences that in retrospect seem wholly inexplicable, it does not come as a surprise that in Sovietology, more a craft than a science, there was equally stubborn resistance against accepting the obvious. In part it may have been a question of prestige; having invested so much intellectual capital in building theories, it was difficult to admit mistakes. Sometimes it was a matter of training and education: having grown up in a certain academic tradition, accustomed to certain methods and approaches, it was not at all easy to relinquish them. On top of all this was the mistaken belief that a scholarly approach meant taking morality out of history and politics.

Questions about the shortcomings of Sovietology were asked after 1990 and suggestions made about how to overcome them. Fleron and Hoffmann argued that Sovietologists had been unprepared for post-Communism "because we had been influenced too little by Western social science rather than too much."[28] In other words, they had read the wrong books and articles. They had been too much preoccupied with the uniqueness of the Soviet regime; there had been too much policy-oriented research, and linguistic skills had been insufficient. They had focused on the top rather than the bottom of the social pyramid and tended to judge regimes by how they treated intellectuals.

What were the new directions that seemed most promising to over-come these shortcomings? What theories should be used to understand the political and cultural revolution in the former Soviet Union? Fleron and Hoffman mention Durkheim, Freud, and Saussure, the re-evaluation of former approaches, theories of colonialization and federalism, theories of traditionalism and modernism, but above all Clifford Geertz's classic "Deep Play: Notes on the Balinese Cockfight" ("your view of *perestroika* and post-communism may never be the same again.")[29] The authors freely refer to hermeneutic interpretations, to "synchronic" and "diachronic," to idiographic and nomothetic approaches, to cognitive traditionalism, and other concepts well known to students of the social sciences. If these concepts and theories were not known to the Sovietologists earlier on, this is a matter of regret. But would Saussure's and Geertz's classic essay on cockfights have made a decisive difference in understanding the reasons for the decline of the Soviet empire—or the conflict between, say, Gor-bachev and Ligachev, or Yeltsin and Khasbulatov? This, to put it cau-tiously, is doubtful. The desperate search for a miracle concept (or concepts) among authors as yet undiscovered and books as yet unread reminds one of the alchemists' quest for the philosopher's stone. The alchemists, it will be recalled, never succeeded in manufacturing gold from other substances, and it can be taken for granted that their successors will be equally unsuccessful.

The failure of mainstream academic Sovietology has been interpreted by some as a by-product of the general crisis of political science (and of much of social science and social history). It ought to be recalled that this was the era of the "triumph of theory" (and of pseudoscience) in these disciplines, of the cult of relativism, of faddish new terminologies, of abstract model building, and the antics of the Modern Language Associa-tion and other such groups. Many fields were affected as a result, and it would have been a near miracle if the study of Soviet politics had been uncontaminated. There is some truth in this argument as emphasized earlier on. But why did the study of Russian literature by and large escape the destructive fashions affecting other fields of literary scholarship? Why, on the other hand, was the record of the study of Soviet economics less than brilliant, even though these fashions played hardly any role at all? Acci-dent may have played a certain role; perhaps there were connections and reasons that have not yet clearly emerged. At present the outside observer can only register what happened and pose questions to be answered at a future date.

IV

The fact that all was not well in the field of Soviet studies was no secret in the 1970s and 1980s; controversies in the professional journals bear witness to this effect. Trying in 1986 to provide an interim balance sheet on the impact of the revisionist school, I noted that far from clarifying issues, it had obfuscated them, and that, in any case, [it] now belonged to the past.[30] Even earlier, there had been skeptical voices from inside the revisionist camp—for instance, with regard to the value of the pluralism concept, according to which it was unsuitable with regard to Soviet politics. The passion for comparison was decried, and it was suggested to focus on the uniqueness of Soviet society.[31] But by and large, it was not accepted that Sovietology had strayed far from Soviet realities until the very subject of the discipline—the Soviet Union—disappeared.

The first detailed, closely reasoned attack on the record of mainstream Sovietology under *glasnost* was made by Martin Malia, a historian of the older generation.[32] He became known to a wider public as the author of the essay signed "Z", in which he predicted the failure of Gorbachev's reforms. Later yet he was an ardent supporter of the Yeltsin regime and expressed great confidence concerning its long-term prospects.[33] "From under the Rubble" (which we mentioned earlier on) is a devastating account of how economists, political scientists, and sociologists specializing in the Soviet Union had gone wrong over a long period—and why: how American economists had failed to take into account not only the unreliability of Soviet statistics, but, more importantly, the low quality of industrial output; how political scientists with their value-free categories had increasingly blurred the Soviet Union's historical specificity under a vocabulary that spoke in universal political and social terms; how the emphasis on "development," "authoritarianism," and "pluralism" had resulted in the image of Sovietism as a road to modernity and progress—as another species of a modern economy and multipolar polity; and how revisionist historians had shifted their attention to a particular kind of social history that led to the rehabilitation of Sovietism and even "soft Stalinism."[34]

> And so, by the mid-1980s and the onset of *perestroika*, revisionist historical writing had spelled out period by period, and in concrete terms, the basically positive evaluation of Sovietism given in different ways by economics, political science and sociology. And the implied conclusion of this whole interdisciplinary joint venture was that a mature Communism, since it had grown into an advanced industrial urbanized superpower, was ready for a liberalizing reform that would make of Russia a wholly "modern" society. So Gorbachev's *perestroika* was received by most Sovietologists with enthusiasm and was happily processed through a panoply of predictive models for portents of success. But *perestroika* did not rejuvenate Communism, it killed it.[35]

Malia does not deny that Sovietism engaged in development of sorts with its concomitants of urbanization, but such modernization was wholly driven by the political purposes of Communism—hence its sterility. It was capable of imitating and multiplying industrial models taken from the West, but it did not have the capacity to innovate on its own—hence its decline and ultimate downfall.

The Malia "state of the art" survey caused greater annoyance among the fraternity than previous critiques, as it coincided with the breakdown of the Soviet Union. Only a few months earlier, Jerry Hough, appearing before a congressional committee, had argued that economic reform in the Soviet Union was going ahead with amazing speed and that Soviet political problems had been grossly exaggerated—modern countries did not break up: Gorbachev was secure.[36] Those in the West who had any doubts in this regard had no understanding of Russia's past and present. A few weeks after, the Soviet Union had ceased to exist.

Malia had seldom commented on current Soviet affairs prior to 1989; thus it was easy for him to point to the mistakes of those who had come on record when he kept silent. But such arguments hardly invalidated the substance of his views. He was clearly mistaken on certain issues, such as his polemic against Richard Löwenthal's concept of modernization theory. Löwenthal had not argued that Sovietism was a good model for development in backward Third World countries; nor had he subscribed to the concept of convergence.[37]

Malia branded revisionist historiography as "Neo-Menshevist." A similar view was expressed by William Odom, who claimed that the Russian (and other European) Social Democrats had been convinced that Marxism was basically sound as a theory of development, that Lenin was merely a Social Democrat gone astray and thus not beyond redemption. Their interpretations of the Soviet experience fostered the debate in American universities about whether Stalinism emerged organically from Leninism or whether it was a discontinuity, a break with Leninism. The dispute is alive and well in many classrooms, conferences, and academic journals; and these inheritors of the mantle of Menshevism continue to find evidence of political pluralism in Leninism that was blighted by Stalinism."[38]

This is not in accordance with the historical record. While Trotskyism and various old and new left sects shared such opinions, most Mensheviks never did, at least not after 1921—and there was no Sovietology before that date. In fact, the Mensheviks, with all their internal disputes, were not only the best-informed critics of Soviet Communism, but also the ones most consistently correct in their assessments. It has been said about Russian literature of the nineteenth century that "we all came out of Gogol's *Shinel* [overcoat]". With even greater justice it could be said that all serious Sovietology came out of the mantle of Menshevism, including those practitioners who were not aware of it.

Malia also wrote, "In short, there is no such thing as socialism and the Soviet Union has built it."[39] This was, at the very least, a premature statement. Is it really necessary to reiterate that the success of market economics in the former Soviet Union is by no means a foregone conclusion? Elsewhere in Europe the socialist idea had produced the welfare state. As time passes since the downfall of the Soviet empire, celebrations of the final victory of capitalism appear more and more premature.

V

The Cold War had been one of the main bones of contention in the ongoing debate on the character of Soviet policies and relations with the outside world. As the Cold War ended, the question of its origins, place in history, and the reasons for its end again come to the fore. This discussion started with George Kennan's famous dispatches from Moscow in 1946, advocating containment, and the articles in which Walter Lippmann popularized the term "Cold War." Lippmann declared that containment was too costly and eventually came to observe (in November 1947) that "the Russians have lost the Cold War and know it."[40]

There were opponents of the Cold War in the West from the very beginning, mainly Communists and fellow travelers, but also pacifistically inclined commentators and, generally speaking, those who believed that diplomacy had not been given a fair chance to settle the dispute with the Soviet Union. Following its experience in World War II, it was only natural that Moscow regarded Eastern Europe and the Balkans as its *cordon sanitaire*.. If, in the course of establishing its sphere of influence, it imposed its political system on Eastern Europe, this was regrettable but had to be accepted in the interest of world peace.

Only in the 1960s did a systematic reappraisal of the origins of the Cold War begin. Its influence on the profession and the media was considerable for almost two decades. There were differences in the argumentation of the Cold War revisionists, sometimes significant ones, and it is impossible to do justice to the various schools of thought by generalizing.

By and large, however, the reassessment was along the following lines: the breakdown of the wartime alliance and the outbreak of the Cold War were partly, or mainly, the fault of the West, above all the United States.[41] Soviet demands were not unreasonable. The Soviet system was basically conservative, and the Soviet Union had no interest in world revolution. Furthermore the Soviet Union was far too weak after the war to engage in military adventures. While Soviet policy was essentially peaceful, or at least not aggressive, Stalin's crudity and mistakes played into the hands of American hawks, who were out to have their confrontation. As most of these writers saw it, American capitalism aggressively promoted a policy of the open door. This and the hysterical fear of Communism, utterly divorced from reality, were the mainsprings of U.S. strategy, not the alleged battle between freedom and enslavement. Seen in this light, the history of the postwar era, particularly after Stalin's death but even before (Stalin's offer on Germany in 1952!) is a chain of opportunities missed by Washington. By that time the military-industrial complex had developed a vested interest in the continuation of the Cold War.

This is also the line taken by post–Cold War revisionism, which can be summarized briefly as follows. For a variety of reasons America needed an enemy in the postwar world and found it in the Soviet Union, which most of the time was on the defensive rather than being an aggressor. There was no need for Americans to get so worked up about an enemy who was, as events proved, an empty shell with a decrepit economy and insufficient political will to keep it from falling apart. In brief, the alleged Soviet threat had been entirely, or almost entirely, a figment of American imaginations.[42] The basic flaws of such latter-day revisionism are the same as those of the earlier species: it is ahistorical, inasmuch as it assumes that the Soviet Union in 1950 or 1960 was the same as in 1990 and that the correlation of forces on the world scene was the same. It assumes, secondly, that since Soviet foreign policy was not more aggressive in the postwar era, the Western defense effort was unnecessary, failing even to consider the possibility that Western defense had something to do with Soviet restraint. Lastly, it focuses almost entirely on what American policy makers did, ignoring the Soviet side, including the evidence that came to light after *glasnost*.

The revisionist credo – the absence of aggressive designs on the part of the Soviet Union – was based on hope rather than knowledge, for no one abroad could know at the time what Moscow's true intentions were. Western critics of revisionism did not claim that the Soviet Union's course was one of relentless expansion; they argued that it was dangerous to lead the Soviets into temptation through giving the wrong signals, as in Korea. After the disintegration of the Soviet Union and East Germany, documents were uncovered according to which detailed blueprints existed for offensives into Central and Western Europe and the occupation of these areas.[43] It could still be argued that military action against NATO was quite unlikely, but it cannot be claimed that the idea never crossed the mind of strategic planners.

Some revisionists tended to put less emphasis on American villainy and more on misunderstandings: Western leaders and their advisers tended to misunderstand Soviet motives. Furthermore, there was a constant spiral of escalation – hardline Western politicians were providing indirect assistance to the hawks in the Kremlin, and vice versa. There were similar nuances concerning Soviet strength. In the beginning most tended to stress Russia's weakness; and when the Cold War ended, it again became fashionable to argue that the West had always overrated Soviet strength. Western policy, as Strobe Talbott noted, was based on "grotesque exaggerations" of what the Soviet Union could do.

But while the Cold War lasted, most revisionists took a very different line: the Soviet Union was a "giant" (the title of one of Richard Barnet's books). It had militarily reached parity with the United States, perhaps even overtaken it. Under the circumstances, Washington had no alternative but to compromise with the Russians. Frightening scenarios abounded: soon there would be Soviet submarines and surface ships armed with cruise missiles off the American coast.

According to the same scenario, the world was moving away from capitalist democracy; Communism was growing stronger, especially in the Third World but also in Europe (the rise of Euro-Communism). In these circumstances, it seemed almost suicidal to make the promotion of democratic institutions and human rights the cornerstone of American foreign policy. Stephen Cohen wrote in 1983 that Soviet society was remarkably stable. It was ridiculous to assume that it faced a crisis; the dissidents, were of little consequence and in any case did not know what they wanted. Eight years earlier, Andrei Sakharov, not a politologist by profession, had written that his country was moving toward a major systemic crisis arising from its inability to live up to its promises. Some Western observers argued that the Soviet people and those of other Communist countries were happy with their lot and supported their governments. As doubt appeared about Soviet strength in the 1980s, a growing number of voices claimed that the Communist leaders felt besieged and that, for this reason, it was wrong to drive them into a corner.

In the 1970s, following the breakdown of détente and contrary to revisionist predictions, Soviet foreign policy became more adventurous from Angola to Afghanistan. These operations were dismissed as exceptional and unimportant and probably reactions to Western policies that were perceived as a threat in Moscow. Western writers of this school could never quite make up their minds whether Soviet leaders were strong, conservative, and purposeful but peaceloving—or weak and gravitating toward paranoia, in which case due consideration had to be taken of their fears and general psychological lability.

When the Cold War ended, revisionists accused Western hawks of having misled Western public opinion all along, and of having invented the concept of the irreversibility of Communism, thus magnifying a nonexistent danger. But this concept had been invented by Brezhnev, a Soviet leader considered moderate by the revisionists, and found its classic formulation in the "Brezhnev Doctrine." The Soviet army had shown in the case of Czechoslovakia that the doctrine was no mere abstraction.

Who was right and who was wrong in the dispute on Soviet military strength and political ambitions? That the idea of world revolution had been buried long ago was no secret among Western hawks, but it was equally obvious that Soviet policy was engaged on a course of expansion, wherever it could be pursued without risk. Whether such expansion was basically defensive in inspiration—as some claimed—was an interesting scholastic question but of little practical importance.

Many Westerners believed with George Kennan that the Soviet empire had reached the stage of overstretch. But there was no sign that this nightmare caused sleepless nights for Soviet leaders. Nor could it be reasonably argued that the Soviet Union was militarily weak. It spent a far higher part, as compared to the United States of its GNP on rearmament. Only under Gorbachev did it become clear how high the share had been: most Western estimates, including those of the CIA, had greatly underestimated it. World War II showed the military strength of the Soviet Union; but for the existence of the Eastern front the outcome of the war might have been quite different. Was there any reason to assume that the Soviet army in 1953 or 1963 was any weaker than it had been 1943? It was precisely for this reason—overwhelming Soviet power—that some Western leaders counseled against firm responses to Soviet moves—for example, in Czechoslovakia and Afghanistan—invoking the threat of incineration of Western cities. It was only a small step from warnings against the "inordinate fear of Communism" (Carter) to invoking the specter of genetic disaster.

The motives of Cold War revisionism were mixed. Among the moderate were many men and women of good will guided by what seemed to them common sense. In any quarrel, personal or collective, truth and justice were never entirely on one side. Hence the need to understand the other side and to compromise. The same people would not, on the whole, have suggested a similar approach to the Nazi regime—but such a comparison seemed to them anathema. To a large degree, revisionism was generated by the old left and above all by the students' revolt and the Vietnam war. To some extent it was the outcome of the academic fashions of the late 1960s, according to which the Soviet Union was becoming pluralist and democratic in some way. In addition, as George Urban put it:

> There were, furthermore, those in Western Europe, and especially the U.S., who were too uneducated to have theoretical or methodological axes to grind, but had so profound a hate for American institutions and presidents— especially Richard Nixon and Ronald Reagan—that they thought to clothe all things Soviet in a favorable light on the basis that this will outrage Nixon or "undermine the confidence of the military-industrial complex."[45]

The motive of self-hatred has been singled out, but at least as important was ignorance, both in the academic world and in government. The Cold War had become boring and unfashionable. As for the historians preoccupied with the Cold War, the majority had no special knowledge of Soviet affairs, but were specialists in American diplomatic history. The result was often disconcerting and sometimes funny; it was as if a sports reporter commented on a match in which he could see one boxer or one football team only. This generation lacked an instinctive understanding of Sovietism, as it did of fascism, of Muslim fundamentalism, or indeed of creeds and political systems radically different from America's.

In the late 1970s Cold War revisionism ran out of steam; as the zeitgeist changed, so did the comments. The grosser forms of attacks against American imperialism became rare, partly because everything in this direction had been said, but also because the earlier allegations now seemed exaggerated, if not altogether misguided. A post-revisionist school appeared on the scene, trying to apportion praise and blame more fairly.[46] In some ways the problems facing this school were the same that had confronted an earlier generation of Cold War critics; most of them were diplomatic historians specializing in American affairs. They could write with confidence about Gromyko and his underlings, but with a few notable exceptions they had little knowledge of the essence of the Soviet regime and were at sea when dealing with the mainsprings of Soviet domestic policy, Communist doctrine, and its impact on foreign policy.

The post-revisionists, too, made a considerable effort, at least during the early period, to dissociate themselves from Western "Cold War" historians who had squarely put the blame for the events of 1947 to 1950 on the Russians. It was only in Gorbachev's day that John Gaddis, the best known representative of the post-revisionist school, was to write that President Truman had been right when he had warned Congress in March 1947 that the world faced a struggle between two ways of life, one based on the will of the majority and the other based on the will of a minority, forcibly imposed on the majority: "The idea of freedom proved more durable than the practice of authoritarianism, and as a consequence, the Cold War ended."[47]

Even five or ten years earlier this would have been a very controversial statement. Truman's views had been considered blindly anti-Communist, naïve, and self-righteous. Everyone knew that the conflict was mainly about balances of power and spheres of influence. As Gaddis put it in 1992: "Many of us had become too sophisticated to see . . . that the Cold War really was about the imposition of autocracy and the denial of freedom." "Sophisticated" is probably the wrong word in the context, but the author's meaning was clear.

Twenty years earlier, Gaddis had been less categorical in defense of Truman. While dissociating himself from the revisionists, he stated, "[N]either side can bear sole responsibility for the onset of the Cold War."[48] If perhaps somewhat greater responsibility should be assigned to Stalin than to Truman, it was because there were greater domestic constraints on Truman than on Stalin. Stalin was immune from the pressures of parliament, public opinion, the press, and even ideology.[49] This is perfectly correct, but it also means that if the American Congress and public opinion had been more inclined to give in to Soviet demands, Truman (and his successors) would have been well advised to follow suit.

How did the Cold War revisionists react once the Soviet Union ceased to exist? Lafeber concluded that there had been not one Cold War but four.[50] Ronald Steel wrote that the Cold War had lasted so long because this had served the interests of the United States and the Soviet Union in Europe.[51] Noam Chomsky observed that the situation in Latin America was far from satisfactory, a correct, but irrelevant statement.[52] Lundestad and Alperowitz added that the United States was in decline.[53] Richard Barnet agreed: the United States had paid dearly for its Cold War victory.[54] Yet others took a long time to recover their breath.

All these arguments had little to do with the revisionists' writings during the Cold War. They had claimed for many years that the Cold War was both dangerous and unnecessary, that it was largely America's fault, that it could be ended almost any time – and that there was not the slightest chance that it could be won. Even Arthur Schlesinger had been convinced that there was an international conspiracy of hardliners who in "weird lockstep are marching the rest of us down the road to extinction." A few years later, Schlesinger concluded that the proponents of liberal society were proved right. After seventy years of trial, Communism turned out—by the confession of its own leaders—to be an economic, political, and moral disaster.[55] True revisionists would not go remotely that far, because the progressive character, even if submerged, of the Soviet empire had been one of their fundamental articles of faith. It had been a much needed countervailing force against American imperialist aggression.

More than one generation of American students had been taught the subject on the basis of a textbook entitled *America, Russia and the Cold War*, written by Walter Lafeber, a prize-winning moderate revisionist.[56] Covering the 1980s, the author describes President Reagan as vague, ignorant, and confused, and having a low approval rating. Under Reagan, U.S. policy was taking a turn back to 1950. His ideas were derived, at least in part, from a 1940 movie called *Murder in the Air*. American foreign policy was inconsistent and contradictory.[57] Reagan committed many mistakes and suffered failures in various parts of the world. It was a very depressing picture indeed; the chapter covering the years from 1977 to 1990 is entitled "From Cold War to Old War." An unprejudiced reader was bound to reach the conclusion that such shortsighted and unwise leadership could only lead America to disaster.

But then, quite suddenly, an earthquake occurred, not in America but in Eastern Europe, and instead of two superpowers there was only one. The Cold War was over. The threat of nuclear holocaust was removed, at least for the time being. What had happened and why? To this question, diplomatic historians, alas, could not provide a plausible answer.

Kennan wrote that it was ridiculous to argue that the Republicans had won the Cold War—it had been a bipartisan effort.[58] The Cold War had indeed broken out under President Truman, although Churchill and Bevin had urged stronger resistance against Soviet encroachments even before.

What was one to make of Strobe Talbott's arguments? A few years earlier he had written a book expressing horror with regard to Reagan's policy with regard to the Russians.[59] He referred to the famous "evil empire" and "decay of Communism" speeches, the primitive anti-Communism displayed, the bitter hostility, and the stupid assumption that a position of strength could be attained in the contest with the Russians. Reagan was the first president who willfully and persistently set about to break with the past, and this effort was doomed to failure. The impact of the American hard line was to make the Russians angry.[60] As Seweryn Bialer reported from Moscow, members of the Russian political class displayed feelings of rage and a mood of defiance; they were about to teach Reagan a lesson.[61]

But the concern shown by Talbott was misplaced: Reagan was not impeached and replaced, and his foreign policy did not cause fatal harm to the United States. A very few years later, he walked down Pennsylvania Avenue with Gorbachev, who seemed neither enraged or defiant, but in an excellent mood.

One of the main bugbears of the doves had been Reagan's SDI ("Star Wars") initiative in 1983, a fantastic scheme that they said would never work, would ruin America financially, and would impel the Russians to build up their military arsenal. Perhaps they were right with regard to the technical feasibility of the program—this may not be proven for a long time. But leading Russian foreign affairs experts made it known in later years that SDI had contributed to "changing Soviet arms policy and ending the Cold War." Among them were Aleksander Bessmertnykh, former Soviet foreign minister and Anatoly Chernayev, Gorbachev's foreign policy adviser.[62]

"Hawks" and "doves" are imprecise terms; furthermore, not all policy suggestions made by hawks were prudent, and not all the proposals of the doves were stupid and self-defeating. But in the light of the historical record it is impossible to argue that the Cold War lasted for so long because Western hawks provided much needed arguments for their Soviet counterparts—and vice versa. It could be maintained with much greater justice that a firm Western line persuaded the Soviet leaders in the end that the attempt to overtake the United States in the military field was hopeless and had ruined their country. This is what the record tends to show and what many Russians now believe.[63]

Western doves did not bring the end of the Cold War any nearer with their insistence on conciliation and concession. A case in point is the opposition of some doves to the activities of Radio Liberty and Radio Free Europe. These Munich-based stations provided a free flow of information to the East and contributed more than any other Western source to the emergence of a critical attitude beyond the Iron Curtain and the erosion of Soviet ideology. These radio services were under constant pressure; Senators J. William Fulbright and Frank Church wanted to abolish them (and almost succeeded). Instructions were given not to broadcast any material that would embarrass the Soviet and East European leaders; and for a while Solzhenitsyn was not permitted to appear. In fact, the policy guidelines for the radio stations that were established to promote the cause of democracy in Eastern Europe read as follows in the 1970s: "RFL/RL have no mandate to advocate the establishment or disestablishment of any particular system, form of state organization or ideology in the areas to which they broadcast."[64] With instructions like these, it seems a miracle that the radios survived at all. When liberty came at last, they received almost unanimous congratulations from leaders, ranging from Václav Havel to Lech Walensa for the crucial role they had played in the overthrow of the Communist regimes; even Gorbachev recommended that they continue to operate. If the doves had had their way, these stations would have ceased operations long ago.

They viewed the disintegration of the Soviet Union and the other East European countries without enthusiasm. There was justified apprehension among all thoughtful observers in the West. With the disappearance of Soviet or Yugoslav supremacy, many nations and mini-states claimed and to some extent obtained statehood. There was reason to fear that some of them would try to expand their territory, fight one another, and mistreat their minorities and that, generally speaking, disorder might ensue in parts of the former Soviet Union and Eastern Europe. These concerns were legitimate, but re establishing Stalinism or Titoism was neither a feasible nor desirable option.

The preservation of international law and order was not, however, the main concern of this school of thought. They felt as if a horse on which they had gambled for a long time had stumbled and not finished the course. They claimed that as a result of the Cold War, America was in a state of steep and fatal decline. The consequence (as Barnet had claimed for years) was "political and moral exhaustion" or, as Lundestad and Alperowitz put it, "social decay."[65] Others argued that as the result of America's victory in the Cold War its position in the world had been fatally weakened (Ronald Steel and others) and that Europe, specifically Germany, had emerged as the big winner of the Cold War. These conclusions did not come as a surprise; most Cold War critics had argued all along that America was weak and in a state of advanced decline. At the same time, it was widely claimed among revisionists that with its victory America had become too strong and thus in a position to cause great mischief. For consistency, one would look in vain in these arguments.

Perhaps America was in decline, as the critics claimed, but the shining examples quoted, Germany and Japan, which had spent far less on defense, also found themselves in considerable difficulties as the Cold War ended. Some European countries that had spent hardly anything on defense had an unemployment rate of 15 to 20 percent. Perhaps there could have been other reasons for the economic recession of the early 1990s? And even if one accepted the reasoning of the Cold War critics, it could still be argued that the Cold War had acted as a Keynesian stimulus to the economy (as World War II had done before). Perhaps the Cold War had even acted as a countervailing factor to American decline? Some thoughtful Cold War revisionists came close to accepting this argument, even though they believed that the money invested in defense could have been used for more productive purposes domestically. Nor was it readily obvious why the Cold War critics should be so concerned about America's loss of political influence in the post–Cold War world. They had never been great believers in American political supremacy in the first place, fearful of the excesses of American imperialism running the world.

That the Soviet Union lost the Cold War will not be seriously disputed in the years to come. But the controversy will continue a long time as to who started it and whether it could not have ended earlier–if only the West had not engaged in an arms race, if it had been more conciliatory and refrained from criticizing Soviet human rights records and other provocative Soviet behavior. There is hardly any important period in history on which there is not some dissent. It is therefore almost certain that Communism will also find some apologists in the West in the years to come. The

Soviet experience, they will argue, does not prove anything, because the country was too backward and its tradition too inauspicious for the success of what was basically a promising idea.

VI

The Russian contribution to the Cold War debate came, by necessity, late in the day. Up to 1988, the old party line prevailed–Soviet foreign policy had always promoted peace and progress, and Western historians were, by definition, mendacious, or at least muddle headed, and the servants of imperialists and warmongers. In 1988 *Pravda* published a very restrained article by Gaddis, stating his post-revisionist position, which was however immediately "refuted" by a party historian.[66] In 1988 and 1989 Soviet historians such as Dashichev and Semiryaga published articles critical of Soviet foreign policy during both the prewar and the postwar periods.

However, mainline Russian historians, especially those working at the Academy of Science, continued to defend Soviet foreign policy, albeit with certain reservations. The present writer participated in a conference in Moscow in 1990, cosponsored by the Soviet foreign ministry. The overall line taken by the Soviet participants was then that, while Stalin and his successors had made major mistakes, so had the West. The allocation of responsibility for the postwar conflict and tension would take a long time.[67]

Gradually, Soviet historiography of the Cold War began to change but less than expected compared with other aspects of the Stalin and post-Stalin period. "Patriotic" considerations probably played a major role in Soviet reluctance to engage in self-criticism. Furthermore, the senior members of the profession had been trained in the Khrushchev and Brezhnev eras. They had faithfully followed the party line and could not simply dissociate themselves from their earlier writings. True, they expressed regret that owing to lack of access to the archives they had not been able to make a significant contribution to analyzing Soviet decision making after 1945.[68] But this, needless to say, was not the only, nor the basic reason for the failure of Soviet historiography.

Soviet historians writing under *glasnost* found Western revisionism absurd. Their sympathies were, by and large, with the post-revisionists. A. M. Filitov argued that a balanced approach was needed in Russia, not a turn by 180 degrees from "unmasking imperialism" to "Soviet ultra-revisionism.[69] Historians were ready to give up some clearly untenable positions, but they still believed that the truth lay somewhere between the Western and the old Soviet position. This goes for the origins of the Cold War as much as for its end. Filitov found it still difficult to make a clear break with the old line; he agreed with Arthur Schlesinger that Communism in the form in which it was built in the Soviet Union had suffered bankruptcy. But Communism in Filitov's eyes was one thing, and the "straitjacket" of the Cold War was another. When Filitov mentioned the defeat of "Communism," he put it into quotation marks. As he saw it, the dismantling of Communism was delayed by the Western policy of continuing the Cold War. N. V. Zagladin, son of a former prominent member of the Central Committee, had no hesitation in stating that the Soviet Union was defeated economically as well as politically. The fact that the chaos that ensued was not in the best interest of the West was a different question altogether.[70]

The beginning, middle, and end of the Cold War are bound to be debated in the Soviet Union for many years to come—probably with even greater passion than in the West, where all possible versions and theories have already been discussed. According to an old Italian saying, "Quando la nave è perduta, tutti san piloti" (When the ship is lost, all became pilots).[71]

7
How Many Victims?

One of the cardinal features of the totalitarian dictatorships of the twentieth century was internal terror, the huge number of "enemies" – and potential enemies–interned and executed. Measured by the standards of Germany and Russia, Fascist Italy was almost a humanitarian society. Not more than a few thousand were exiled or arrested, and not more than a few dozen were executed after 1923. But in the case of Nazi Germany and Soviet Russia repression affected millions of people. The gas chambers became the pronounced feature for which the Hitler regime is now mainly remembered, and the gulag archipelago was an intrinsic part of Soviet policy under Stalin and, to a lesser degree, under his successors. The invention of the concentration camp goes back to the pre-totalitarian age, but totalitarian dictatorships certainly perfected it.

The extent of these crimes–the number of victims who were killed or suffered death or long years of imprisonment and forced labor–has remained a bone of contention to this day. The same is true in all cases of mass murder in our times from the massacres and deliberate starvation of Armenians in World War I to the massacres in Cambodia under the murderous rule of Pol Pot.

Figures quoted in the case of the Armenian deaths range from 100,000 (Turkish sources) to 2 million, (Armenian sources); those referring to the Cambodian killings, from 1 to 2 million. In both cases, well-known public figures (Arnold Toynbee on Turkey and Noam Chomsky concerning Pol Pot) claimed that the number of victims was grossly exaggerated. Many civilians were killed in the Yasenavats concentration camp by Croatian fascists during World War II. Independent historians mentioned the figure of 400,000; the Serbs, 700,000; and some Croats argued that there was no massacre at all. The issue became a major bone of contention between

Serbs and Croats in postwar Yugoslavia, and it contributed to poisoning relations and heightening the tensions that ultimately led to the disintegration of Yugoslavia.

The reasons for these discrepancies are not difficult to fathom: genocide often took place at a time of war or civil war or other internal upheavals, when statistical systems were not developed or incomplete and relevant documents were lost, deliberately destroyed, or did not exist in the first instance. The greater the crime, the less likely that written orders to commit the crime ever existed. Thus, a written order issued by Hitler to exterminate European Jewry has never been found and probably never existed.

Fifty years after the event, some historians of the Holocaust reached the conclusion that the number of those killed at Auschwitz was closer to 1.5 to 2.5 million than to the 4 million, previously estimated. This new estimate did not have any bearing on the total number of Holocaust victims, which has been estimated at between 5.1 and 6 million by all serious researchers. There is no certainty even now, however, that the new figure for Auschwitz is closer to reality than the earlier one, because no complete documentation exists. In the final analysis, both figures rested on an estimate, and those who opted for the lower figures simply preferred to err on the side of caution.

Germany had probably the most developed, comprehensive, and reliable statistical apparatus at the time, and there exist accurate figures for major actions such as Babi Yar in Kiev, where Sonderkommando 42 of the SS, with the support of the German army, killed 33,771 Jews within a few days in 1941.[1] However, by and large, even those who organized the mass murders had no idea how many victims actually died. When, in the middle of the war, Himmler asked Korherr, the chief statistician of the SS, to submit a report providing details as to how many European Jews had actually been deported to the east and killed, the statistician had to operate with approximate figures. The extermination camps were outside Germany. They did not employ official statisticians, their daily reports were by necessity inaccurate, many documents were destroyed, and on top of all this, orders from above dictated that no traces be left—ruling out, among other things, an accurate statisticical record.

Hence it did not come as a surprise that after the war there were considerable divergences in estimates of how many victims had been in camps and how many had been killed in mass shootings.[2] A broad consensus has been reached by serious students who engaged in research on this terrible subject. Outside this consensus are those for whom, for political reasons, the historical facts were unacceptable, especially the neo-Nazis and their sympathizers. As far as they are concerned, genocide never happened. After all, no extermination camp had ever been found intact; perhaps the victims had all committed suicide or disappeared in some other mysterious way, before, during, or after the war. In addition to the objective difficulties of collecting and analyzing statistics, there are people who have a reason to deny or belittle the extent of every case of genocide.

The number of Russian soldiers killed in the Russian-Finnish war of 1939 and 1940 was given at the time as 48,700. But this was under Stalin; more recent publications give a much higher number– 131,000.[3] There is reason to assume that even this figure is somewhat too low. Estimates concerning Soviet soldiers who perished in World War II produced a number that seems to have been arrived at carefully: 8,668,400. It is almost certainly too low.[4] The total population of the Soviet Union at the outbreak of the war was 200.1 million; at its end, 167 million.[5] There is reason to believe that whole categories of victims have either not been included, or not listed fully in estimates of the losses; among the possible exclusions are Russian prisoners of war who died in Germany and reserve officers and soldiers who died in the defense of Moscow, Leningrad, and Stalingrad.

It had, of course, been known that a great number of people had perished in the purges of the 1930s and later in the gulag, as well as during the civil war and collectivization of agriculture. But there were no official (or unofficial) Soviet figures prior to *glasnost*, and estimates published in the West diverged widely. Thus, the distinguished Russian émigré economist Naum Yasny wrote in 1951 that there could not have been more than 3.5 million gulag inmates, whereas the book by Dallin and Nikolayevsky, also published in the 1950s and widely considered a standard work, quoted estimates ranging from 9 to 15 million. Putting more reliance on the lower figures, Robert Conquest, author of another standard work, adduced estimates between 5 and 9 million victims. In the polemical exchanges among Western academics in the 1970s and early 1980s estimates ranged from "tens of thousands" to more than 10 million. According to Solzhenitsyn and the Russian samizdat writer Antonov-Ovseenko, the number of the victims was 15 million or even higher. Under *glasnost* even higher figures were quoted in Russia, ranging up to 60 even 100 million. But these figures included the whole Soviet period, and not only people who were actually killed through state terrorism but the entire demographic shortfall, that is to say, people killed in wartime, children who had not been born, as well as victims of starvation and epidemics.[6] Some of these figures were simply guesswork, some wild, and some plausible; others were attempts to reach more or less accurate figures by way of deduction based on economic or demographic data that were broadly speaking known. But there is no certainty that the figures are even remotely correct. All that is known was that many people disappeared in the late 1930s and during the other purges, but no one could say with any confidence exactly how many. As it appeared subsequently, even the members of the Politburo did not know. If Stalin received detailed weekly or monthly reports about arrests and executions, the documents have not been preserved (except in the case of certain regions) or were not found.

Outside the Soviet Union the purges and the gulag had been followed with fascination and horror even without exact figures. The information came from survivors, both Russians and foreigners, who had been released from the camps; some of them found their way to the West during the war or thereafter. Only faithful communists denied the very existence of the Gulag, and it is not certain that they believed what they proclaimed.

II

In the 1970s and 1980s, some Western Sovietologists claimed that the importance of purges and forced labor had been grossly overstated, both quantitatively and qualitatively: quantitatively, because the number of those involved had been much smaller than widely thought, qualitatively, because there had been no "great fear," as had been claimed by "Cold War historians" in the West. One such revisionist writer argued that the purges had mainly to do with quarrels in the Politburo; another suggested that the purges were a "radical, even hysterical reaction to bureaucracy." The entrenched officeholders were destroyed from "above and below in a chaotic wave of voluntarism and revolutionary puritanism."[7] Stalin's role was not altogether dismissed, but it was certainly downgraded in comparison with earlier writers; such issues as tensions between the "center" and the "periphery" were thought to be of far greater importance, and economic considerations were also adduced. Stalin had more or less stumbled into the terror. A similar interpretation was given out by the German revisionists about Hitler and the Final Solution, except that in the German case the main culprit was said to have been the bureaucracy, whereas in the Soviet Union the terror had been directed against the bureaucracy.

Eyewitness accounts about purges and the gulag were not trusted by the revisionists, since some of these witnesses were too close to events and others were too distant. Still others, including Khrushchev (who wrote in his memoirs that there were some 10 million inmates in the gulag), were "self-interested parties." True, many thousands of innocent people had been arrested and executed, and Stalin was not to be exonerated. But his main crime was apparently not paying enough attention to what his underlings were doing.

A similar line was taken by Robert Thurston, an American scholar who reached the conclusion that there was no pervasive fear and that the majority of people were not terrorized. Moreover, with the appointment of Lavrenti Beria as head of state security in 1938, the tortures were believed to have ceased; after that date the elite was no longer harassed, and criticism from below was encouraged. The total number of victims was considerably smaller than commonly assumed, if only because the NKVD was itself much too small to arrest so many people and keep them in camps. In short, after 1938 the Soviet Union was almost back to normal.[8]

The timing of the publication of these essays and books (1983 to 1985) was unfortunate, for within a year or two after their appearance, a wave of revelations from inside the Soviet Union brought abundant evidence of how great the impact of the purges had been. True, from inside the Soviet Union also came voices claiming that the "liberals" of *Memorial* and other such groups were falsifying history, that most people had enjoyed living through the magnificent 1930s, that some regrettable mistakes had been made, but that in the history of other countries worse crimes had been committed. These arguments were pressed both by neo-Stalinists (like Nina Andreyeva) and as well by ideologists of the extreme right.[9]

Not surprisingly, Western advocates of the don't-let-us-get-emotional thesis were in no hurry to retract their earlier views about the terror or to modify them, though they did become more cautious in their formulations. They regarded the revelations of 1988 and 1989 as a gross overreaction that sooner or later would give way to a more sober and scholarly approach. J. Arch Getty admonished his colleagues to show a more critical attitude toward dubious sources and praised Soviet historians for having paid much attention to *istochnikovedenie*, the evaluation of sources.[10]

It is always praiseworthy to view sources critically, but such criticism, needless to say, should not be limited to sources opposed to the Soviet regime. While Rybakov's novel, *Children of the Arbat*, criticized both by Russian antireformers and by Getty, never claimed to be academic history, the author had lived through the period he described. Thus, as an eyewitness and a survivor he had intuitively a better understanding of it than Western academics, who had no firsthand knowledge of either time or place or the people they were writing about. He was certainly in a better position to judge whether people had been afraid or not.

While the revisionists kept their silence for a while, the demographers and political scientists tried to make sense of the new figures that were coming out of Russia.[11] Unfortunately, the new facts and figures were still of doubtful provenance and in any case quite incomplete. Those that came from critics of the regime were mere estimates or extrapolations, though in some cases they were based on internal Soviet reports. The figures that emanated directly or indirectly from the KGB archives were suspect for a variety of other reasons.[12] The KGB archives and its 10 million files are closed and, in all probability, will remain closed for the foreseeable future. The same is true with regard to the military archives of the Ministry of Defense. There is every reason to assume that many KGB files were burned or shredded, some in Stalin's time, particularly in October 1941, when the German armed forces reached the suburbs of Moscow. Some were very likely destroyed after the Twentieth Party Congress (1956), and some under *glasnost* in the summer of 1990 and especially in the wake of the coup of August 1991.[13]

The most detailed figures were contained in a number of articles by V. N. Zemskov and A. N. Dugin, writers not widely known either in the Soviet Union or abroad, but they happened to be the only ones who had first access to the relevant KGB files. Both authors were openly polemical in their approach. According to their version, they had discovered top secret statistics about the yearly number of gulag inmates not in the KGB archives (where they belonged) but in the central state archives of the

October Revolution–an unlikely place to keep documents of such sensitivity. It is possible that the two authors made a lucky find; it is equally possible that the statistics were planted by the KGB. And it also possible that while the statistics were genuine, they were still inaccurate. The findings of Dugin and Zemskov were mostly published in the periodicals of the rightwing antireform camp, another circumstance that did not inspire confidence.[14]

According to KGB spokesmen in 1989 and 1990, altogether 642,980 men and women had been executed from 1921 to 1954 and between 3.6 and 3.7 million had been "repressed" for political reasons. These figures were first given in a secret letter to Khrushchev dated February 1, 1954, signed by Roman Rudenko (of the Nuremberg trials fame), the attorney general of the Soviet Union, and also by the ministers of justice and interior. If so, how does one explain Khrushchev's reference to 10 million in his autobiography? Various arguments have been advanced to explain that figure and why Khrushchev was mistaken, but none of them has been very convincing.

The following are Dugin's figures on the number of inmates of labor camps:

1934	510,307
1936	839,406
1938	996,367
1940	1,344,408
1942	1,415,596
1944	663,594
1947	808,839
1950	1,416,300
1953	1,727,970

To this one should add the number of residents in labor colonies, usually those with a sentence of less than three years, which was not inconsiderable: it was 457,000 in 1936 and 1,145,000 in 1950. However, the total number of inmates never exceeded 2.6 million at one time; in fact, prior to 1948 it never exceeded 2 million. Furthermore, most of the inmates of the camps and colonies had not been sentenced under paragraph 58 of the Soviet criminal code–that is to say, for political reasons.[15] If that were true, the number of political prisoners should be measured in hundreds of thousands rather than millions, and it would be impossible to fathom how Rudenko had reached a figure of 3.6 million, even if one assumes that some (not many) prisoners were kept in prisons rather than camps and that the rate of mortality in the camps was high.[16]

These figures were endorsed by the leading KGB official, Kryuchkov, but they encountered skepticism both inside Russia and the West. According to René Ahlberg, a leading German student of Soviet affairs, "nobody in the West will be impressed by the methods by means of which Zemskov and Dugin try to belittle the crimes of Stalinism."[17]

This prediction was overoptimistic because in the absence of objective, reliable figures and, above all, in the absence of free access to the archives, the figures were in fact taken quite seriously. Some Western Sovietologists saw them as confirmation of their view expressed prior to *glasnost*, that their Cold War colleagues were exaggerating the impact of the terror.[18] Zemskov argued that the figures he discovered *must* be correct because if they were not, it would mean that the KGB employed two sets of statistics all along—a true set and a set designed to mislead. Although this assertion stretches credulity, there is a time-honored tradition of faking statistics in the Soviet Union, and such practices are by no means unthinkable. In fact, no act of commission is needed to fake statistics; they can be adjusted simply by *deleting*.

Figures of a similar magnitude—3,853,000 arrests and 827,995 death sentences between 1917 and 1990—were quoted in 1993 by Major General Anatoli Krayushkin, head of the archives of the Ministry of State Security.[19] This senior official also argued that the figures must be correct, but he made two important reservations: his figures referred only to crimes against the state (that is, those covered under paragraph 58). Furthermore, they did not include people who had been killed or perished without legal investigation and a court sentence, such as the kulaks deported during the collectivization of agriculture, or the national minorities deported before, during, and after World War II.

III

Inside Russia, *glasnost* revelations about the extent of the terror under Stalin (and also before and after) had a great political impact. But they also provoked protests and contradiction by the old Bolsheviks. The new information was anathema for them, inasmuch as it put into question everything in which they had believed. Hence the denials, the outcry against "democratic lies and defamation." Total denial was impossible under the circumstances, however, simply because too many people had been involved. The general line of the Russian "revisionists" was that the extent of the purges had been grossly exaggerated, that most of the victims had been guilty of one crime or another, that there had been regrettable mistakes, many of which were later rectified (for instance, the dismissal of many officers in 1937 and 1938 and their reinstatement in 1939 and 1940.)[20]

The neo-Communists became involved in many contradictions. They wanted to prove at one and the same time that the executions and the gulag had been absolutely necessary and that the excesses and mistakes had been committed by people like Dzershinski and Menshinski—(former heads of the political police) that the spiritual fathers of the gulag were Frenkel, Berman, and Kogan (former leading figures in the gulag administration).

But this was straining credulity well beyond the breaking point. If the Poles, the Latvians, and the Jews, not the Russians, were responsible for the gulag, they should be credited also with its allegedly positive aspects.

One such author notes with astonishment that Molotov, Kalinin, and Voroshilov had their wives detained and Kaganovich had his brother executed, but they did not protest. How does one explain their silence? Obviously, the crimes of their families were so manifest that there could be no doubt whatsoever.[21] It does not occur to the author that the husbands and brothers should also have been punished, as should Stalin in view of his lack of vigilance and good judgment.

The inspiration of Russian revisionism is obvious. It claimed to be the truth, but with rare exceptions it does not bother to present the trappings of scholarship, very much in contrast to Western (mainly American) revisionism, which was primarily based on the Dugin–Zemskov findings and began a counteroffensive in 1992.[22] Neither Western nor Soviet revisionists deny that a large proportion of the Communist leadership and the state bureaucracy was arrested, many of them executed, and that "eventually millions of Soviet citizens were drawn into the expanding terror."[23] But they still assert that the number of those affected was much smaller than the figures adduced by Western authorities such as Robert Conquest and Soviet dissidents such as Solzhenitsyn, Roy Medvedev, and Antonov Ovseenko. Neo-Stalinist Kuzmin asks: "Where are the millions of the falsifiers such as Solzhenitsyn and Medvedev?"[24]

The revisionists feel certain that the KGB documents constitute solid archival evidence and permit a sharp narrowing of the range of estimates of victims. For the first time, they believe, the scale of the repression can be documented; expressions such as "we now know" occur frequently in these writings. It is conceded that the figures might not be quite complete, but they still are thought to give a "fairly accurate picture."[25]

To sum up a complex series of figures: the picture that emerges is that in March 1940, at the end of the purges, there were 1.3 million inmates in the gulag. Of these, only one-third, about 400,000, were in the gulag for political reasons. The Russian neo-Communists who base their analyses on the same archives give even lower figures– 105,000 in 1937 and 185,000 in 1938 – no more than 200,000 at the height of the purges.[26] They claim the maximum total population detained during the great purges to have been around 3 million, but the majority was not there for political reasons but because of common crimes or infringement of labor discipline or other such reasons. They were not considered victims of repression.

The number of those sentenced to death between 1930 and 1953 (again a KGB figure) for "counterrevolutionary and state crimes" was 786,098, of which 681,692 were killed in 1937 and 1938. On top of this 1,053,829 persons died in the gulag between 1934 and 1953.[27]

The statistics give a rough indication of which groups were most affected. Many of the figures show that more men were arrested and exiled than women, that the educated elite was proportionately much more

affected that the "common people" (this had been known before), and that
the non-Russian minorities were not more severely hit than the Russians.
What should one make of these KGB statistics, which are said to prove that
high pre-*glasnost* estimates were wrong?

It is possible that these new figures are more or less correct, but in the
light of circumstances and historical experience, it is unlikely. A comprehensive masterlist of all victims never existed. The lists that do exist are in
the hands of the Russian security services, which are not a disinterested
party; obviously they do not want to besmirch the good name of past
generations of Cheka officials more than necessary. As two Russian researchers put it: "The guardian of the materials on the repressions is the
direct successor of the organization that inflicted the repressions, and
moreover, the files of the victims are examined in the very same building
where they were tortured and executed."[28]

Such reflections are rejected by revisionists as mainly aesthetic (or
moralistic). Do the circumstances of the repression affect the truthfulness
of the documents? Even if the new figures cannot possibly be precise, do
they not allow a narrowing down of the estimates concerning the number
of victims?

The value of these figures in that respect is doubtful, as a number of
examples will show. Trotsky and other victims of the NKVD (the precursor of the KGB) are certainly not included in the statistics, because their
"executions" took place outside the territory of the Soviet Union. But these
victims, it will be argued, are statistically irrelevant, since their numbers
are counted in dozens, not millions. What of the Polish officers killed in
1940 in Katyn and other camps—perhaps 15,000 to 20,000—(and of the
Italian, Hungarian, and other officers killed during the war?). They
certainly do not appear in the KGB figures for death penalties and executions for the respective years. Again, it could be argued that these crimes
were of no major statistical importance—perhaps they were exceptions.
There could have been more such exceptions, however, in the sparsely
populated (or unpopulated) regions of Siberia or Kazakhstan. Katyn is
located a few miles outside the major Russian city of Smolensk, and some
1.5 to 2 million Kazakhs disappeared in the 1930s. According to official
statistics, a high percentage of them emigrated, a claim that is most
unlikely, not to say impossible. According to independent writers, Kazakh
and Russian, some 1.5 to 1.75 million perished. Perhaps the Kazakh case
was also unique, but it was certainly not statistically insignificant. How
many other unique cases were there? To this question there cannot be an
answer now; perhaps there never will be.

From the KGB archives detailed figures have been culled, probably
quite selectively, concerning the number of death sentences. But no one
knows how many were "liquidated" without death sentences or perished as
the result of inhuman conditions. It is quite likely that some of the earlier
estimates of the killings and the gulag population (20 million and up) were
too high. The country would have come to a standstill if such a great part of

the working population had been liquidated or detained. But this still leaves an enormous margin of uncertainty, as the differences of opinion between leading revisionists indicate. According to Alec Nove, there were some 11 million "excess" deaths between 1927 and 1937; according to Steven Wheatcroft, 4 to 5 million.[29] With regard to the number of wartime victims not killed as the result of enemy action, only the roughest estimates are possible. Their number must have been high, perhaps very high. In the light of these and other uncertainties, the claim that the "long awaited archival evidence" tends to confirm the orders of magnitude indicated by the pre-*glasnost* revisionists can be substantiated[30] only if one adopts the psychology of the man looking for his lost keys not where he dropped them but where the streetlights are shining. A search in such conditions might still result in findings of some interest, but it will not justify sweeping conclusions.

The pre-*glasnost* debates were not primarily about exact figures of victims, which, everyone admitted, could not possibly be established. They were primarily about the origins of the terror, its consequences, and its place in Soviet history. What new light has been shed in this context by the findings in the KGB archives? Roger R. Reese, having investigated the impact of the great purges on the Red Army, reaches the conclusion that it was much less than previously thought, for instance by John Erickson and Robert Conquest.[31] He maintains that only 7.7 percent of the Red Army officer corps was affected, some 34,000 altogether (not a small number; it is about equal to the entire officer corps of the U.S. armed forces in 1938).

The Russian revisionists give a far lower number: 12,461 officers dismissed altogether. Out of these, the 8,122 who were arrested were described as mainly drunkards, thieves, politically doubtful elements such as Germans, Poles, Jews, Balts, and members of other minorities.[32] It is not known how this figure was established; Reese's statistics are based not on archival findings but on publications in Russian journals. Reese notes that earlier Western authors were not much mistaken with regard to the total number of victims, but they underrated the size of the officer corps, which was much larger than previously assumed.

The figures also show what had been known earlier on, that the junior officers were much less affected by the purge than their seniors. As far as marshals, admirals, and generals were concerned, the rate of attrition was 50 or even 80 percent. The fact (or the allegation) that only 7.7 percent were hit is a quantitative and potentially misleading statement. It is like saying that a corpse was in reasonably good shape, but the head had been severed from the body, or like noting that Soviet literature was not really affected by the terror because only a few eccentrics like Mandelstam, Babel, and Tsvetayeva were killed or driven to suicide, whereas many Stalinist hawks thrived. The arrest, and in many cases execution of the senior command staff, did have a tremendous impact. One specific consequence should be recalled: it created the impression abroad that the Red Army had been decapitated. It made it much easier for Hitler to decide to attack the Soviet Union. At the same time, the Western allies, all other misgivings apart, came to regard the Soviet Union as an unreliable and probably incompetent ally.

To what extent can the new figures concerning the Red Army be trusted? They originate in the periodical *Izvestiya*, published by the Central Committee of the Communist party of the Soviet Union prior to August 1991, and the *Voenno-Istoricheskii Zhurnal*, a publication of the Russian Ministry of Defense. Neither can be regarded as a disinterested publication that could be accepted uncritically. True, the army did not initiate the purges, and there has been much resentment ever since about KGB interference and the meddling of "politicians." But revelations about the purges are bound to bring much unsavory material to light about the behavior of army commanders who denounced their fellow officers, or at the very least failed to defend them. Thus the desire to rehabilitate those who were "unjustly repressed" collides with the wish not to provide more grist for the mill of the denigrators of the army (and Russia) at home and abroad.[33]

Two general comments on the "revisionist counteroffensive" seem called for. First, the new figures are not small by any standard; they are certainly higher than those quoted by the same writers prior to *glasnost*, when reference was often made to "a few hundreds or thousands" or even "tens of thousands." Thus Wheatcroft, a leading member of this school, revised his estimate of the mortality of the 1932 to 1933 famine upward by 1 million.[34] The figure of 681,000 executed in 1937 and 1938 compares with a few dozen (at most) of political executions in Italy from the beginning of fascist rule to Mussolini's fall. It compares with 10,000 inmates in Nazi concentration camps in 1937. It compares with fewer than 100 victims in Hitler's "Night of the Long Knives" (June 1934). Never before in modern history had there been so many victims in a time of peace.[35] In other words, even the "low estimates" are not low by any meaningful standard. Secondly, there is no remotely accurate information about the number of victims of the civil war, the collectivization of agriculture, the deportation (frequently fatal) of nationalities before, during, and after World War II, and other crucial events.

In the pre-*glasnost* debates the number of victims had not been the only bone of contention. Western revisionists had come out in favor of low figures, but the main emphasis in their publications (as noted earlier on) had been on such issues as the origins and the causes of the terror. To what extent did they modify their views in the light of the *glasnost* revelations?

A certain change is unmistakable. The whole tenor has become more cautious and even conciliatory. The earlier, "traditionalist" interpretations are no longer dismissed out of hand as unscholarly and unworthy of serious consideration. On the contrary, it is now (1994) argued that "most of us would vigorously deny being a revisionist altogether," that "[we] do not claim to supplant the totalitarian model."[36] Accusations of "Cold War attitudes" no longer feature prominently. On the contrary, it is stated that no one wants to belittle Stalin's enormous role in the terror and that much research still remains to be done. On Stalin's responsibility there is still some vagueness; it is said to be "something less than a hundred percent." One page further on it is stated that there are "two halves to the story"; although Stalin lit the match, the cataclysm also required dry tinder and favorable winds to become what it did.[37] But this had never been in doubt. Nor are the revisionists now very eager to emphasize the function of the terror as a democratic backlash against a dictatorial bureaucracy.

Compared with the 1986 revisionist version, this is a major retreat. It was then claimed that Stalin's interventions were ad hoc, that he merely sparked off an uncontrolled explosion. The whole question of Stalin was then thought to be of secondary importance, the real issues at stake being high-level personal rivalries, "disputes over development or modernization plans, powerful and conflicting centrifugal and centripetal forces, and local conflicts." The terror was deemed to be as (earlier noted) a "radical, even hysterical, reaction to bureaucracy in a chaotic wave of voluntarism and revolutionary puritanism."[38]

These claims, welcomed in 1985 and 1986 by some as a major break-through and dismissed by others as arrant nonsense, are no longer re-peated in 1993 – admittedly with a few notable exceptions. Even now it is argued that Stalin was an ordinary mortal, who "stumbled into everything from collectivization to foreign policy," that "Stalin's crimes were of the unplanned, erratic kind."[39] Or as Roberta Manning put it: "The great purges appear to be a far more complicated set of events than earlier scholarship and *belles lettres* alike would let us believe."[40] Stalin is com-pared with Eichmann, a comparison that would have been unthinkable in 1985 because it constitutes an unscholarly value judgment. It is an unfortu-nate comparison in any case, since Eichmann's crimes were hardly of the "unplanned erratic kind." And to top it all, Hannah Arendt's misleading phrase about banal and ordinary evil is disinterred on the occasion.

To summarize: A substantial retreat from the pre-*glasnost* position has taken place, but the temptation is still strong to preserve whatever can be saved; nor does the retreat extend to the issue of the number of the victims.[41]

IV

The Nazi experience provides some interesting examples for the obfuscation of figures. The first concentration camps were established soon after the Nazis came to power. There exist fairly accurate figures for the early years: 7,500 inmates in 1936 (an all-time low) and 10,000 in 1937. After the annex-ation of Austria and Czechoslovakia and following *Kristallnacht*, the number increased to 60,000. By the outbreak of the war, it was down to 26,000. The three main camps, Dachau, Sachsenhausen, and Buchenwald, had 5,000 inmates each, and there was one camp specifically for women – Lichtenburg.

With the outbreak of the war, many new camps were established, especially outside Germany, and the number of inmates rose immensely. Some were labor camps, others extermination camps, and Auschwitz combined the two functions. Thus, after 1939, accurate figures no longer existed or became meaningless. It was not helpful to know that at a certain date, 500,000 people were in the camps, if within a week (or month) a third or half of them had been killed. In the early years, the concentration camp authorities had instructions to inform the family of each victim of his death (usually giving no cause of death or a false one). During the war, however, they received orders from Himmler not to inform relatives, not to count the number of Jews massacred, and generally speaking to falsify and obfuscate numbers.[42]

It was not, however, only a matter of statistical falsification. Systematic attempts were made to destroy the physical evidence. To give but one example, two special units were dispatched to Kiev in July 1943 when the Russians were advancing, to exhume the bodies in Babi Yar and to cremate them. Several hundred people were employed, and the cremation continued for four weeks.[43]

Although the estimate of the number killed at Auschwitz was reduced fifty years after the event, the figures for such places of mass killing as Solovetsky, Vinnitsa, Katyn, Kharkov, Odessa, and Kuropaty are now thought to have been too low.[44]

If the Soviet population census could be falsified, if the location of cities and villages on the maps could be "moved," it was certainly not impossible to "edit" the numbers of those executed and the number of gulag inmates.[45] In any case, the figures were not small in absolute terms; according to Dugin some 11.8 million Soviet citizens passed through the camps between 1934 and 1953 (both criminals *and* political prisoners). This figure, as mentioned earlier, does not include categories such as the victims of collectivization and the deportation of nationalities during the war. Nor does it include the prison population of the Soviet Union, which fluctuated during the years in question between 155,000 (in 1944) and 434,000 (December 1940).

How many people were needed to run the terror machinery? It has been argued that it would have been physically impossible to keep many millions of detainees in the Soviet camps, because there were not enough guards. It is not known how many camp and prison guards served at the time. Estimates vary between 6 percent and 25 percent of the total camp population. According to seemingly reliable estimates, there were about 300,000 prison guards. It is known that the Nazis operated their terror apparatus in Germany with few people, certainly much fewer than commonly believed.

A few figures should suffice: when the KGB was dissolved in 1991, it counted 513,000 full-time employees, as compared with 130,000 serving in its Russian successor organization.[46]

The Gestapo counted a mere 32,000 members toward the end of its existence (1944). There is reason to believe that before the war it had been considerably smaller. It is known, for instance, that Gestapo Düsseldorf, with a catchment area of some 4 million inhabitants, counted altogether 291 officials in 1937, some of which, furthermore, were engaged exclusively in administrative work. In a city such as Essen, which had 650,000 inhabitants (a left-wing region prior to 1933, like the Ruhr in general) had 43 Gestapo officials.[47] Nor did the Gestapo rely heavily on informants. Full figures are not available, but the following facts are probably quite typical: in central Franconia, with a population of 2.7 million inhabitants, there were 6 officials dealing with 80 to 100 regular informers and a larger number of "spite informers" denouncing personal enemies. (The latter category seems, in fact, to have been more important for Gestapo work.) In the city of Frankfurt, about 1,200 cards were found of people who had acted as informers at one time or another, many apparently only once.[48] It is instructive to compare the numerical strength of the Gestapo with the Stasi establishment in East Germany. In Rostock district, there lived in 1989 some 900,000 people. The regional Stasi consisted of 3,600 members, not counting border inspectors and several other auxiliary units, and they had some 10,000 unofficial, part-time collaborators, most of whom were informants.[49] Roughly speaking, the number of Stasi staff and informants was at least ten, perhaps twenty, times as high as that of the Gestapo.

The power of the Gestapo lay not in numbers but in the fearful impression of omnipresence and omnipotence, the belief that no one could escape its scrutiny.[50] The KGB was a far larger institution than the Gestapo; in 1940 it accounted for some 13 percent of all capital construction in the Soviet Union. It could have expanded further, if necessary. Given the remote location of the camps and the enormous difficulties of escaping, these guards could have guarded with equal ease 2 or 8 million prisoners.

Perhaps one should at present concentrate on the fate of people in smaller communities and associations where the margin of error is bound to be smaller. One such study has been made by Sheila Fitzpatrick, who, on the basis of the Moscow and Leningrad telephone directories, tried to check the rate of attrition among senior staff of the Commissariat of Heavy Industry. She found that the "dropout rate" was three to four times as high as among the public at large (of 163 listed in 1937, 98 were missing in 1939). Those further down were much less affected. As far as the public at large was concerned, there was hardly any change at all,[51] but the public at large is a huge, amorphous body about which we know little.

Vitaly Chentalinsky, a Russian author who investigated the number of Soviet writers affected by the purge, reached the conclusion that of 2,000 writers who were arrested, 1,500 disappeared in prisons and the gulag.[52] These were not necessarily the most famous. Some of the best known, such as Sholokhov, Pasternak, and Ehrenburg, were under investigation but were saved precisely because Stalin thought that these "engineers of the human soul" were not expendable.

These figures account for perhaps 10 to 20 percent (or more) of all Soviet writers, but figures alone say nothing about the impact these arrests and executions had on those who survived or the consequences of the terror for the general level of Soviet literature.

The official KGB figures revealed in the Soviet Union in 1989 and 1990 could be correct as far as they go, in terms of covering certain places and categories of murder. But given their origins, and above all the impossibility to verify them, it would be wise not to attribute much importance to them. If, as in the case of the murder of Sergei Kirov in 1934, one seems now no nearer to knowing the truth than ten or fifty years ago, it is unlikely that the whole truth will ever be known about purges and the gulag.[53]

Revisionism on the left has its mirror image in a new revisionism of the right, which is stated with equal emphasis.[54] Its best known representative in the West is the German historian and philosopher Ernst Nolte, who asserted that the Communist terror and the gulag had been more original (*ursprünglich*) than Hitler's extermination policy; that there was a causal connection between the two (in other words, Hitler's fear of Bolshevism was the paramount factor in his policy); and that, in one way or another, he received his inspiration from the Russians.[55] It can be shown without difficulty that while Russian anti-Semitism (such as the *Protocols of the Elders of Zion*) had a certain impact on early Nazism, Hitler did not need Lenin, Zinoviev, or Stalin as mentors; neither is mentioned in *Mein Kampf*. In his *Tabletalk*, Hitler stated, *expressis verbis*, that Stalin continued the tsarist tradition and had virtually jettisoned Communism. Hitler certainly did not act as if Bolshevism was a mortal danger to Germany and all mankind; his declaration of war against the United States and other such decisions do not make sense on the basis of this assumption. Nolte discovered the text of a speech by Zinoviev in 1919 according to which it might be necessary to destroy 10 million enemies of the Soviet regime so that Communism should triumph. While the civil war was bloody, it could hardly be argued that the murder of 10 million was official Bolshevik policy at the time. Zinoviev was given to hysteria and hyperbole; isolated (often apocryphal) quotations can be found for advocating almost any thesis and are meaningless.

The Bolshevik Revolution was not the first in history to lead to a prolonged debate about terror. The executions in the French Revolution, above all during the first half of 1794, were discussed for a long time after the event. These discussions did not, however, concern the extent of the terror, but its reasons and consequences. The numbers were never in dispute: some 16,000 perished under guillotine; perhaps 10,000 died in prison; and there were more victims as the result of the civil strife in various regions such as the Vendée. There are detailed local figures: 289 were executed in Marseilles and 302 in Bordeaux, to give but two examples. Lists of individual names have been preserved. The debate in France related to motives and consequences. According to the Jacobin school of thought, dominant in French historiography from World War I to the late 1960s, the terror was unavoidable, even though excesses and mistakes had been committed. Radical changes could be carried out only if the enemies of the revolutions were destroyed. Thus Robespierre and St. Just, the incorruptible, remained the main heroes of the left.

But it was difficult to show on the basis of detailed investigations that those executed were indeed the chief enemies of the revolution. Marie Antoinette, to be sure, was no sympathizer, but even if we assume that Danton was a deviationist such as Bukharin, the great majority of those killed (probably 80 to 90 percent) were neither nobles nor clergymen but simple people who, for one reason or another, often by accident, found themselves in prison sentenced to the guillotine. Far from strengthening the revolutionary movement, the terror brought about its downfall.

Nevertheless, the French left did not condemn the terror per se; it was a tragic episode. In retrospect, both Robespierre and Danton had been heroes and victims. The French social historians—an interesting parallel with Western social historians of the Soviet period—thought that the whole issue of the terror had been exaggerated. The terror provided much fascinating material for novelists and playwrights, but had it really been that important in the long run? The social historians focused on the *long durée* (the long rhythms), not on political events (*histoire événementiel*).

But then, some twenty years ago, a paradoxical development took place. In the 1920s and 1930s, Bolshevik violence had been justified in France with reference to the terror of 1794. In the 1970s, on the contrary, the revelations about the gulag led to a rethinking on the terror initiated by Robespierre and St. Just. And since the publication of Solzhenitsyn's books in France coincided with the eclipse of Marxism and the Communist party in France, the traditional explanations and justifications for the terror went out of fashion.[56] There was, however, a basic difference, for the rethinking in France did not lead to a total rejection of the French Revolution.

8

The Nationalist Revival

The failure of the Soviet economy sealed the doom of the system—but only in the long run, not necessarily in 1991. It could have muddled through a number of years longer, and while it is unlikely that a gradual transformation toward a market economy could have taken place in the Soviet Union as in China, such a possibility cannot be ruled out altogether. The collapse of the system came about because of the loss of self-confidence among the rulers: the fact that they put up surprisingly little resistance against the forces challenging them. This phenomenon will be investigated for many years to come.[1] It has to do with the erosion of ideological belief and the disappearance of utopian hopes, as well as with closer contacts with Western ideas and realities. There are various reasons why nations, political systems, groups, and individuals rise and decline. Some are objective and can be measured; others are subjective and accidental, and there is no statistical accounting for them.

The single most important factor was the emergence (or re-emergence) of ethnic nationalism in the non-Russian republics. Little attention was paid to the nationality issue by the Soviet leadership and not much more by Western students of the Soviet Union. There were some experts in the United States and Europe specializing in these fields, but by and large Sovietology was confined to Russian studies or at best the study of specific areas of the Soviet Union.[2] Among Soviet experts in the West it was widely believed that the topic of nationality studies was of peripheral, not central interest. The "disintegrationists," those who thought it was of crucial importance, potentially the Achilles heel of the Soviet system, were not many.[3]

Among political scientists the tendency prevailed to view events in the republics as a reflection of what was decreed in Moscow (or an extension of what was happening in the Russian Socialist Republic) "leading them to write authoritatively" about the local scene without troubling to look into the specifics.⁴ At the same time, students of Islam and the Middle East tended to regard Central Asia as a mere extension of Muslim society and politics, which was equally erroneous.

Such criticism mainly refers to approach and method. To what extent were Soviet experts in the West influenced by Western theoretical thinking on nationalism, and in what way did it have an impact on their conclusions? The writings of some of these experts in the 1970s and 1980s show familiarity with the books and articles of Karl Deutsch, Anthony Smith, Ernest Gellner, and other theoreticians. It certainly shows in the language they used, with frequent references to ethnopolitics, ethnonationalism, ethnofederalism, primordial and instrumental mobilizational strategies, and so forth. Except in terminology, the influence was by and large not overwhelming, however. Gellner and Smith were mainly preoccupied with the past, and being part of the "British" (in contradiction to the American) tradition, had few predictive ambitions. If Sovietologists such as Gail Lapidus and Mary McAuley tended to attribute to the Soviet system greater legitimacy and integrative power than it proved to have, this had probably little to do with their theoretical-methodological orientation. The historians among the experts, such as Alexandre Bennigsen, Helène Carrère d'Encausse, Anders Wimbush, and the Baltic specialists, with their pragmatic approach, were more skeptical about the success of Soviet nationality policy than the political scientists, with their emphasis on theory. The reason was, no doubt, that these historians were dealing with regions such as Central Asia and the Baltic, where the failure of national integration had been particularly obvious.⁵ If a political scientist demonstrated in a book published in 1990 why the non-Russian nations would not rebel, he could argue in retrospect that there was, after all, no full-scale rebellion, except perhaps in the Baltic countries, and the Soviet empire collapsed not because of a rebellion but because of the eclipse of the center.

Thus of all the factors bringing about the downfall of the union, nationalism was, by and large, the one to which least attention had been paid. True, Soviet leaders were not altogether unaware of the growth of national (and nationalist) awareness. Andropov referred to it when he was secretary general of the party. The head of the Institute of Ethnography at the Academy of Science had noted in the 1970s that "in our country there has been a headlong growth of national self-consciousness, part of a worldwide ethnic renaissance."⁶

This observation certainly contradicted the general assumption in Moscow (also fairly widespread in the West) that modernization and urbanization were bringing about an erosion of "ethnicity," a term that had not been widely used, except among some experts, before the 1970s. A few Western "disintegrationists" did refer to the Soviet Union as the last (and therefore doomed) empire and to the "yellowing of the Red Army." But these studies mainly referred to demographic trends in the Muslim republics of Central Asia. It is difficult to think of anyone who predicted that the Ukraine and White Russia would secede. Such predictions would have seemed altogether farfetched even in 1989, because the majority in most republics (except the Baltic countries) was by no means in favor of secession. Although this issue was not on the political agenda, disintegration came suddenly and gathered momentum quickly, as central power in Moscow weakened. It is unfair to blame the experts for not recognizing something that did not manifest itself at the time; their mistake was to have underrated or altogether ignored the explosive potential of what was still widely called the "nationality question."

In retrospect, Soviet scholarly thought on nationalism has been called "dogmatic, derivative, repetitious, arcane, inflexible, removed from reality, and generally incapable of comprehending the tectonic political movements already at work in Soviet society."[7] All this may be correct, but it should have been added that the system seemed to work reasonably well, and most Western observers shared the conviction of the Soviet leaders that national divisions, while bothersome, were not the most critical issue facing them. If the Soviet leaders had succeeded in building a prosperous society, the prospects for separatism would have considerably diminished. It is also true that the primitive Soviet pamphlets about "nationalism as the worst enemy of the working class" do not look that ridiculous now, after years of ethnic conflict and thousands of victims.

What caused the revival of nationalism? And could it have been contained by a more enlightened leadership? In the Brezhnev years as under Khrushchev, the emphasis was, on the whole, on the great strides made by the Soviet people. Brezhnev and his successor Andropov made it clear in their speeches that they did not want to force integration. Some Communist leaders believed that the federation of states constitutionally in effect since 1922 had become an anachronism and that a more centralized framework was needed. But others advised caution, saying "it would be dangerous to accelerate artificially the rapprochement between nations."[8] The Soviet Union was a multiethnic society, and though the coming together of the various nationalities was an objective long-term goal, one had to tread carefully. Some Soviet experts and leaders were in favor of encouraging assimilation more actively. The 1961 party program stated *expressis verbis* that the party had solved the problem of relations between nations. Brezhnev, on the occasion of the fiftieth anniversary of the foundation of the Soviet Union (1972), said even more emphatically that the nationalities question had been solved "completely, definitely, irrevocably."[9] Soviet leaders seem to have believed that while certain tensions would remain for a long time, longer than tensions between classes, these constituted no threat to the survival of the regime, provided certain concessions were made to the local elites. Nationalities were appeased, especially in Central Asia and the Caucasus, where local leaders were given virtually a free hand to establish their feudal fiefdoms, as long as they followed the economic guidelines issued by Moscow (at least in broad outline) and said the right things on the right occasions, paying verbal tribute to the Soviet Union and its wise leadership.

But the Kremlin seems to have realized in the 1970s that the local leaders were systematically hoodwinking their bosses in Moscow with reports of enormous economic achievements, and that mismanagement and corruption there had gone well beyond what was considered normal and permissible.[10] On one of his last visits to Central Asia, Brezhnev sounded angry complaints that the Central Asian (and the Caucasian) republics were not just lagging behind in their economic performance but had failed to make a significant effort to make any headway and to mend their ways. There were hints that Russian subsidies to Central Asia were becoming too heavy a burden. At the same time, leading figures in Moscow complained that "operation headstart" for the non-Russians had gotten out of hand and that Russians were not adequately represented in the non-Russian republics. An "arithmetic approach" to appointments was deemed inappropriate – a growing number of people opposed "affirmative action." The fact that thousands of Russians had been leaving the Central Asian republics since the early 1970s because they felt uncomfortable among the native population must have been known in Moscow. Speeches made by the then head of the KGB indicated awareness of possible undesirable repercussions of the Afghan war on Soviet Central Asia. There seems to have been less concern about the Caucasus, and little, if any, about Moldova and the Baltic countries. No significant attempt was made to restrict the appointment of local cadres. The Kazakhstan riots, in Alma-Ata in December 1986, were a warning sign, if any was needed, of what might happen if a senior local party leader (however inefficient and unpopular among his own people) was replaced by a Russian.

But there still was no full realization in Moscow of the fact that the survival of the regime in certain crucial parts of the union depended on giving a free hand to the local satraps. Any attempt to clean up, to do away with the grosser abuses of power and inefficiency, was bound to lead to a nationalist backlash. The Kremlin had become prisoner of the system it had installed.

When Gorbachev came to power the nationality question did not figure high on his list of priorities. Most experts realized that the Soviet Union had not functioned well as a melting pot except perhaps in the case of some small nationalities that had virtually disappeared. There seemed to be no reason to fear that the situation was in any way critical.[11] There had been a few dozen dissenters among the Ukrainians and the Balts, and a handful in the Caucasus, but they had no significant support at the time.

Western experts, even the better informed among them, tended to accept the view that the nationalities would not rebel as long as the system remained more or less stable. As long as Moscow's power was unbroken, there was little chance that they would attain independence. The Gorbachev era might bring far-reaching reforms that were long overdue, including important changes in the status of the republics, but the disintegration of the empire seemed utterly impossible.[12] Such a perception seemed only natural, for virtually no one in the national republics expected independence and sovereignty in the near future. A great majority of non-Russians would probably not have favored it in free elections, except in the Baltic countries and the Western Ukraine. Even the most ardent non-Russian nationalists knew that there was no chance of attaining independence unless the center was fatally and decisively weakened to the point that it lost all control. There was no objective reason to assume that this day was near.

The disintegration of the Soviet empire as the result of the secession of the non-Russian republics will be studied in minute detail in the decades to come. Only the main stages of this process are of relevance in the present context. Could this process have been halted and perhaps even reversed? The Alma-Ata riots of 1986 remained, more or less, an isolated incident. True, fighting and ethnic pogroms did take place, but they were between local nationalities or between Communists and nationalists,[13] or between members of opposed clans rather than directed against Russians. The Russian exodus from Central Asia continued, but it was measured in tens of thousands rather than in millions.

The first clashes in the Caucasus were likewise between the local nations. Examples are the demonstrations in Erevan and other Armenian cities in favor of reuniting Nagorno-Karabakh with Armenia, and afterward the anti-Armenian pogroms in Sungait (February 1989). Russian military forces intervened in April 1989 in Tbilisi, putting down demonstrations for Georgian independence and, on a more massive scale, attempting to restore order in Baku (January 1990). The Tbilisi demonstrations, in which some twenty people were killed, had originally been directed against the separatist Abkhasians and other minorities. In Baku many more were killed, but the intention of the Russian forces was to restore law and order and to stop the attacks against the Armenians.

The movement aiming at full sovereignty and secession from the Soviet Union appeared first in the Baltic countries in the early days of *glasnost*. A public demonstration took place on August 23, 1987, in Vilna in protest against the Molotov–VonRibbentrop pact of August 1939, as the result of which the Baltic countries had been forcibly incorporated into the Soviet Union. In June 1987, the Lithuanian Movement for reconstruction (Sajudis) was founded. Its first actions in Lithuania (where Russians made up less than 10 percent of the population) included further demonstrations against the Molotov–VonRibbentrop pact. In August 1988, a crowd of 250,000 participated. In August 1989, a living chain extended 370 miles from Tallinn to Vilna. Ecological concerns and the preservation of the native cultural heritage (language, folksongs, and so on) also played a central role in these demonstrations. There was an attempt by Russian forces, probably with the knowledge of the Kremlin, to suppress the nationalist movement by force in Vilna in January 1991. The effort was on a small scale and half-hearted, and it had little support even among the

Russians. In February 1991, in a Lithuanian referendum, 90 percent of the population voted for independence; in March of that year, 77 percent and 73 percent voted for independence in Estonia and Latvia, respectively. These secessionist movements were part of a general East European movement toward independence from Moscow. Lithuania, Latvia, and Estonia had been sovereign countries between the two world wars; and the majority of the population had never been fully integrated into the Soviet Union. They had always stressed their specific national character, and on a social level there had been little mingling with the Russians.

The situation in other parts of the Soviet empire was different, with the few exceptions that have been mentioned–especially the three western *oblasti* of the Ukraine, which had not been part of Russia since the Middle Ages and which were incorporated only in 1939 and again in 1944 and 1945. The negative attitude in these localities toward union with Russia was as ardent as in the Baltic states. In the first free elections in March 1991, more than 80 percent of the electorate in the western Ukraine voted for independence. In the rest of Ukraine, the results were quite different: 80 percent pronounced themselves in favor of the union. The language issue, which was of considerable importance among the Georgians, for instance, did not play a paramount role among Ukrainians.

The other notable exception was the Moldavian republic, or Moldova, as it became known. The movement toward a merger with Romania was mainly supported by the intelligentsia, but only after the Baltic and Caucasian republics had declared their independence. Some 70 percent of the population of Moldova followed suit in a plebiscite in early 1991. In Georgia, 99 percent voted for independence in March 1991. In October 1990, the radical advocates of full sovereignty under Gamsakhurdia had won the elections.

The observer of the Soviet scene groping for an explanation for the events that took place in 1990 and 1991 faces a series of riddles. How can we explain that almost 80 percent of Ukrainians voted for the survival of the union on March 17, 1991, whereas an even greater majority voted against it on December 1 of that year?[14]

In the case of White Russia, it seems even more difficult to find an explanation. No strong independence movement had ever existed. Nevertheless, on August 26, 1991, White Russia declared independence, a few days before the Caucasian and Central Asian republics.

One could think of a number of obvious reasons. In the same measure as the central power became weaker, separatism became stronger. This seems to be true with regard to the attitudes not only of the republics vis-à-vis Russia, but also those of the smaller minorities vis-à-vis the republics. Separatism fueled the war over Nagorno-Karabakh and in Tajikistan, the conflict in Abkhazia and in Ossetia directed against Georgia, the civil war in Moldova in the summer of 1992, the rebellion in Azerbaijan, and the fighting between North Ossetia and the Ingush. Nationalist tensions that had been suppressed for decades now came to the fore. There was clearly something akin to a bandwagon effect.

But all this does not explain the stampede that brought about total disintegration. With equal justice one could have expected growing pressure on the part of the periphery on the center, the demand for concessions, wider power for the republics, and a new federal structure. There seems to have been the instinctive feeling that while there had been certain benefits in belonging to a powerful association such as the old Soviet Union, even as a junior member, there was no benefit at all derived from membership in a club that had fallen on evil days. Furthermore, the old Communist establishments in the republics were afraid to lose all influence (and all their positions) unless they matched or outdid the nationalists in separatist fervor. So they changed the names of their parties, made themselves independent from Moscow, and in most cases successfully managed to cling to power.

In 1990 and 1991 full independence must have seemed genuinely attractive. It meant the realization of old dreams, recognition by the world community, and support by the industrial world. If small countries such as Portugal and Norway were sovereign, should countries of equal or larger size and population in Eastern Europe not have equal status? The Ukraine is as populous as France, Britain, and Italy and is rich in resources; the fact that it had no full independence must have seemed an outrageous anachronism. At a time when so many republics left the union, to stay behind appeared unseemly, showing a lack of courage and patriotism.

The illusions did not last long. All European and most Central Asian republics experienced after 1991 the very same economic difficulties Russia did (which the republics had hoped to bypass), aggravated by specific local problems–decline in production, productivity, and exports; enormous inflation; a drought in Lithuania; and lack of fuel in the Baltic countries and Armenia, where the economy almost came to a standstill. Ukraine experienced a monthly inflation rate of 30 percent, and industrial output fell by one quarter in 1992; the situation further deteriorated in 1993 to 1994. In most republics, the proverbial light at the end of the tunnel could not be seen. Local entrepreneurs preferred to invest abroad rather than at home, where prospects seemed so grim.

At the same time, a swing back could be observed from the nationalist camp to the old Communist leadership, together with a marked decline in nationalist enthusiasm outside the Caucasus. People were preoccupied with their own survival, and interest in politics, which had been at a high pitch in 1990 and 1991, declined.[15]

Despite their problems, the republics were not about to rejoin the Union. New administrations were now in place, and many officials had a vested interest in the new status of full sovereignty. Nor was troubled Russia a powerful magnet.

Some observers of the East European and ex-Soviet scene maintained that the nationalist wave was inevitable in the transition from authoritarian systems (with their weakly developed civil societies) toward democracy.[16] Others referred to the revolution of 1848, the *Völkerfrühling* (spring of nations), when nationalism and democracy had shared, broadly speaking, the same aspirations. Yet others believed the upsurge of nationalism was the victory of the eighteenth century over the twentieth. But as European history has shown, nationalism has identified itself with equal ease (probably more often) with dictatorships than with the cause of democracy. If the national liberation movement was largely democratic in the Baltic countries, it was by no means so with regard to all other parts of the former Soviet Union.

As one observer put it, 1988 did show that nations large and small had kept their historical memory of their former rights, flags, and national symbols, as well as the conditions under which they had joined or were forced to join Russia or the Soviet Union.[17] But did this increasing national consciousness inevitably lead to the total disintegration of the union? Some may argue that history shows that the attempt to transform an empire into a commonwealth invariably fails: If the British and the French failed, why should the Soviet Union have succeeded? But there have also been cases in history when assimilation has taken place and other instances where a separate identity has not caused the ruin of the nation and the state. The Soviet Union was in some essential respects different from the colonial empires, not because the old Russia had been less repressive toward its non-Russian subjects but because it was geographically contiguous. Furthermore, there were very few British in India or Nigeria, but a great many Russians lived in Latvia and Kazakhstan. The relationship between Russia and Ukraine or Byelorussia was not really that between metropolitan country and colony; the same is true even with regard to the Caucasian republics. The social, cultural, and linguistic differences between Russians and Ukrainians were less than those between German- and French-speaking Swiss or Canadians, between Finns and Swedes in Finland, or between Flamands and Walloons.

If the Soviet Union could collapse in 1991 like a house of cards, a number of preconditions clearly existed. One was the weakness of the center, which made no determined effort to hold at least some of the republics together. Another was the conviction of the republics that they would be politically and economically better off if the association with Russia came to an end. Ukrainians and Armenians were relying on the support of their countrymen abroad; the Azerbaijanis hoped that Turkey would help; and the Baltic states expected assistance from Europe and America. Such delusions might not have been a *conditio sine qua non*, but they certainly played a role everywhere: not a single republic had a realistic picture of the difficulties ahead.

Lastly, there was the general lack of appreciation on the part of the Moscow leadership that the "nationality question" had acquired a new urgency and radical reforms had become imperative. If, as some observers had argued, influential circles in the Kremlin had opposed *glasnost* and *perestroika* in the first place, it was precisely because they feared that this would release forces over which they would soon lose control. In fact, the behavior of the Politburo, the Central Committee, and lower party organs between 1985 and 1988 showed little such concern. They seem to have genuinely believed in traditional Marxist-Leninist doctrine, according to which underlying the nationalities' complaints was mainly economic hardship. Once the economic situation in the republics improved, nationalist deviations would become less acute and the internationalist spirit would grow in strength. Most of the Moscow party bosses failed to understand the mainsprings of the resistance to Russification.[18] There was not much tolerance in Moscow with regard to the wide use of native languages, local environmental concerns, or the resentment caused by the cadres policy and the appointment of Russians to key positions. The first party secretary in every republic was usually a native, but the second secretary, a Russian, would often be more powerful.

Concerning the imposition of the Russian language as the means of communication, there was no significant difference between Brezhnev and Andropov, or between Gorbachev and Ligachev. In fact, under Lenin the attitude had been more liberal in this respect.

When coming up against difficulties, the tendency in the Kremlin was to temporize and postpone decisions. This was not unnatural, for there was no solution, for example, to the Nagorno-Karabakh problem that would not have antagonized at least one of the sides in the dispute, nor was there any way to do justice to the Crimean Tartars or the Volga Germans without harming the interests of the Russians and Ukrainians who had settled in these regions after the expulsion of the Tartars and the Germans. In fact, there were no solutions to most national conflicts as long as ethnocentrism prevailed, except temporizing and muddling through.

The year of national mass mobilization was 1988: the native language became the official language in all republics. Beginning in November 1988, all republics declared their sovereignty; from that date on republican laws took precedence over all-union laws. This shift led to independence declarations by the three Baltic republics (between March and May 1990) and the three Caucasian republics (between August 1990 and April 1991). When the abortive coup occurred in August 1991, almost half the republics had already de jure declared their secession from the union. These declarations were not merely abstract. More and more young men in the non-Russian republics who were called up to serve in the Soviet army simply ignored the summons. The great majority of the republican Communist leaders defected to join the national fronts (first in Armenia in 1988) or establish their own independent parties. This strategy proved to be successful; in most republics, the former leading party members succeeded in keeping their positions or, after a brief interval, recaptured them.

What has been said about political and cultural discrimination under the old regime refers above all to the Baltic and Central Asian republics. It is less true with regard to Caucasus, which had a considerable degree of autonomy even in the 1970s and 1980s. As for Ukraine and White Russia, the Slavic republics, there was, if anything, reverse discrimination.

Gerhard Simon, a leading student of the non-Russian republics, noted in 1986 that the representation of Ukrainians and White Russians in the Kremlin consistently exceeded their percentage in the population.[19] There were no purges among the local officials, and generally speaking these republics received preferential treatment.

To stem the nationalist tide, a number of measures were taken by the Moscow authorities. They promised a return to "Leninist norms" in their policy toward nationalities. A special section dealing with interethnic relations was established in the Central Committee in 1987. Its first task was to prepare an extraordinary Central Committee plenum on nationality policy. This meeting took place in September 1989. The resolutions passed provided for greater autonomy (including foreign relations), the return of the nationalities expelled by Stalin to their old homelands wherever possible, various "affirmative action" initiatives, and (as mentioned earlier) the right of each republic to declare the native language the official language of the republic.[20]

The Soviet leadership decided to give ill-defined new powers to the Soviet of Nationalities (one of the two houses of the Supreme Soviet). Nationalities issues also figured prominently at the Tenth Party Conference and the Twenty-eighth All-Union Party Congress, the very last to take place. But the new "platform" of the parties came too late and offered too little. It was probably of more interest to the smaller nationalities than to the republics. Most of their basic, far-reaching demands were ignored or even emphatically rejected. Russian radicals like Sakharov as well as leading academic experts were warning that the time of empires was past, that the concept of the "older brother" had to be given up, and that unless the Soviet Union would transform itself into a federation of equal republics, it would not survive the twentieth century.

These ideas did not percolate to the top leadership, which was taken by surprise by the stormy nationalist upsurge. Gorbachev opposed the nationalists, and the other leaders resisted change even more strongly. He did not accept the idea of a new union treaty, replacing the treaty of 1922, until early summer of 1990. After that date Gorbachev and some of his colleagues seem to have realized the urgency of change, and in November 1990 the first draft of a new treaty was published. A second draft was circulated in March 1991—just before the referendum of March 17, in which Soviet citizens were asked whether they favored the preservation of the union as a federation of equal, sovereign republics in which human and national rights would be fully guaranteed. Although 76 percent of the votes favored this proposition, the Baltic republics and three others—(Armenia, Georgia, and the recently renamed Moldova—boycotted the referendum.

In April 1991, negotiations were begun in Novo-Ogaryevo near Moscow, but without significant progress. On August 20, 1991, the Russian Federation, Kazakhstan, and Uzbekistan were scheduled to sign a draft of a new union treaty, but the attempted coup, which occurred the day before, put an end to attempts to reform the old order. One of the motives of the organizers of the coup had been the wish to prevent further weakening of the center; as they saw it, Gorbachev had made too many concessions.

Resistance to the coup, it ought to be noted, came not from the capitals of the republics. Their leaders reacted cautiously because they seem to have been afraid. Would the Soviet Union have survived if the coup had succeeded? Perhaps for a few months or even years. It would have meant a wholesale purge, military intervention, and ultimately a civil war.

The defeat of the rebels was followed by declarations of independence on the part of all republics. An attempt was made to preserve at least a very loose framework (the GUS) covering most former republics. But the Baltic countries and Georgia refused even to discuss this proposal, and the measure of success among the rest was minimal. On December 25, 1991, Gorbachev resigned as president of the Soviet Union–the day after the union ceased to exist.

Could the disintegration of the union have been prevented? The answer to this question depends largely on the analysis of the crisis that brought about the downfall of the empire. One informed student counts seven possible interpretations.[21] Another says that in the final analysis it boils down to one: the components of the union, the "national bricks," were too disparate to serve as a stable foundation for a common home, unless held together by a totalitarian frame.[22] There is the "economic" interpretation as well as the thesis that puts all the fault on "extremists" unwilling to accept a reasonable compromise, the ideological foes ("enemies of *perestroika*"), and the "hidden hand" or the mafia and foreign intelligence services. There usually is a small grain of truth in every interpretation. Separatism seldom occurs among very rich nations, because too many people have too much to lose; but the Soviet Union was not a very wealthy country, nor was there any prospect that it would be in the forseeable future. Extremists did play a certain role; they always do at a time of crisis. The leaders of the non-Russian nationalist movements were not all pure idealists; personal ambitions and interests did play a certain role. Foreign political factors were involved, not the intelligence services but, on the contrary, the disappearance of the danger of war (and the winding down of the Cold War), which had served for so many years as the iron bracket keeping the empire together. If there was no serious outside threat, why not give the republics greater freedom?

For the theoreticians of "internal colonialism," events in the Soviet Union did not provide much comfort. In Spain and Yugoslavia, it was not the poorest and most exploited regions that were in the forefront of rebellion, but the more advanced and prosperous ones. In the Soviet Union, this role was played by the Baltic republics, which had the highest standard of living.

According to yet another version frequently heard among reform Communists during the early years of *perestroika*, Leninist nationality policy had been constructive and a possible road to peaceful coexistence, but the deformities in later years had caused much (perhaps irreparable) harm. Again, a grain of truth can be detected. As empires go, early Soviet nationality policy had been relatively enlightened; we have mentioned elsewhere that it was acclaimed at the time even by bitter enemies of the Communist regime. But the right of self-determination had been violated early on in Soviet history, for instance by the Army's occupation of Social Democratic Georgia.

One need not examine in detail all theories, for conditions varied so much from republic to republic that it is unthinkable that one overall interpretation could possibly explain the resurgence of nationalism everywhere.[23] The collapse would obviously not have occurred if the "center" had violently suppressed the nationalist movements. Would the Kremlin have been capable of ruling the country by means of Stalinist methods? This is unlikely, but something less than extreme violence might have been sufficient to keep the union together for years, assuming that the nationalist stirrings were suppressed early on. In that case, there might have been gradual devolution. The politicians in the center and the local Communist leaders would not have been taken by surprise, and a confederation might have come into existence. Since in any case the old leadership of most republics remained in power under a new banner, it stands to reason that these leaders could have opted with equal ease for a closer relationship with Moscow. They opted for separatism and a nationalist platform because in the circumstances this seemed the only feasible approach to save their positions.

Terrorism never succeeds on a large scale in an effective dictatorship, and the same is true with regard to separatist movements. Separatism occurred in Sri Lanka but not in China, in Morocco but not in Iran. In Spain under Franco's old-fashioned dictatorship, there was some resistance among the Basques and the Catalans, but it did not amount to much because the army and the police were firmly in control. The same is true with regard to Yugoslavia under Tito. To this extent events in the Soviet Union and Eastern Europe seem to bear out the old Tocquevillian theory of revolutions (which did not account for the victory of Communism in Russia in 1917 and in China in 1949), according to which revolutions occur not when the situation becomes intolerable but, on the contrary, when bad regimes try to reform themselves.

The events in the Soviet Union bear little resemblance to nineteenth- and twentieth-century revolutions in Europe and elsewhere. They were not uprisings by a political opposition (let alone a class), but a revolt of the periphery against the center. These events have to be seen in the context of global ethnic conflicts and instability rather than revolution, and this leads one back to the question of ethnicity and nationalism and their mainsprings and manifestations.

Historians, political philosophers, and sociologists have debated at great length the cultural chasm thesis, theories of uneven development, the role of the intelligentsia in modern nationalist movements, and whether nationalism was a creation of the nineteenth century or whether something akin to nationalism existed well before. The debate about the historical dimension of nationalism is of undoubted general interest, but hardly of much relevance in the context of the fall of the Soviet empire.

The majority of the intelligentsia did not play a paramount role in recent decades among Ukrainian and Georgian nationalists, probably not even in the Baltic republics. In any case, this is not a question of crucial importance. The spread of higher education in the republics and the growing number of members of the intelligentsia who could not find commensurate work in other parts of the union increased, but this factor did not play a decisive role either.

Was the question of language a central component in the revolt against the center in the Soviet Union? Language as a manifestation of cultural identity played an important role in Georgia and the Baltic republics, but it was not of overriding importance in the Ukraine (except in the three western Ukrainian districts).[24]

Were the separatists motivated by the fear of losing their national identity unless they obtained full independence? If there was a danger of assimilation, it had been more pronounced thirty or forty years earlier. By 1990, it was obvious that the Soviet Union was not an effective melting pot, in contrast to what Lenin, Stalin, and their successors had assumed.

Investigations into the social, economic, and cultural background of the ethnic revival in the Soviet Union have not so far greatly enhanced our understanding of why it occurred. To what extent was it part of the worldwide ethnic revival that has taken place since the 1960s?[25]

Why did it lead to the breakup of the Soviet Union but not of England or Spain? It could be argued that reaction is most violent where repression has been harshest; this thesis could explain the containment of Scottish nationalism, but not the state of affairs in Spain. The cultural differences between Catalonia and Spain are at least as substantial as those between Russia and Ukraine. Manifestations of Catalan culture were more severely suppressed under Franco than Ukrainian culture in the Soviet Union before Gorbachev. Yet the Catalans did not secede, whereas the Ukrainians did. A seemingly promising initiative to explain nationalism in the Soviet Union was the "rational actor approach" used, for instance, by John Armstrong in an influential essay in 1965. This approach was based, roughly speaking, on certain commonsense assumptions, such as the fact that some republics were more highly developed than others, that some were more willing to cooperate with the Russians than others, and that some, as seen from Moscow, were more vital than others. Hence the conclusion that it would be rational from the point of view of the Soviet leadership if it concentrated on retaining the more cooperative among the younger brothers and the more important ones, while cutting its losses elsewhere. However, almost twenty years later, Armstrong noted that his observation of the behavior of the Russian leadership had sufficiently chastened his expectations of a functional rational policy and that he no longer expected such an outcome.[26] He might perhaps have added that while the outcome largely depended on the policy of the leadership, it also depended on the non-Russian republics, and their behavior did not follow the rational model either.

Since the great majority of modern states are polyethnic and since even small ethnic communities have demanded sovereign rights, the upsurge of ethnicity has led (and will lead) to conflict within and between states. Compromises are difficult not only because of intolerance but in view of the intermingling of ethnic groups in most parts of the world. Acceding to the claims of one group almost always means doing injustice to another. In brief, as long as the heavy emphasis on ethnocentrism persists, the situation is basically incurable, except perhaps by radical measures such as population transfer, now commonly called ethnic cleansing.

If relentlessly pursued, this policy would lead not just to fragmentization into smaller and smaller states, such as existed in eighteenth- and nineteenth-century Germany and Italy, but also to splits and divisions incompatible with the exigencies of modern industrial and postindustrial society.[27] Georgia, an old historical nation, seceded from the Soviet Union, whereupon minorities within Georgia such as the Abkhazians immediately staked their claims for autonomy. But quite often there are deep internal cleavages even among minorities, and the splintering process could continue to the level of tribal clans and other small, subnational units. Thus to give but one example, the Karachaevo-Cherkess national district in the northern Caucasus with a total population of 400,000 split into five quasi-independent republics, two of them Cossack.

The ethnic revival in Western Europe in the 1960s was based on the then fashionable belief that small was beautiful; that small groups too had the right of self-determination and sovereignty; that without full independence nationalities did not count for anything in the modern world; that from the point of view of economic viability, small nations as well as large could survive, just as small firms could coexist with giant corporations. It was argued, furthermore, that large and powerful nations were a priori more dangerous than small ones, simply because they tended to be more aggressive and could afflict greater damage on their smaller neighbors. In any case, the movement toward nationhood seemed natural and inevitable, and any attempt to prevent it was tantamount to oppression and the violation of elementary rights.

Most of these arguments now appear less convincing. While every ethnic and national group has the right of self-determination, of becoming a political nation on the level of abstraction, there is no sacred obligation to exercise this right. In view of the multiethnic character of so many countries, aggressive insistence on full independence and the unwillingness to make concessions has frequently led to bloodshed and constant strife. The prospects of democracy and political freedom are certainly not brighter in homogeneous nations than in multiethnic societies.

Small countries have been as aggressive as big ones, and in the age of the proliferation of means of mass destruction, the danger to world peace has enormously grown. Small may be beautiful, but the murder of little children, the mass rape of women, and "ethnic cleansing" are not. Nationalism has been compared to the god Janus looking at one and the same time in two opposite directions. But this comparison was more accurate in the nineteenth century than in the twentieth. In recent decades, the face of Janus has been directed more and more toward repression and destruction. Even if the trend toward nationalist self-assertion should be inevitable, there is no reason for rejoicing over it. The dangers it involves far outweigh the hopes it may engender.[28]

How strong is this nationalist wave? Having underestimated it for so long, there is now a tendency to overrate its long-term staying power, especially with regard to the new "non-historical" nations. The record of nationalism in Asia and Africa since independence has been disappointing by and large. Independence has not necessarily resulted in the pursuit of happiness. The hopes of the citizens have been often disappointed, and national strife has been frequent and destructive. How long will the appeals to nationalism remain effective if the political systems in these countries are unable to justify at least some of the hopes originally placed in them? Europe has learned the bitter lessons of two world wars caused by aggressive nationalism; hence the movement towards unity. If resistance against political unity has resurfaced, there is at least the comfort that such particularism will only condemn Western Europe to political impotence; military aggression has become unthinkable.

This, in briefest outline was the global context in which the breakup of the Union of Soviet Socialist Republics occurred. Since the political system keeping the union together had failed, the center was bound to collapse or at least suffer temporary eclipse. In these conditions, old and new nationalist movements found it easy to make political headway. Had there been a civil society, all-union opposition parties might have developed and the republics, large and small, might have been satisfied with the establishment of a confederation that would have protected common interests while giving much greater rights to the republics. In the absence of other political forces, however, the nationalist fronts became the only vehicle for pressing demands, and nothing short of full secession seemed acceptable. Even regional cooperation among the seceding republics was restricted in Central Asia and the Baltics, and there was none among the Transcaucasian republics. If the Russian leadership failed to keep the links even with Byelorussia and Ukraine despite cultural and other ties, it seems in retrospect that even a more astute policy would not have saved the Union in 1990 and 1991; only repression could have succeeded.

Could the union have been reformed twenty years earlier? This belongs to the kind of question that will keep practitioners of counterfactual history busy for a long time to come. It seems improbable, but the possibility cannot be ruled out altogether. But in this case, the whole political system would have had to undergo basic changes.

The consequences of the fall of the Soviet empire will not be clear for many years to come, not until a new order emerges in Europe and Asia, which may not occur for a long time. Further splits are a distinct possibility; so are, in a longer perspective, new mergers.[29]

The collapse of the "prison house of the peoples" did not inaugurate a new dawn of national liberation and a season of great hope. On the contrary, the euphoria was very shortlived as the republics that had left the union were facing difficulties even greater than the Russian Federation. As a result, those who had insisted on separation in the Caucasus as in Central Asia were again looking for a rapprochement with Moscow after an interval of only a few years, without great enthusiasm, to be sure, but for pressing economic and political reasons.[30] Inside the Russian Federation, the experience of not only the Caucasian republics, but also the others, tended to dampen the eagerness of minorities that had initially demanded full autonomy. Among the Russian leadership, a new assertiveness emerged with regard to the "Near Abroad" (meaning the republics that had seceded from the Union). Among Russian extremists this manifested itself as the demand to reincorporate all (or most) of the republics. Among the moderates it showed itself in the wish to protect millions of ethnic Russians living outside Russia and, generally speaking, to consider the "Near Abroad" a sphere of special Russian influence, something akin to an undeclared Russian Monroe Doctrine.[31]

If seventy years of Soviet rule did not solve the "national question," neither did the breakup of the Soviet Union. And it will all depend on the prudence and moderation (or its absence) on the part of the Russian leaders and those in the "Near Abroad" whether the years to come will be a period of peaceful coexistence or of national strife and irredentism.

9

East Germany: A Case Study

The downfall of the East German regime and reunification came as an enormous surprise to most politicians, political commentators in West and East, and, not least, the experts among them. True, strong doubts about an impending radical change had also been voiced by Western diplomats in Prague only a few weeks prior to the "velvet revolution." But in the case of East Germany, there was near unanimity. Honecker had been the best pupil in the Communist master class. The German Democratic Republic (DDR) had been a showcase, –nowhere had Communism been as successful and its achievements as striking. As Egon Bahr, one of the leading Social Democratic authorities on things German, had said in December 1988: "The old idea that there could be no peace in Europe as long as Germany was divided was fundamentally wrong, based in part on self-delusion, in part on fraud. To deny the partition was leading to nowhere, whereas there was promise in accepting it."[1]

In retrospect, the rootedness and popularity of the regime were not above suspicion. Its relative prosperity depended to a considerable degree on credits and other assistance given by Bonn. The East German intelligentsia and artists had been largely alienated–many had moved to the West, and even the achievements in sports had a great deal to do with the systematic use of anabolic steroids. Above all, what was going to be East Germany's fate at a time when its chief protector was showing signs of weakness? Against this fear, it was argued that Germany was not Poland, where Communism's feet of clay had appeared ten years earlier. The self-confidence, even arrogance of the East German leadership seemed unbroken.

The case of East Germany is of great symptomatic interest because more about it was known (or could have been known) before the wall came down, and more about the past is known now than elsewhere in Eastern Europe. This makes the misjudgments more difficult to understand even in retrospect.

The country was relatively open. Many tens of thousands of West Germans visited the DDR each year, and vice versa. It was a small country, and secrets were difficult to hide. West and East Germans spoke the same language, and it stands to reason that members of a family meeting from time to time would not hide their feelings from the visitors of the West, or they would at least give some indication of what they really felt.

There had been awareness in the West with regard to an incipient Soviet crisis; there certainly was with regard to Poland a decade earlier. Could it be perhaps that there was no crisis prior to the summer of 1989 in East Germany and that the turning came suddenly without any forewarning? Was it not true that dictatorships always appear stronger than they really are—up to the moment of their downfall? There is a grain of truth in this contention, but it does not suffice by way of explanation. For, as in the case of Russia, it should have been clearer that appearances in the Soviet bloc were deceptive, that behind the façade of stability there was much latent dissatisfaction, that the roots of the regime were more shallow than assumed, and that its sudden demise was far from unthinkable. If the Gorbachev miracle had been possible in the Soviet Union, about anything was possible in the Soviet bloc. This should have been the main lesson, but it did not register.

The East German state came into being in 1949 in the Soviet occupation zone of Germany. During the 1950s and 1960s, it was reconstructed, broadly speaking on the Soviet pattern. But whereas the East German government received the support of the overwhelming majority of the population (between 99.7 and 99.8 percent) at carefully staged elections, its legitimacy still seemed doubtful. From the end of the war to 1961, some 3 million Germans (out of a total population of about 20 million) fled from East to West, even though the superiority of the DDR was a basic tenet of official doctrine. East Germany was the only Communist country from which escape was physically possible in any significant numbers—hence the erection of the Berlin Wall in 1961. The official argument was that the wall was needed to defend East Germany against a big military attack said to be impending. The true aim was, of course, to stabilize the situation inside the DDR and between the two German states.

This target was broadly speaking achieved. Up to the 1960s, West Germany had claimed to be the only legitimate German state, and Bonn broke off relations with every country (except the Soviet Union) that recognized the DDR (the Hallstein Doctrine). After the building of the wall, Bonn had to retreat from this intransigent line. A basic change took place in 1969 and 1970, culminating in a series of treaties regulating relations between the two German states on an equal basis. If Bonn had hoped that these treaties (*Ostpolitik*) would lead to a marked improvement in relations, such expectations were realized only to a limited degree. Although minor concessions were made by East Berlin, the basic policy of the DDR was not *rapprochement* – let alone reunification – but *Abgrenzung*, keeping its distance from the Bundesrepublik. East Berlin wanted West German economic help but was not willing to make far-reaching political concessions. The only major exceptions in this context were certain alleviations as far as travel was concerned. Up to 1988, every fourth citizen of the DDR had been permitted to visit the West at least once. Some 40,000 had been allowed to emigrate to West Germany in 1984, admittedly an exceptional year in this respect. *Ostpolitik*, which had been initiated under the Social Democrats, continued under Chancellor Helmut Kohl, who met Honecker in 1987 to discuss further "small steps" to normalize and improve relations between the two countries. The opposition Social Democrats were ready to go considerably further than the Christian Democrats in making concessions to the DDR, going beyond realpolitik toward finding common ground. They suggested direct contacts between the West German and the East German parliaments and even appointed a commission to examine common ideological ground between their party and the East German Communists, a decision they were to regret in later years. They also demanded the abolition of the official West German research institute (Salzgitter), which recorded political crimes committed by the DDR authorities.

These initiatives were both undignified and pointless. By and large, there was no significant progress as far as relations between the two countries were concerned – partly for the political reasons already mentioned, but also because East German economic weaknesses made closer collaboration difficult. Trade between the two countries actually declined after 1985.

There was a growing inclination in West Germany after the building of the wall to accept the DDR as what it claimed to be, not only a separate state, but also a separate (socialist) nation. While Bonn had originally based its policy on the eventual reunification of the two Germanys, this idea came more and more into disrepute. Conservative historian Golo Mann first called it a *Lebenslüge* (an innate lie); Willy Brandt was to echo him a few years later. The opposition of conservatives like Mann was based on the fear that a united Germany would be neutral and turn its back on the West, whereas the proponents of a "third way" – Social Democrats like Gaus and Egon Bahr – found precisely this prospect appealing. Although leading West German politologists like Bracher and Schwan emphasized the declining importance of the nation state as the result of European unification, they had no intention of embellishing the merits of the DDR, as did many politicians and leading journals like *Die Zeit* and *Der Spiegel* as well as academic experts.

The normalization in relations between the two German states was the inevitable by-product of détente. If Bonn had insisted on its exclusive right to represent the German nation, it would have been denounced as "re-vanchist" not only in the East, but also among its Western allies. By a consistent hard line, little if anything would have been achieved in practical political terms; the DDR certainly would not have collapsed. On the contrary, West Germany would have been isolated. The changes that began in the late 1960s were a matter of realpolitik. But can one explain how the exigencies of realpolitik came to affect the general assessment of the DDR with regard both to its present state and its more distant prospects so radically and with such misleading consequences? There certainly was no conspiracy to depict the DDR in a false light–such a conspiracy among politicians, media, and experts would have been unthinkable in a democratic society. Nor was there a giant deceptive maneuver on the part of the DDR; deception may have played a minor role but it was by no means decisive.[2] Reorientation was, to use the hackneyed term, a reflection of the zeitgeist, which in the final analysis, was stronger than the facts. There was always a surfeit of facts pointing different directions, and it was only too easy to select those that fitted best into preconceived notions. As a result, Bonn's diplomatic representatives, such as Gaus, who spent seven years in East Berlin, and Bölling, failed to see the writing on the wall as totally as the professors developing their hypotheses in the groves of academe.

There had been commentators counseling rapprochement between the two German states with the intention of bringing about a change in the character and behavior of the East German regime even before Willy Brandt became chancellor and his Ostpolitik was adopted as official German policy.[3] These commentators assumed stabilization of the East German regime was in the best interest of the West Germans, because only from a position of strength and confidence would the East German Communists be prepared to discuss closer relations with Bonn and alleviate the lot of their own population. Thus West Germany had to be as much interested as the Communists in the preservation of the status quo in the DDR.

However, the detailed, systematic ideological underpinning of the reassessment of the achievements of the DDR came only with the emergence of a new discipline in 1968 and 1969–"Germanology" (*Deutschlandforschung*). East German affairs had, of course, been studied before, but under a different name and from a different point of view. The institutes and periodicals, usually sponsored by the government, referred up to 1968 to the German Democratic Republic as SBZ (Soviet occupation zone) rather than the DDR as a sovereign state. This practice was changed because it was thought to be insulting to the East Germans. In the 1950s, the DDR had widely been regarded as a provisional entity, but by the late 1960s the belief gained ground that the DDR was there to stay–possibly forever.

This belief was accompanied by two corollaries. First, the situation in the DDR was steadily improving from an economic point of view–according to some it was now among the ten most important industrial powers in the world. Second, the situation of the average citizen had improved; there was less oppression, the regime had become more popular, and something akin to a specific East German state and national consciousness had developed. Hence the need to replace the propagandistic approach that had prevailed in East German studies in the 1950s by a strictly academic and objective one.[4]

The central figure in the emergence of Germanology was Peter Christian Ludz, a political scientist who had been influenced by the then fashionable view in American universities according to which the age of totalitarianism had ended in Eastern Europe and was replaced by something called (for want of a better term) "consultative authoritarianism."[5] Ludz was a believer in comparative studies, and owing to his initiative huge and detailed comparative studies were published with the financial help of the Bonn government.[6] The merit of these publications was their wealth of facts and figures, but in one decisive respect they were incurably flawed. As Ludz saw it, they had to be "system-immanent"; in other words, the situation in the DDR had to be measured not by Western yardsticks but by East German. They had to be taken at face value. The reports on the situation in West Germany (and the facts and figures contained therein) were subject to the usual critical approach, whereas the surveys on East Germany were based on material published by the East German Communist party; that is, they were uncritical and often untrue, misleading, and propagandistic. Whole institutions were not covered in such comparative analyses simply because they did not figure in DDR publications. An important example is the state security service (Stasi). Ludz argued that the use of terroristic means was becoming more and more infrequent, as the Communist leadership could rely more and more on consensus on the part of the population. But this was, at best, a vision of some future age. For the time being, the Stasi was still an essential part of the regime, and also, as it subsequently appeared, one of the biggest employers, with almost 100,000 full-time employees in 1989 (up from 12,000 in 1953) and many hundreds of thousands of part-time collaborators. The Stasi had penetrated every sphere of East German society, and to write about the DDR while omitting this powerful and feared organization was to miss one of the most essential features of the regime.[7]

The impression gained from the products of the new science of Germanology was that East Germany had made great strides in its quest for social justice and the well-being of its citizens. Although it had not achieved production records and such a high standard of living as the Bundesrepublik, it was not to be forgotten that it had begun from a lower point. The Western allies had provided a flying start to Bonn's recovery (the Marshall Plan), but East Germany had borne the brunt of Russian demands for war reparations.

This specific argument lost validity as time went by. How to explain the continuing lag if East Germany's membership in the East European trade association (COMECON) gave it such tremendous advantages, as official propaganda constantly claimed? It was also maintained by many publicists and Germanologists that in various respects positive lessons could be learned from the East German experience. The DDR was much more traditionally German than West Germany, which had been subject to the influx of Western (American) mass culture. It was a poorer but happier country, and relations between human beings were warmer.[8]

Sometimes the impression was created that life in the small towns of East Germany retained the *Gemütlichkeit*, the comfort and cozyness, of the nineteenth-century Biedermeier period, as reflected in Spitzweg's pictures of small town life, in stark contrast to the boring, shabby, Stasi-penetrated and dominated society that happened to be the reality. Western newspaper reports, television documentaries, and even schoolbooks conveyed an image of East Germany exuding stability and satisfaction that was far prettier than it really was. As Kurt Sontheimer, the author of one of the most objective West German texts, later conceded, he and his co-author had started from the premise that the developments in the DDR were irreversible, that a socialist consciousness had developed, and that the great majority of DDR citizens had adjusted themselves to the existence of this state.[9] It is, of course, perfectly true that not everyone in the DDR was actually unhappy; human beings show an infinite capacity to adjust themselves even to execrable conditions. Western writers failed to see that such adjustments did not make a bad system normal. Other authors had gone much further in embellishing the realities and were unwilling to admit after the collapse that they had been wrong.

The view that the German question (reunification) was no longer topical was the prevailing consensus among West German politicians and experts. Following the rise of the Social Democratic–Liberal coalition, support for institutes and publications critical of the DDR ceased. They were thought to harm the process of reconciliation that had been initiated by the government. Nevertheless, a society for *Deutschlandkunde* ("Germanology") came into being in 1978. Assuming that the German question had not yet been solved, the society tried to sponsor critical research independent of considerations of realpolitik. Not all experts in the society shared the consensus. There were some exceptions among those in the legal profession (such as S. Mampe and S. Brunner), perhaps because they tended professionally toward a more conservative approach, and also among scholars specializing in the DDR economy.[10] Leading legal experts opposed the suggestion made by leading politicians (including Willy Brandt) to change the preamble of the constitution, which referred to German reunification. Although political leaders of all parties–including Franz Josef Strauss–declared that they could not envisage reunification in the forseeable future, the lawyers knew that one must not lightly change a constitution.

Economists tended to take a more realistic view of the DDR because they had to stick to facts and figures and were therefore more acutely aware of the real situation–the incapacity to modernize and to compete outside

COMECON, the low standard of living, and the great and growing economic bottlenecks. Politologists could engage in speculations about the more pragmatic orientation of the younger generation of DDR leaders and other such subjects. The economists, even those sympathetic to the DDR, could not stray too far from realities. Thus a committee headed by Karl C. Thalheim, the leading expert on the DDR economy, reached the conclusion in 1987 that only radical reforms could save the DDR regime, but that such reforms would not be tackled since they affected the very essence of the planned economy.[11] But the full implications of such reports were not realized by the politicians and the media, nor was it clear whether a deterioration in the economic situation would have any immediate political consequences.

When did the last act of East German history begin? Perhaps a date somewhere in 1987 should be chosen as a starting point. It seems obvious in retrospect that as the reform movement in the Soviet Union gathered speed, the East German government should have adjusted its policies to the new trend in Eastern Europe; but it did not. Perhaps it thought that the new line in Moscow would be only of short duration–Gorbachev would not last long. Or they might have persuaded themselves that what was needed in the Soviet Union was not necessarily applicable in their own country, simply because their economy was functioning better and the hold of their regime was firmer. In any case, they did not at all like the talk about the "Common European home" emanating from Moscow. As a member of the Politburo, Kurt Hager, said in April 1987, the fact that a neighbor is refurbishing his apartment does not necessarily mean that you ought to copy him. The East Germans seem to have been genuinely annoyed by events in Moscow. There was criticism, usually by implication and sometimes even by censorship. For the first time in the history of the DDR a Soviet journal (*Sputnik*) was banned. There was no sign of alarm, even of unease or apprehension, however, in East Berlin. East German leader Erich Honecker repeated that whether Kohl and the West Germans liked it, the DDR (and the wall) were there to stay. The East German leadership should have been worried, among other things, by the rapprochement between Bonn and Moscow. Kohl visited Moscow in October 1988, and when Gorbachev came to Bonn in June 1989, he was given a much more rapturous welcome than in East Berlin.

Perhaps the curtain for the last act was lifted only in July and August 1989, when there was a sudden increase in the number of East German citizens trying to leave their country by legal and illegal means. On August 8, the West German embassy in East Berlin was closed because 131 East Germans had shown up, applied for visas and refused to leave the building. Other West German embassies began closing for similar reasons: six days later, the West German embassy in Budapest; on August 23, the embassy in Prague; and on September 19, the embassy in Warsaw. It seemed a concerted operation, well prepared, but in fact it was quite spontaneous. Meanwhile, on August 19, 660 DDR citizens had used the opportunity of an assembly on the Hungarian–Austrian border to escape to the West. On September 11, Hungary opened its western frontier for East German refugees despite protests from East Berlin. The East German government felt it had to compromise: the refugees from Prague were permitted to leave for the West. The trains carrying them passed through East German territory, generating more demonstrations.

Thus by August and September 1989 at the very latest, it should have been clear that the East German system was in deep trouble. It is next to impossible to point to any specific immediate causes. In May, there had been municipal elections with the usual 99 percent supporting the Communist government. There were widespread allegations of fraud, but there had been the same results in all previous elections. The supply situation was, by and large, neither better nor worse than in earlier years. Perhaps there was a feeling among the dissidents that in the new world political climate, the Communist leadership would find it difficult to put down oppositionist activities with the customary brutality, but they could not be certain. Their members were still detained (albeit for shorter periods than before), and their protests and demands continued to be rejected.

In Bonn there was no greater awareness that momentous events were about to occur in the East. One of the few West German political figures who showed instinctive awareness that something was acutely wrong in the DDR was the left Social Democrat Erhard Eppler, who had by that time left active politics. He belonged to those who believed in the necessity of a stable, self-confident East German government. But in a paper written in 1987, he had raised the possibility that the DDR would destabilize itself. On June 17, 1989, he gave the traditional address in the Reichstag on the occasion of the anniversary of the June insurrection in 1953. He said that if there was no change in DDR policy, there was a real possibility that the majority of the citizens in the DDR, who were still hoping for reform, would turn into a majority hoping for the end of Communist rule. He also noted a certain unease among DDR rulers– "There seems to be among the DDR leadership growing anxiety with regard to their survival" – and said that the West Germans had no obligation to prevent the East Germans from ruining themselves.

Most other West German politicians did not share this assessment at the time. In Bonn it was business as usual; the bureaucracy had prepared for the EEC summit in Madrid in late June. After that date, politicians went on their annual holiday, except for those who had to attend the summit meeting of the leading industrial nations in Paris in mid-July. But after that their diaries were left clear for a number of weeks. Eppler's party colleagues certainly did not share his views. Bahr, Peter Glotz, and most others continued to argue that the demand for reunification was an anachronism and probably a wicked one. The citizens of the DDR would not permit anyone to take their state away from them. Willy Brandt was more astute than others. He had been a leading proponent of the *Lebenslüge* thesis, but he was also among the first to change his mind as he realized that there was a genuine mass movement in the East opposing the regime and that the days of the DDR were counted.

The protest inside East Germany gathered speed. On September 4, several hundred people protested in front of the Nikolai church in Leipzig; on September 25, their number had risen to 8,000; on October 2, there were 25,000 (3,000 according to the Stasi); on October 9, 70,000; on October 16, 100,000; on October 23, 300,000. Demonstrations in Dresden and other cities began a little later and were not quite on the same scale, but almost everywhere mass marches and meetings took place. In East Berlin about 1 million participated on November 4, demonstrating in favor of freedom of speech and assembly and for free elections.

Honecker had been ill throughout most of August and September and returned to work only on September 25. The supreme party and state organs were paralyzed, but it was not the result of the leader's absence. The leadership must have been at least vaguely aware of the precariousness of the situation, but they went through the motions as usual. On October 7, the fortieth anniversary of the foundation of the DDR was celebrated; Honecker and Gorbachev embraced and kissed. The day after, Gorbachev said in a press conference that those acting too late were punished by history.

Ten days later, Honecker requested to be released for reasons of health from his post as first secretary and chairman of the State Council. Two other key figures resigned, and Egon Krenz was unanimously appointed to replace Honecker. The new leadership appealed to the people to cooperate in a reform program, and freedom of travel was promised. On November 2, most of the Politburo resigned; on November 8, the whole government. The Socialist Unity (Communist) party surrendered its power monopoly and announced that the first free election would take place in June 1990. Honecker and company were now excluded from the party, and criminal proceedings were opened against him as well as other figures of the old regime. On December 22, the Brandenburg Gate was opened for the first time in twenty-eight years.

This in briefest outline was the sequence of events that led to the downfall of the Communist regime. The deliberations and decisions that followed, leading to German reunification, have been the subject of many accounts; they are only of marginal significance in the present context.

II

The causes of the collapse of the East German regime, the extent to which local leaders were aware of their predicament, and the reasons that so many outside experts were mistaken in their assessment can be discussed on the basis of a greater quantity of reliable information than has been available in the case of the Soviet Union.[12]

Economic factors certainly played an important role in the breakdown of the DDR. The system was ineffective, and it was run rigidly and irresponsibly by corrupt people of no great intelligence.[13] Although the system worked badly, its productivity was low, and it did not catch up with the West (or the Far East), the results were still somewhat better than elsewhere in COMECON, and poor economic performance does not explain the sudden collapse. There was corruption in the East German state, but probably not more than in many other East European countries, and, in any case, the extent of corruption became known only after the collapse.

There were some differences of opinion in the party leadership between conservatives and (mild) reformers, but there was no open split because the latter kept their ideas more or less to themselves. The party, some argued in retrospect, was fatally ill.[14] It was a party of careerists, not idealists. Since it had so many members – 2.3 million out of a population of 16 million, the party was neither an elite nor a transmission belt to keep the masses in line. People belonged to the Socialist Unity Party (SED) because they were expected to do so. This had been the case for many years, however, and no one had considered it an indication of specific weakness. The leadership was elderly and cut off from the real problems facing society, but this was not a unique feature either, typical only of the DDR.

Warning signs could be seen in other directions. The number of people excluded from the SED was 11,000 in 1988, more than in any previous year. The number of inner party trials (23,000) was also higher than in earlier years. The number of DDR citizens not returning from journeys abroad was twice as high in 1988 (834) than in the previous year.[15] The number of applications to leave the DDR was also steadily rising.

But whether a few thousand left a party numbering more than 2 million, whether a few hundred did not return from a journey abroad, were not very important facts per se. They were only straws in the wind. People were less afraid than before. And it should also be recalled that each such case of "defection" would be known and discussed at the work place, in the residential quarter, and elsewhere. Such news had a ripple effect.

Another indication of growing dissatisfaction were the letters of complaint sent to the Central Committee and to Honecker personally – some 148,000 between 1986 and June 1988.[16] A letter sent to a trade union newspaper in September 1989 notes that the coverage of daily life by the SED media created the impression that they were talking about an entirely different country. People were in a bad mood; there was no enthusiastic acclaim for government policy. Daily life had not improved. It was difficult or impossible to plan a holiday, to get a spare part for a car, to obtain fruit or vegetables or children's clothes. The rulers were shielded from the people by the police. If a member of the government went for a visit outside East Berlin, highroads, streets, and railway stations were sealed off.[17] There is some reason to believe that open dissatisfaction was stronger in the south of the republic – the heavily industrialized regions of Saxony and Thuringia, once the main bulwark of the regime. It was a frequent cause of complaint that the party membership as a whole was totally excluded from political decision making; but had the situation ever been essentially different?

If there was a gradual or sudden change in the attitude of the citizens of the DDR, when did it take place and how? There is the evidence, by necessity impressionistic, of close observers of the East German scene, and there are also the results of polls carried out by the East German Academy of Social Sciences. These empirical data were not published and probably were never meant for publication–and thus more reliable, since there was no need to embellish them.[18]

Nevertheless, there were fairly narrow limits to the latitude enjoyed by the researchers who prepared the polling questions. It also stands to reason that those who replied were far less reticent about telling the truth in 1988 and 1989 than ten years earlier. Given these reservations, the results of the polls are still of some interest. An analysis shows an apparently stable society in 1987 with a great measure of contentment. In 1987, a clear majority not only endorsed the "peace policy" of the government, but expressed satisfaction with the ecological situation at least as far as their immediate surroundings were concerned. True, even then there was much less enthusiasm among the younger people than among their parents' generation.[19] In 1977 and 1978, more than 40 percent of those asked replied that their working and housing conditions had improved within the last few years.

In 1988, growing skepticism and even pessimism clearly appeared from the data. The main complaints concerned the supply of goods and the environment; these were considered the main problems by 74 percent and 84 percent respectively of those asked. Income and length of working day bothered only 34 percent and 24 percent. It was reported by 62 percent that supplies and ecological conditions had actually deteriorated during the previous five to six years. About 53 percent felt acutely endangered by the growing pollution. Only 23 percent believed that there would be significant improvements during the years to come, and 65 percent did not think that the DDR would reduce the nation's distance behind the leading industrial nations by the year 2000.

Two further observations are relevant. First, freedom to travel to the West did play a substantial role all along among the complaints, but it was apparently not the paramount issue. Second, alienation had increased among the younger generation, who showed a much more pronounced tendency to enjoy themselves than their elders did. Neither the work ethic nor voluntary social work interested them. If the evidence is accurate, this trend shows that the SED had lost ground in its ability to indoctrinate, trying to form a new type of socialist individual. On the other hand, it could be that the eagerness of the middle aged was also more limited than the figures tend to show. They may have felt more reluctance to tell the truth.

According to the polls, there was a certain decline in contentment of the population during the 1980s, even though objectively there was no substantial change in the situation–the supply of goods and the ecological disaster were not significantly worse in 1988 than five or ten years earlier.

Even in early 1988, a small majority of those asked (52 percent) did not indicate acute unhappiness. On a scale of 1 to 5 they opted for 3.5; they were "partly content, partly unhappy." What the polls did reflect was the loss of hope and a declining willingness to put up with shortages and pollution.

According to these research data, the change in mood occurred only after September 1989, when the media could report more or less freely about living and working conditions, and when countless revelations were made about the failure of forty years of SED rule. The data are of some interest, but how reliable are they? Polls are not always reliable even in democratic societies; and while the East German data were not manipulated, it was obvious that the great majority of those asked would still not express extreme dissatisfaction with their life. Saying that they were not altogether happy was probably the limit to which they could safely go. Any stronger statement of dissatisfaction would probably have been reported to the Stasi. It could be that the change in mood came quite suddenly, or, to be precise, that it affected the majority of the population rather suddenly. The DDR survey data do not offer conclusive evidence however. When thousands of young people decided in 1989 to travel to Hungary, Poland, and even Czechoslovakia in the hope of leaving the DDR, they exposed themselves to considerable risk. It is inconceivable that they acted on the spur of a moment. Such a far-reaching decision must have been years in the making. No survey data can give definitive answers on how such a decision was made and why, once a minority had pioneered this kind of action, many others were ready to join in by fleeing or taking to the streets.

III

To what extent was the party leadership aware of the ferment in the population? In June 1989, the regional party secretaries were informed by the Stasi that the enemies of the DDR had intensified their activities and that the party should therefore take the offensive – meaning, presumably, both increased propaganda and attempts to remedy the main complaints among the population. On August 31, 1989 (after the events in Hungary and Czechoslovakia), a meeting took place in the office of General Erich Mielke, the internal security minister, in which the chief Stasi commanders reported about the mood among the populations of various cities. General Hähnel reported that a large part of the population of Berlin unfortunately listened to the West German media; Colonel Anders dealt with the activities of the church in Dresden; General Schwarz made it known that a few hundred young people from the Erfurt area had left for Hungary, but not the kind of people he would miss.[20] Then came the turn of Colonel Dangries, who painted a picture that was less rosy. When the minister asked for his assessment of the general situation in Gera, he replied that it was stable. But there were various problems, above all the exodus from the DDR, which provided food for thought.

MINISTER: And if there should be tomorrow another June 17 [the date of the workers' revolt in 1953]?

COLONEL DANGRIES: This won't happen; this is, after all, what we are here for.

MINISTER: Do you understand the meaning?

DANGRIES: Yes.

But Dangries went on pointing to the expectations among the population. It would be exaggerated to say that the mood was one of pessimism, but there was general dissatisfaction. General Hummitzsch, who spoke after him concerning Leipzig, said, "We are masters of the situation," but added, "Sometimes in a certain situation a single spark is enough to trigger off something." The Stasi commander from Chemnitz, Karl Marxstadt, said that the situation there was as good and as bad as in Berlin. In summing up, he said that the state of affairs was more or less under control.[21]

While the Stasi was aware of many details (above all, activities inside the Protestant church and its periphery) and local officials were not badly informed, they were reluctant in their summaries to paint too dark a picture, perhaps because this would have reflected badly on their efficiency. They reported, by and large, what they thought their superiors wanted to hear. But the impression is also created that the Stasi was overorganized and had too many employees who were preoccupied much of the time in espionage within the party. In the end, no clear warning emerged from this vast organization.

Twelve days later, a paper was submitted to the Stasi minister reporting on the mood among party members. This account was far more pessimistic than the earlier report. Party members of long standing were deeply anxious about the situation and about the future. They had reached the conclusion that the SED leadership did not want to know about the many problems facing the country and that the media were lying.[22] As a result, discipline at work was declining. The leadership was made responsible for the existence of the critical problems, and it was thought that it was incapable of remedying them. There was hardly a difference anymore between party members and those outside the SED.

By mid-October, even the most optimistic Stasi commanders must have realized that they were no longer in control. On October 21, there was yet another session in Mielke's office, in which he said that one ought to find out "who was who," to identify the ringleaders inciting the masses. Could the Stasi not have known this after all the years of close observation of groups and individuals? In their report to the Politburo on October 23, they could say nothing that had not been reported in the media earlier on. In another circular to the Politburo, dated November 7 – one of the last on record – it was claimed that young people, above all, were prominent in "heating up the atmosphere." Among them were many who were drunk or had criminal records. By that time, any television viewer in West Germany and indeed the whole world knew that young people did play a prominent role in the demonstrations. The "drunkenness" seems to have been the invention of the Stasi, which could not think of other explanations. All in all, however effective the Stasi had been as an instrument of repression over the years, it proved to be useless as a seismograph. Honecker did read the Stasi reports, but as he said in an interview after the fall, he did not give great credence to them because they contained little that he had not read in the Western media.[23] It is doubtful, in retrospect, whether warnings would or could in fact have been heeded, had they been given in time.

The East German uprising in 1989 was spontaneous, not a revolution from above, as in the Soviet Union. Whereas in Russia the reform movement started in the capital and was restricted, by and large, to a few big cities, in the DDR the decisive impetus came from Leipzig, Dresden, and some other urban centers, mainly in the south of the republic, with Berlin remaining relatively quiet.[24] The fact that the dissident movement was deeply penetrated by the Stasi (more than in the Soviet Union), which had some 80 to 100 agents in leading positions, did not in the end make any difference at all.

IV

The postmortem on the record on the professional DDR watchers began almost immediately after the downfall of the Communist regime. Some of them (like some politicians and journalists) had believed in the stability of the DDR right up to its fall. They now claimed that the mainstream Germanologists had been more often right than wrong, but that nobody had been in a position to predict the exact date of the explosion. There were not enough hard facts available about the "real thinking and feeling of the population," and the motives and strategies of the rulers were not calculable either.[25] This is correct up to a point, but it had not prevented the "mainstreamers" in West Germany from claiming that SED rule was stable. In truth, the optimistic (and wrong) assessment by the mainstream Germanologists was based on certain assumptions that had been mistaken, such as the belief that the system had not been flawed per se, but had merely taken a wrong turn toward bureaucratic socialism at some past stage. The mainstreamers conceded that they had underrated the latent instability of the regime and the creeping political and psychological alienation of the population, and it had overrated the ability of the regime to reform itself. They were aware of the constant violations of human rights, but in contrast to their more critical colleagues, they did not constantly refer to it: "We did not want to repeat the obvious." This argument, too, would have been more credible had they stressed the repression as often as the achievements of the SED. They claimed that they had merely favored objective comparisons between the democratic and Communist systems, in a self-critical spirit and without prejudice. It remains to be investigated how a seemingly oppressed, depoliticized and atomized society gradually mustered the courage to protest against the system.[26] Lastly, some of yesterday's mainstreamers pointed to a "theory deficit," a term beloved among left-wing German social scientists, which had prevailed in their ranks for a long time. Perhaps the modernization concept, while basically correct, had to be modified? Was it not true that state socialism such as practiced in the DDR was still one of the approaches to modernizing a society ("a shortcut to the universal emancipation of humanity"), which had failed because it had been too authoritarian and bureaucratic?

This explanation, too, does not seem persuasive in retrospect. There had been plenty of theoretical models to justify mainstream thinking about the DDR, only most of them, beginning with Ludz's writings, had been partly or wholly wrong, whereas some of the despised "empiricists" had been far more correct. It could always be claimed that mainstream Germanology had produced specialized studies that were of lasting value about all kinds of aspects of life in the DDR. They still had been wrong as far as essentials were concerned, however, and that this was largely the result of being "value-free" and equidistant. When Helmuth Schmidt was chancellor, he complained in 1978 in a speech at the annual conference of German historians that as a result of a surfeit of "theory" many Germans still had a fuzzy picture of what Nazism had been like. The same was true, at least to the same degree with regard to the character of the Communist system in the DDR.[27]

Egon Bahr had been the most vocal and consistent advocate in West Germany of a rapprochement with the DDR. After the downfall of the regime, he submitted an explanation that was certainly original: he had always believed that Communism was a disease from which Europe and Russia had to be liberated.[28] He implied that a policy of concessions offered to help stabilize the SED regime was likely to hasten its downfall, whereas a more critical approach might have had the opposite effect.

Similar arguments have been adduced in the case of the Soviet Union: détente precipitated the ruin of the regime. Whether détente did indeed have this effect or whether it prolonged the survival of the Communist regime is the kind of counterfactual history that can be endlessly discussed. However, even if the claim is true, it still remains highly doubtful whether these were the secret intentions of the architects of détente in Washington and Europe. Democratic systems are not capable, on the whole, of engaging in such long-term Machiavellian strategies.

A great deal of painful soul searching was needed, and since the willingness to admit mistakes is certainly not more developed among German academics than among human beings in general, it was only to be expected that rearguard battles would be fought to demonstrate that, after all, they had not been entirely wrong and that in any case their critics had been even more mistaken.[29]

The attempts to salvage the record of mainstream research on the DDR are unlikely to succeed, but there remain some crucial questions to be answered. As one researcher asked: How had the regime lasted for so long, if the situation was really so bad?[30] This kind of question was more likely to be asked by those who had opposed the totalitarianism concept than those who had accepted it. Hans Modrow, the last DDR leader and an old Communist, said in retrospect that the DDR was in many respects still Stalinist. This was precisely what many mainstream West Germans had steadfastly denied. They had accepted as normal a situation—the dictatorship—that was basically abnormal. They had been deeply convinced that while antifascism was right, anti-Communism ("primitive anti-Communism") was indefensible. While it is true that all kinds of people had opposed Communism for the wrong reason, this still did not mean that Communism was right and its critics wrong. Anti-Communism, as Thomas Mann had said early on in the Cold War, was the greatest folly of the twentieth century—it was also endangering world peace. For according to the prevailing consensus during détente, the preservation of the status quo was absolutely essential for the maintenance of world peace. And this involved accepting the reality of the other side even if one did not fully agree with it. This was the zeitgeist prevailing among most politicians and the media. Mainstream research on the DDR never lagged far behind: it had supported cold war attitudes in the 1950s, became détente-oriented in the 1960s and 1970s, and a believer in status quo in the 1980s.

Some have argued in retrospect that it was impossible to imagine in the 1970s and 1980s that German reunification was still feasible, because there was no indication of overwhelming support for it inside Germany. The other powers certainly were not enthusiastic about this prospect. The East German regime did not fall because it was opposed to German unity—official Bonn had de facto long ago accepted the division. Even if reunification (as Gunter Grass and others believed) was a bad idea, even if there should be grave difficulties in the process of reunification, this cannot be construed as justifying the East German system. On the contrary, some may argue that the policy of the regime had caused such a fundamental mess that there was no way out of it except at the price of considerable damage and human suffering. As in Russia, there may well be in the DDR a wave of nostalgia for the "good old times."

One could think of several reasons that contributed to the misjudgments of West German experts. One was the fact that most of them visited East Berlin rather than the other cities and villages in the DDR. But East Berlin had always been a show window, even more so than Moscow. However, this could not possibly have been a decisive factor, for enough was known about the rest of the DDR. Thousands went to Leipzig, Dresden, and Weimar, which were also show windows, but on a considerably lower level. Cottbus, Rostock, and Eisenhüttenstadt were only an hour or two away from Berlin and these were not in zones closed to foreigners.

Mention has been made of the pressure exerted by the DDR authorities on the West German media: those who were too critical were punished;

those sharing a more friendly attitude were rewarded in various small ways—or at least not expelled. This was also true to some degree with regard to academic experts. There was, of course, no open censorship, but if Western specialists wanted to have access to archives, libraries, and other such services, self-censorship might have appeared prudent, unless, of course, they agreed with the DDR authorities in the first place. It is most unlikely that a highly placed DDR official would have been ready to give an interview to a Western expert known for his negative attitude toward the regime. The opportunities for "objective" (or friendly) experts were, of course, greater. This is true with regard to all dictatorships and to a lesser degree other governments; it is a factor that is too often forgotten.

If Western experts were misled, it was only to a small degree owing to the cunning of DDR propaganda. Far more important was the fact that some of their basic assumptions and attitudes had been wrong for more than twenty years. And it is, of course, also true that there were certain essential factors in the situation that simply defied measurement, analysis, and assessment. There was no possible way to know whether deep down in their hearts the people of the DDR were really content, let alone how firm and rooted their contentment was. Nor could it be predicted how the leadership would react at a time of crisis.

But no superhuman powers of prophecy were needed after 1987 to realize that prospects for the DDR had greatly deteriorated. Once *perestroika* was under way throughout the Eastern bloc, the chances for survival for the DDR were bleak. If it rejected reforms, it was doomed because it depended for its survival on Moscow. If it opted for reform, its chances were equally dismal because the regime was brittle, unyielding, highly centralized, and could not bend. Carrying out basic change would have required giving up the monopoly of power: East Germany would have ceased to be the DDR. True, there still was the possibility, at least in theory, of a "Chinese solution,"—economic reform coupled with political repression. But East Germany was not China, and the idea seems not to have been seriously considered by the SED leadership.

If mainstream West German thinking about the DDR was so far off the mark, it would be unrealistic to expect more accurate predictions from experts in Western Europe and the United States. To a considerable extent, they received both their inspiration and their facts from West Germany. If a leading West German captain of industry with decades of experience in Eastern Europe told a meeting of experts in New York in the summer of 1989 that the most important factor that had contributed to the improvement of relations between the two German states was the increased self-confidence of the SED leadership, who were they to doubt such wisdom?[31]

If the CIA, with its superior resources, reached the conclusion that average per capita income in the DDR was about as high as in Britain and much higher than in Spain or Israel, the academic experts must be forgiven for not straying very far from such assessments.[32]

Although American media did not pay much attention to the DDR, interest among scholars was substantial. There were regular country-wide seminars in New Hampshire, meetings in Madison, and conferences in San Francisco and elsewhere. Scores of experts met, exchanged views, and spoke about their findings, which, with a very few exceptions, were not different from those of the West German Germanologists.

As A. James McAdams, a leading American expert on East German affairs, put it in 1989, the successes of the SED had been so great that they might become an obstacle in dealing with new challenges. In a paper written on the occasion of the fortieth anniversary of the DDR, he predicted that there was much reason to assume that East German Communism would prosper over the next forty years. Visiting East Berlin, one was immediately struck by the "air of quiet self-satisfaction" among party officials that had not been apparent a few years earlier. Our visitor was deeply impressed; for the Soviets, Honecker had become not just a senior statesman, but the leader of the USSR's most important ally: "East Germany epitomizes the successful construction of socialism outside the Soviet Union's borders." With the emergence of a much stronger, more self-confident East German state, the advantage (in Germany–Germany relations) had slipped out of West Germany's grasp.[33]

Other Western observers were somewhat less sanguine with regard to the DDR's economic achievements. Martin McCauley, a British expert, noted that the good years were over, that while the economy was growing on paper, living standards were stagnating, and to compensate for the dimming of self-confidence there had been a militarization of society. This fact seems to have escaped the attention of McAdams, despite countless on-the-spot interviews in the DDR. However, McCauley gave importance to the Volkskammer, the East German parliament, which had no political clout whatsoever; whereas one looks in vain in his book for a description of the Stasi, which, all other functions apart, was one of the biggest enterprises in the country, with almost 100,000 full time employees in 1989 and several hundred thousand part-time assistants.[34]

In 1992, the DDR successes noted by McAdams became a mere "illusion of success." He still believed that there was nothing in 1989 that could have prepared politicians in West or East Germany, let alone the onlooking world, for the kind of disorder that was to engulf the Germanys as the result of a single decision made outside East Germany's border. This decision was the removal by the Hungarian government of the barbed-wire fences on its borders with Austria on May 2, 1989. McAdams concedes that he had been wholly convinced that two separate German states would exist during his lifetime, as many a German policy maker had assured him.[35] In retrospect, he would have been better off if he had talked to fewer policy makers.

It is only fair to add that these views were shared at the time by virtually all leading figures in German studies in the United States. Some went considerably further in their belief in the achievements and stability of the DDR. After the fall, there was neither in America nor in West

Germany a rush to engage in public self-criticism among the experts. On the contrary, there was an intensive search for alibis and a reluctance to admit errors. True, the DDR had disappeared, but it was clearly too early to draw far-reaching conclusions: perhaps the merger of the two Germanys would end in failure, or cause all kinds of complications for the rest of Europe and the world. Perhaps at some future date the record of the DDR would be judged more justly, and its positive achievements recognized. Perhaps it would have been better if East Germany (or the whole of Germany) had opted for a "third way" between West and East, between Communism and capitalism, as Gaus and others had suggested for many years. However, even if socialism does get a second chance in Germany, it will be a very different system from the one prevailing in the DDR between 1945 and 1990. Such a second coming could in no way act as retrospective justification of the mainstream DDR watchers, who for many years and with disastrous consequences saw only what they wanted to see.

And lastly, what did the Russians know at the time about the true state of affairs in East Germany? What I have written so far has been reviewed by Ivan Kuzmin, the resident of the KGB in East Berlin during the critical years. (He was also a noted specialist in German studies with a doctorate from Humbold University.) He agrees with the general thrust of my observations and conclusions. Erich Honecker and his paladins lived in an unreal world, a fool's paradise of festive torchlight parades and reports about great achievements in socialist competition. He did not want to hear the warnings of his own intelligence, and his subsequent allegations that they did not give him trustworthy information are simply not true.[36] According to Kuzmin, the Soviet diplomats, military leaders, and intelligence agents stationed in East Germany had no illusions about the true state of affairs. One year before the breakdown, the KGB reported that contracts with West Germany were getting out of control and that "objectively" the trend was leading toward the restoration of a unified German nation. Since 1986, German Communist leaders such as Stoph and Krolikowski had asked for Soviet help to replace Honecker with Krentz. According to Kuzmin, the leadership in Moscow had no wish to get involved, and the alarmist KGB reports during the second half of 1988 and early 1989 fell on deaf ears.

The version of a highly placed source is of interest. But was the East German crisis the responsibility of one senile leader and his incompetent advisers? Would Krentz have made that much of a difference? Could the DDR have been reformed? None of these possibilities seems likely even in retrospect, and for this reason the inaction of the Moscow leadership does not appear to have been a decisive factor in retrospect.

What, then, were the lessons of the collapse of the German Democratic Republic? In an interesting essay Albert Hirschmann has noted that the events in East Germany came as a total surprise to spectators and actors, which suggests that "our capacity to comprehend large scale political and social change remains utterly undeveloped." He believes that the real mystery of the 1989 events was the transformation of a purely private activity—the effort of scattered individuals to move from East to West—into a broad movement of public protest.

But is it so difficult to understand that, given the dramatic changes in other East European countries, a young generation in the DDR should have come to believe that there was such a chance in their country too? And that, in any case, the risks in the case of their failure were not as great as in the past? If there was a mystery, it was in Moscow, not in East Berlin or in Leipzig. Once the Soviet leadership had decided not to fight for the survival of their East European empire, the fall of the East German regime was only a question of time. East Germany was neither North Korea nor Vietnam; it could not survive in isolation. The flight of East German citizens turned into a mass flight, and this was bound to lead to protest demonstrations on the parts of those who wanted to stay. Once the Communist leadership had shown weakness facing the defection of so many citizens to the West, there was a good chance that it would no longer show much determination opposing their demands regarding change inside the DDR. And even if there would have been repression, there was much reason to assume that it would not be on a massive scale. The East German protesters felt, instinctively perhaps, that the fate of their country had been decided in Moscow, and they were not mistaken.

10
Conclusion

Accident played a considerable role in the beginning and the end of Soviet history; accident will play a similar role in the future. But for Lenin the Bolsheviks might never have come to power. What would have happened in this case? A return to autocratic tsarism and a constitutional monarchy seem not very probable in retrospect. Some kind of authoritarian regime seems far more probable, perhaps a military dictatorship, which, with luck, might have eventually given way to a democratic regime as it did in Turkey and Spain.

Could there have been a development worse than Leninism, which ultimately turned into Stalinism, followed by the Khrushchev and Brezhnev era? Nothing is a priori impossible, but such a scenario puts a strain on one's imagination. A Russian kind of fascism seems improbable in retrospect and not just in the absence of a charismatic *führer* or *duce*. In contrast to Germany or Italy, Russia was not ethnically a homogeneous country. A purely nationalist-racialist ideological appeal would not have sufficed to generate patriotic enthusiasm, and in any case, mass communications were not sufficiently developed in Russia in 1917 and 1918 for the establishment of an effective fascist regime. For these reasons, there was a greater likelihood of the emergence of either an old-fashioned autocratic regime, with some modern elements, or a very imperfect democracy. There is the possibility that the Russian empire might have disintegrated in 1917 as the result of the weakness of the center. But this seems not very likely in retrospect. After the secession of Poland, the Baltic countries, and Finland, the demographic predominance of the Russians was strong; there existed nationalist movements in the Caucasus, but in the Ukraine, nationalism was weak and in Central Asia it did not have a powerful appeal either.

Would a non-Bolshevik government have been able to provide a minimum of effective rule and economic development? The administration on both the central and especially the local level had not been that inefficient even under the tsar. There had been economic progress before 1914 as in most other countries, quite irrespective of government policies, which helped economic development in some respects and hindered it in others. Would such a regime have been capable of resisting the onslaught of Nazism in 1941? At this point, at the very latest, exercises in counterfactual history become impossible. No one can say whether but for the existence of the Soviet Union (and the largely mythical threat of Communist revolution imported from the east), Nazism would have come to power in Germany in the first place. Instead, a nationalist-authoritarian regime might have prevailed, which (among other options) might have made common cause with Russia against Western Europe.

What if fascism had prevailed in Russia? It would have crushed the labor movement, dragooned the peasants (short of the collectivization of agriculture), militarized the economy and society in general, and persecuted national minorities, Jews, and intellectuals. Heavy industry would have been nationalized to a significant degree. The annexation of Eastern Europe would have been pursued, and everything would have been done to turn Russia into a great power. In short, as George Lichtheim put it in an essay written in 1964, fascism would have done what Stalin did in any case: "It is true, the ideology would have been different: There would have been no Marxism, just plain Russian National Socialism. But it is arguable that this is going to happen anyhow."[1]

But Communism did prevail. Why did it last so long? Earlier on, attention was drawn to the enthusiasm in the Soviet Union in the 1920s for the building of a society of a new type and higher quality. When discussing this issue with younger Russians, I have often sensed skepticism: Did anyone ever really believe in Communism? People did believe, including some who later became staunch, inveterate critics. Boris Souvarine was one of the bitterest enemies of Soviet Communism and one of the most knowledgeable. He related many years later what he had seen in the Soviet Union in 1920 and 1921: Moscow made a very favorable impression on a French delegation, bearing out the evidence of Pierre Pascal.[2]

> The Russian summer fascinated us. War Communism seemed no more than a bad dream. It was replaced by the NEP which provided a great stimulus to trade, brought about the reopening of shops and the filling up of the show windows. The streets were lively with women in colourful blouses, and merry, playful children. The Bolshoi Theater and the MKHAT were full. Lastly, at the risk of appearing ridiculous—the Russian soul, the famous Slavic charm, which is not a fabrication but a reality to which I always was sensitive. How not to submit to the charm of the Russian language and Russian music? All this has, of course, nothing to do with Communism but it influenced the impressionable guest. It also influenced not a few Russians.

The anticlimax in our day would not have been so dramatic if expectations had not been so high in Russia and abroad. In 1937 the Soviet Union celebrated the twentieth anniversary of the revolution. Sidney Webb called it on this occasion the greatest act of emancipation that humanity had seen. Romain Rolland hailed those "building the new world of which we have been dreaming, you who are free and equal." Heinrich Mann named the revolution "the embodiment of a country which has attained to extraordinary heights within the shortest period of time . . . a fairytale to the stranger." The "Red Dean" of Canterbury, Hewlett Johnson, called it "majestic" and "stupendous" – the new democracy was a marvel, and culture had made immense progress.[3] The Webbs, in their famous *Soviet Communism: A New Civilization*, maintained that it was the morality of Soviet Communism that marked it off from all other civilizations.

E. H. Carr, who usually wrote in more measured terms, announced in 1946 that the world stood on the threshold of a renewal of an East–West movement of men and ideas, of which the penetration of the Western world by ideas from the Soviet Union was the most conspicuous feature – *ex oriente lux*. Even the critics of the Soviet Union professed to love and admire it.[4] It is easy to fill whole libraries with quotations of this kind and they reflected no doubt genuine feelings of admiration and hope. One could not easily think of any other movement in modern history to which such high expectations were attached. Fascism at its most exalted invoked the rebirth of the nation; Communist youth were singing about the "building of a new world."[5]

Some Russians have come to believe that the Communist order was saved from earlier ruin first by the "Great Fatherland War" and later on by the discovery of new oil fields and the massive exports of oil. World War II was a supreme test for the regime, but it also permitted Stalin to mobilize patriotic energies and sentiments against a ruthless invader, out to destroy not just the Communist order but the Russian state and reduce the Russian people to slavery.

Communism survived owing to the state-of-siege and emergency mentality, but in the absence of a real enemy this could not have been maintained forever. Thus Stalin and Hitler may well have prolonged the allotted life span of the Soviet regime. At the same time, however, as the result of successive waves of terror, the overcentralization of the economy and administration, and the destruction of all initiative from below, Stalin made basic change in the house he had built extremely difficult, probably impossible. Some argue to this day that Stalin was not Lenin's legitimate heir, but the creator of a pathological and grotesque caricature of Leninism. While Stalinism was certainly not foreordained, it is difficult to imagine any regime after Lenin's death that would not have been a harsh dictatorship. The possibility of gradual democratization, a "political NEP," could have existed only if the Bolsheviks had had the active support of the majority of the population, which they clearly did not have. In a Soviet regime headed by Trotsky or Bukharin, fewer old Bolsheviks would have been killed and the collectivization of agriculture would not have proceeded so senselessly and cruelly. But the country would still not have moved toward greater political and economic freedom. The alternatives were radicalization or collapse.

World War II ended with a great triumph and the extension of Russia's sphere of influence. In the late 1950s and the early 1960s, the Soviet Union was at the height of its power. The bulk of the population lived poorly, but the country had the most advanced missiles, it produced many millions of tons of steel and oil, and its educational system compared not unfavorably with that of the Western world. The general mood was certainly not one of great enthusiasm, but there was also no black despair. Soviet citizens were but dimly aware of living conditions outside their country. All they could see was that their own conditions were gradually improving over the years.

But the regime had become overextended, and it had planted the seeds for recurring revolts in Eastern Europe and the collapse of the union. A more aggressive foreign policy after 1945 would have resulted in a third world war—with nuclear destruction—and was not a rational course of action.

Could the Soviet leadership have given greater freedom to its East European clients, replacing satellization by Finlandization? This strategy, in theory, might have worked, though it would have involved great risks. It would have meant an end to the Cold War, which in turn would have made it more difficult to run the country. For détente, real and lasting, would have involved giving up the Brezhnev doctrine and also a certain amount of liberalization inside the Soviet Union. It is by no means certain that this would have been compatible with the maintenance of dictatorial rule. Would a controlled, gradual transition from a war economy to a market economy (however imperfect) have been possible in the 1960s or 1970s? Would reforms imposed from above aiming at restructuring relations between the various republics have been feasible twenty or thirty years before the collapse?

The prospects were not good. To begin with, there was no real awareness that economic reform and a radical transformation of the federation were imperative. Furthermore, there was no political force other than the Communist party that could have carried out such a policy, and within the top echelons of the party (as well as further down) there was no desire to engage in such a risky enterprise.[6] The watchword of the 1970s was caution, not bold initiative. There was no realization in Russia in 1980 (as there was in China) that, in the words of Hu Yaobang, "in most Socialist countries the Communist parties have failed to establish a successful system."

Had this book been written twenty years ago, a lengthy digression on the Stalin era would have been called for. The question of Stalin—for or against—was still widely debated at the time. Today it is no longer a problem for historians. The case for Stalinism was, very briefly, that with all the enormous cost involved, the Soviet Union was modernized and became a superpower under his leadership, and that, in any case, there was no real alternative. Today this argument seems quite baseless except, of course, if one happens to believe (as the Russian neo-Communists do) that Stalinist policies were correct, and that the breakdown was not his responsibility but the fault of his revisionist successors.

There was a Western school of social historians in the 1970s and 1980s, who argued that their colleagues had misjudged Stalin because they were interested predominantly in developments at the top of the system. Had they judged Stalinism in the general historical context, they would not have passed moralist judgment or "engaged in the glib luxury of allotting praise and blame."[7] But, however intensively one studies Stalinism in its historical context, the price the people of the Soviet Union had to pay does not become any smaller, nor the achievements of the regime more significant. In brief, Stalinism was not only an abomination, it was also a failure in terms of what it set out to achieve – and by any other standard as well. While historians are, in principle, entitled to question any judgment and to reopen any subject, a prolongation of this specific debate seems a waste of time.

The same refers to the discussion in the West about totalitarianism. If the Soviet regime and its political structures had been merely authoritarian in the manner of, for instance, Franco's Spain or Kemalist Turkey, the transition toward a democratic order would have been much easier. It was precisely the absence of a civil society and of all political, social, and economic initiatives except those sponsored and controlled from above that is making such a transition in Russia (and also most other successor states) so difficult. The simple truth that there was no "straight and short road" from Communist totalitarianism to a civil society and that democracy and freedom could be safeguarded only on the basis of new economic, social, and political structures was universally accepted in Russia even by the former exponents of Marxism-Leninism.[8] In the West, such obvious propositions encountered resistance among those who maintained that totalitarianism, if it had ever existed, had disappeared a long time ago.

The failure of experts to recognize the decomposition of the Communist regime and to consider the possibility of its fall has been noted. Such failure was not, of course, total. The fact that the Soviet Union had become a gerontocracy had not escaped the attention of outside observers. It was quite obvious that the regime had run out of dynamism and new ideas. The worsening ecological and demographic situation was not ignored; nor was the slowing of the growth rates[9], but it was a far cry from noting these dangerous trends to predicting the impending downfall of the regime. On the contrary, precisely because the situation had deteriorated, there was hope among mainstream Soviet experts in the West that a new generation of Soviet leaders would be compelled to lead their country to economic, social, and eventually also political reform.

If there was a political science failure, was it not programmed from the very beginning? In other words, had not the practitioners of Sovietology engaged in an enterprise that was well beyond the frontiers of their discipline–and should they have not known this? The answer to these questions is in the affirmative. In one of the early, classic comments on the art of predicting Soviet behavior, Daniel Bell had noted that sociological analysis could not, on the whole, predict political decisions that were based largely on variables such as accident.[10]

Not every observer of the Soviet scene had predicted a brilliant future for the regime. That Communism was doomed was announced in some quarters from the day after the revolution. For years after 1917, many organs of the foreign press, and above all the émigré papers, announced that the downfall of the regime was imminent: Lenin and Trotsky had already packed their luggage and ordered the train that was to take them abroad. Leading economists like Ludwig von Mises and Boris Brutzkus explained why a socialist planned economy could not possibly work. The Smena Vekh group among the émigrés admonishing its members to return to the homeland predicted that Soviet internationalism would not last and would give way to a revival of Russian nationalism.

Not all the criticism and negative predictions in the 1920s and early 1930s came from the right and the "class enemy." Shortly after the revolution, Bertrand Russell and Rosa Luxemburg, supporters of revolution second to none, wrote with deep regret that it was impossible that the Bolsheviks would succeed in building the kind of society they professed to believe in. Kautsky and the Mensheviks predicted even more emphatically that the whole experiment would end in disaster.

During the 1930s and 1940s, such predictions about the ultimate fall of the Soviet regime became less popular. But they never disappeared altogether, even not during World War II when Stalinism was riding the crest of the wave.[11] When many Western observers noted the re-emergence under Stalin of Russia as a world power, G. P. Fedotov, in his article "The Fall of Soviet Power," astutely noted that revolutionary enthusiasm in the Communist party was already a spent force.[12]

Such predictions, while essentially correct, were premature because it still took decades for these trends to unfold. Nor were the writings of Mises and Brutzkus on the theoretical impossibility of socialism of much help.

Andrei Amalrik's essay asking whether the Soviet Union would survive the year 1984 was the most famous of its genre but by no means the only one. Various essays published in samizdat in the early 1970s were on similar lines, some quite specifically predicting the end of the Soviet empire.[13] Predictions ranged from the pessimistic views of veteran foreign correspondents who had lived in the Soviet Union (such as Eugene Lyons, W. H. Chamberlin, and Isaac Don Levine), to that of Boris Souvarine and Bertram Wolfe to less prominent writers such as the Frenchman Michel Garder.[14]

The journalists did not, on the whole, have the theoretical sophistication of a Carr or a Deutscher, and their grounding in political science was sketchy at best. Nevertheless, they diagnosed the situation in the Soviet Union far more correctly, whether because they relied more on personal experience and common sense, or because their disdain for Communism sharpened their political instincts.

Various articles that appeared in professional journals such as *Problems of Communism* and *Survey* dealt with the decay and the possible downfall of the Soviet regime. Bernard Levin drew attention in 1992 to his prophetic article originally published in the *Times* of London in September 1977, in which an uncannily accurate prediction of the appearance of new faces in the Politburo was made, resulting in radical but peaceful political change.[15]

Western statesmen from Adenauer to Reagan predicted the downfall of the Soviet empire. Senator Daniel Patrick Moynihan in a series of articles and interviews from 1979 onward discussed the possibility, indeed likelihood, of the breakup of the Soviet empire, and there were dozens of similar statements, now forgotten, made all over the Western world.[16] Klaus Mehnert referred to the advanced ideological exhaustion of the Soviet Union, and others observed that the country was geopolitically overextended. Various experts on Central Asia referred to demographic trends as a likely cause for the breakdown of the Soviet empire. It has been noted that quite often these prophecies came from outside the guild of professional Sovietologists.

But sometimes writers reached the right conclusions on the basis of doubtful or even false premises. An example is Walter Lippmann's prediction that the Russias had lost the Cold War, before the Cold War had even begun. I wrote in 1971:

> The Soviet Union will not survive 1984: It fails to make further progress in Western Europe. It suffers further setbacks in the Middle East as President Sadat expels 20,000 Russian experts . . . The performance of the Soviet economy deteriorates, Japanese steel production overtakes Soviet output in 1976. Irredentist movements sprout among the non-Russian peoples; high KGB officials read Marcuse and Laing. An open crisis breaks out in Moscow following years of declining self-confidence among the top leadership . . . The liberal faction in Moscow calls for the convocation of a Constituent Assembly . . . "Internal Polycentrism" prevails in the Soviet Union and, preoccupied with their many internal problems, the new leaders decide to devote their energies mainly to consolidating their position at home.[17]

To put these prophetic words into proper perspective, it ought to be added that this was conceived by the author merely as one of six scenarios, and by no means the most likely one. Upon closer inspection it appears that many of the predictions made before 1980 about the coming fall of the Soviet regime were considered by those who uttered them as a somewhat remote possibility rather than a probability–a comforting thought in an otherwise depressing world situation, a reminder that, after all, the unexpected sometimes does happen.

However, for some (such as Amalrik) the idea was much more than a passing thought. Nor was everyone equally wrong. Up to about 1980, the strength of the Soviet regime was widely overrated by critics of the Soviet regime and revisionists alike. But the latter claimed in addition, following Hegel, that everything that was real was also (more or less) reasonable, that the Soviet regime was on the whole successful in its enterprises, and had the support of the majority of the population.[18] Its remaining shortcomings could and would be improved by way of reform.

When Germany collapsed in 1945, there was deep soul-searching among German historians and, of course, well beyond the academic profession, about confronting the ruins of German history, about a national catastrophe, about the immeasurable depth of the debacle, of an *Abschied von der bisherigen Geschichte* – "farewell to previous history." The Nestor of German historians, Friedrich Meinecke, aged eighty-four, wrote a book entitled *The German Catastrophe.*" There was much talk about "zero" (*Die Stunde Null*), a radical break with the past and the need for a new orientation.

There has been no Meinecke in Russia, and one could think of a variety of explanations: his formative years had been in an earlier period, whereas the Soviet historians were all products of the Soviet era. For them, it was infinitely more difficult to find new (or old) theoretical foundations. Among the Russian right, the consensus was that what had gone wrong had been mainly the fault of foreigners, whereas the old Communists argued that things had worked reasonably well prior to *glasnost* and *perestroika*, and that but for the betrayal of individual leaders, the regime would have gone from strength to strength. Among younger and more independent thinkers, there was, of course, a great deal of soul-searching. But prior to 1990 even the more radical among them did not go as far as Meinecke did.

To what extent was ideological bias involved? The question has been discussed earlier on: Western experts who had claimed for many years that the Soviet GNP was more than half that of the American[19] were not necessarily more well disposed to the Soviet regime. They simply registered what seemed to them indisputable facts and they happened to be wrong.[20]

II

For those in the West who had argued over the years that the Soviet Union was making slow but steady progress toward greater freedom and prosperity, the fall of the empire was a dramatic refutation of their theories. The same goes for such well-known interpreters of the Soviet scene as the émigré Alexander Zinoviev, who had put his reputation on what he defined as "scientific predictions" that Soviet society could not be destroyed in a thousand years because it conformed with the "laws" of history and nature.[21]

The full depth of these disastrous misjudgments seems not to have been recognized yet by either Zinoviev or the cohort of Western social historians. Why write on the long continuation of Soviet history as if there has been no earthquake and the Soviet Union had not disappeared? They are still reluctant to pass moral judgment on Stalin and Stalinism they still base their views on scrutinizing the period from below, as if the view from below was more edifying than from above. At most, they will concede that Soviet realities were "exceedingly complex" and that our knowledge of them is very imperfect. This approach provides as good an excuse as any not to pass judgment, which they believe is not the task of the (social) historian, whose position should be above the fruitless quarrels between Stalinists and anti-Stalinists.[22]

To the critics of the Soviet system, the collapse also came as a surprise, albeit a welcome one. But it meant that the "anti-Communist front"[23] was bound to fall apart with the disappearance of the threat that had served as a unifying factor. Some believed that a gradual transformation would have been in the best interest of the peoples of the Soviet Union and of all mankind; others thought that any weakening of the Russian juggernaut was to be welcomed. Such tactical differences quite apart, there appeared basic differences of opinion: some had opposed Communism and the Soviet regime on the basis of a conservative ideology.[24] Socialism was utopian; the capitalist order had shown its superiority. Since the collapse of Soviet Communism coincided with a crisis of socialism in other countries (such as France and Scandinavia) and a (partial) turn to the market in hitherto collectivist societies (including China and India), they believed that the "end of socialism" had come. Furthermore, vociferous sections of the American left turned toward "political correctness" and various other irrational, faddish, trends and this made it even less likely that a revival of serious left-wing thought would occur soon.

Nevertheless, despite the eclipse of socialism in the 1990s, it was clearly premature to write off a body of ideas and political thinking that had existed in one form or another since time immemorial and that would not simply evaporate. Capitalism had certainly outproduced socialism, but with its social and cultural contradictions, capitalism was also in a state of crisis only too obvious to many denizens of the first world.[25]

Furthermore, in the very places where Communism had been overthrown, a backlash occurred within a very short time. Capitalism had never been popular in Russia and in most other East European countries. According to public-opinion polls, some 59 percent of Russians believed in 1991 that socialism in one form or another would continue to play a positive role in the future development of Russia, whereas only 25 percent favored a total rejection of socialism.[26] During 1992 and 1993, these views became even more emphatic. Support for capitalism in the Baltic countries was between 14 and 30 percent in 1990. As an Estonian private farmer put it: "The word 'businessman' has always had a bad sound especially among ordinary people."[27]

The future of a market economy in Russia and Eastern Europe need not concern us in this context. Some of these countries will probably fare better than others, but even those who make progress will do so slowly and following much hardship. If even the integration of East Germany proved to be infinitely more difficult than originally envisaged, how much more painful will economic and social change be elsewhere. The survival—and the return—of many former Communists in leading positions in government and the economy is a further sign that it is premature to write off socialism even in its most inefficient and discredited form.

All this is bound to have a direct impact on the evaluation of the experience of Soviet Communism by future historians. If the reforms fail, with an accompanying pauperization of large sections of society and the enrichment of a few; if central power gets progressively weaker, with a breakdown of law and order or civil-war like conditions; and if aggressive nationalism should run wild, the Soviet period in Russian history will appear in a more rosy light than it deserves. The right and the Communists will argue (as they have done all along) that democracy, free institutions, and a market economy are unsuitable in Russian conditions.

But if this should come to pass, it will still be a far cry from the sweeping claims of Communist propaganda (and of the arguments of Western revisionists) prior to 1987. Like Humpty Dumpty, the Soviet system had a great fall, and no one can put it together again. But they can still adduce various mitigating circumstances. If Communism had prevailed in a less backward country, if the NEP had been continued, if Lenin had been succeeded by Bukharin rather than Stalin, if Stalin's successors had engaged in a reform policy twenty years earlier, all might have been well. There is no limit to this search for might-have-beens. With Ferdinand Braudel it will be claimed that events are the ephemera of history. But if only long-term trends matter, if neither Lenin nor Stalin, neither Gorbachev nor Yeltsin are of great importance, neither was the October Revolution necessary nor was the attempt to build a Communist society.

Writing about the Soviet period in Russian history at a time of unprecedented ferment and instability, when almost anything seems possible, from total disintegration to the reassumption of an imperial mission, speculation about the future seems futile. Some conclusions about the heritage left by the Soviet experience seem inescapable, however. The heritage was such that it almost doomed a new beginning. The Soviet political system had failed, but it had been eradicated only in part. In this respect, there is a similarity to Germany after World War I. There had been defeat, but not total defeat, and as the new regime failed to register quick successes (and failed to provide a new vision), the antidemocratic party could claim that but for the internal enemy that had stabbed the country in the back, Germany would not have been defeated in the first place. As in Germany, the old elite remained, broadly speaking, in place in Russia and the other successor states, certainly in the bureaucracy and in the economy. As in Germany, the center was too weak and there was a traditional longing for strong leadership, and the government was therefore ignored and treated with contempt.

In some respects, the state of affairs was considerably worse in Russia than in Germany. If there was resentment in Germany as the result of the loss of some minor provinces and a few colonies following the Versailles Treaty, Russia's losses were infinitely greater. According to the pollsters, the loss of empire was regretted by 70 percent of Russians within a year after the collapse. Many millions of Russians resided outside Russia and felt insecure. Russia had lost its old identity, but had not found a new one.[28] The mentality deeply ingrained during the Soviet period could not easily and quickly be eradicated. There was exaggerated reliance on the state and excessive expectations as to what the government could do. Political, social, and economic initiatives had been systematically suppressed for many years, and there was no sudden revival—not even on the local level as in China. The preconditions for democratic reform were far from auspicious, and the new leadership in 1988 to 1993 showed signs of confusion.

Whither Russia? Perhaps it will, after all, muddle through, and the experiment in democracy will not end in failure. If it fails, will it be the fault of an indecisive leadership lacking vision and a clear policy or the lack of support from below for genuine reform? In the absence of genuine popular support, could even leaders of genius have succeeded?

III

In his autobiography, Edward Gibbon recalls how one day in October 1764 as he was musing amid the ruins of the Capitol, while the barefoot friars were singing vespers in the temple of Jupiter, the idea of writing the decline and fall of Rome first started to his mind. There was a grandeur to the Capitoline Hill and the Forum Romanum even after it had been used as a quarry for centuries, which the New Arbat with its money changers, street musicians, jugglers, picture vendors, and sectarian preachers cannot provide to a latter day Gibbon pondering the causes of the decline and fall of the Soviet empire. In any case, 1300 years have not yet passed as in Gibbon's case. The Soviet empire, unlike the Roman and most others, came into being as the manifestation of an idea, which was that there existed a shortcut to the perfection of political institutions and a just society that people, incapable of understanding their own best interest, had to be forced to accept. This was Bolshevism, about which Bertrand Russell wrote in 1920 that he was compelled to reject it for two reasons: "First, because the price mankind must pay to achieve Communism by Bolshevik methods was too terrible; and secondly because even after paying the price, the result would not be what the Bolsheviks profess to desire." Thus the revolution was not "betrayed" some time in the 1920s or 1930s, but the despotism was inherent in the system established in November 1917. Soon after his arrival at the Finland station, Lenin called Russia the freest country in the world; not many years later, it had become the least free. It was a monumental undertaking, and it ended in the destruction of the state and the discrediting of the ideals in the name of which the revolutionaries had been fighting. Were the Bolsheviks unlucky? On the contrary, in retrospect their triumphs rested to a considerable extent on a number of fortunate accidents—such as Lenin's strategy in 1917, the disunity of their enemies in the civil war, the halfhearted intervention of the allies in 1918 to 1920, and the racialist policy of the Nazi invaders.

The search for excuses for the historical failure of Bolshevism is a thankless assignment. Perhaps the future will be kinder to its historical role in view of the noble vision and unselfish intentions of its founders. But this would prove nothing, for posterity is as likely to be wrong as past and present observers. While there is no perfect way to judge a political system, the New Testament criterion that "by their fruits ye shall know them" remains as good a yardstick as any.

Notes

Preface

1. The term "Sovietology" is often used indiscriminately, referring to all those engaged in Russian and even Slavic studies, including nineteenth-century history, literature, and music. A hard-and-fast definition would be imprecise and pedantic, for historians specializing in pre-1917 Russia have also commented on contemporary affairs. In the present context, Sovietology applies not to Russian studies in general but to a more narrow discipline—the writings of political scientists, economists, political sociologists, and historians focusing on the current scene, the recent past, and speculation on the future. In the 1950s and 1960s, when many of the basic works on the Soviet Union were written, the term "Sovietology" was hardly ever used.

2. Mirabeau, "Au major Mauvillon." Since time immemorial, there have been ancestral voices prophesying war. Usually, it is more difficult to predict internal revolution than external war.

3. Francois Furet, interview in *Magazine Littéraire* 258 (1988): 18; O. Duhamel, "La Revolution française est terminée," *Pouvoirs* 50 (1989): 121.

4. "We idealized freedom," Yevgeni Evtushenko said in an interview in 1993, "because we did not know what it means. It appeared to us that freedom had only one face, and that it was beautiful. But then it appeared that freedom has a thousand faces and some of them are repulsive" (*Trud*, 10 July 1993).

5. Klaus Mann, in *Unsere Zeit*, July 1934.

6. Vadim Kozhinov, "Vzglyad v proshloe," *Zavtra*, 4 February 1994.

7. Walter Laqueur, *The Fate of the Revolution: Interpretations of Soviet History from 1917 to the Present*, rev. ed. (New York, 1987).

Chapter 1

1. I chose East Germany for yet another reason: the historical evidence is far more amply available for East Germany than it is for any other Communist country.

2. Raymond Aron, *Le Grand Schisme* (Paris, 1948); Aron, *L'Opium des intellectuels* (Paris, 1955); Jean François Revel, *The Totalitarian Temptation* (New York, 1977).

3. Quoted in Julian Steinberg, ed., *Verdict of Three Decades* (New York, 1950), 20.

4. On the development of Lenin's view on the vanguard party, see Leonard Schapiro, *The Communist Party of the Soviet Union* (New York, 1960), chap. 2.

5. Richard Pipes, *Russia Under the Bolshevik Regime* (New York, 1994). But it does not follow that, as Pipes writes, the victory of the Red Army was a "foregone conclusion" (123).

6. These were some of the most frequent symbols of revolutionary romanticism. Perekop was the last important battle of the civil war; Chapayev, the legendary partisan commander, was the hero of a Soviet film shown to this day. *How the Steel Was Forged* (Moscow, 1935, 1973) was a best-selling novel by Nikolai Ostrovsky about the fate of an exemplary young Communist, Pavel Korchagin, in the civil war and after. *How the Steel Was Forged* was reprinted twenty times in the DDR after 1945, but it did not have remotely the same political effect – and even less in the other satellite nations. *Subbotniki* were the volunteers who devoted their rest day to work for the public good.

7. Edward Bagritsky (slightly older than the rest), Mikhail Svetlov, Pavel Kogan, Alexander Zharov, Iosif Utkin, and Aleksander Bezymensky. Mayakovsky was their idol, but the feeling was not always reciprocated. He compared their work to coffee made of carrots.

8. Klaus Mehnert, *Youth in Soviet Russia* (New York, 1933). The author was born in Moscow and was bilingual; he became a leading Sovietologist.

9. Ibid., 82.

10. Ibid., 237. Mehnert was one of the most astute observers of things Russian. He liked this generation and shared its enthusiasm and romanticism. I remember him telling me, after a visit to China at the time of the Cultural Revolution, that a new man was created under Mao. He had seen the future, and it worked. But Mehnert knew Russia much better than China, where he had spent World War II.

11. Ostrovsky, *How the Steel Was Forged*, 421.

12. A translation cannot, of course, convey even remotely the élan of these songs and poems, many of which are still sung today. What became of their authors? Some were fortunate enough to die a natural death before Stalin disciplined them. Some were shot as Nazi or Japanese spies in the 1930s, and some were killed fighting in the war. Those who survived became Stalinist hacks or committed suicide. The fate of the author of the "March of the Enthusiasts," Anatole D'Aktil, is not mentioned in contemporary reference works.

13. Listening to foreign broadcasts became a crime only during the war.

14. Johann Georgi, in *Freideutscher Rundbrief* 3 (1948), quoted in Walter Laqueur, *Young Germany* (New York, 1962) 202.

15. Very few young former Nazis and fascists went on record in later years trying to explain to themselves and to others their infatuation with these movements. Among those who did, there have been more women than men. Some of the essential literature is listed in Michael Rohrwasser, *Der Stalinismus und die Renegaten* (Stuttgart, 1991), 283, n. 54.

16. The author of these songs was Vasili Lebedev-Kumach; the melody was composed by Isak Dunayevsky. The other famous provider of song texts of this period was Solovyov-Sedoi. The fashion lasted for a few years. By 1938, popular music began to devote its attention to the threat of war and patriotic themes.

17. Fedotov's remarkable article, "Tyazhba o Rossii," appeared in the Paris periodical *Sovremennie Zapisky* 62 (1936). It was reprinted in G. P. Fedotov, *Tyazhba o Rossii* (Paris, 1982), 289.

18. Dziga Vertov (1896–1954) was the great master of the early Soviet propaganda film. *Enthusiasm* was one of the first Soviet talkies.

19. The recurrent claims that Stalin planned an offensive war against Germany later in 1941, or in 1942 at the latest, remain unconvincing.

20. This was the subject of a polemic between two well-known émigrés during the war: Mark Vishniak's "Pravda Antibolshevizma" (*Novy Zhurnal*) and Pavel Milyukov's "Pravda o Kommunizme." Vishniak argued that the Russian soldiers were courageously fighting despite Communist rule; Milyukov took the opposite view. Both were writing from afar; in retrospect, Vishniak was closer to the truth.

21. In the late 1960s and early 1970s. See Chapter 3.

22. This was one of the most scandalous apologies for the Moscow trials and, generally, a beatification of Stalin that cannot be justified even in view of the fact that Stalin was America's ally at the time. The scandal has been described in detail in C. R. Koppes and G. D. Black, *Hollywood Goes to War* (New York, 1987), 98–109. The movie got three and a half stars out of four in the current edition of Leonard Maltin's *TV, Movies and Video Guide* (New York, 1993), which calls it "fascinating propaganda . . . well done," and the British *Time Out Film Guide* (London, 1989) calls it "interesting either as an expressive object or as pure movie . . . quite beautifully put together by Curtiz."

23. Vladimir Lvov, "Ne sotvori sebe kumira," *Literaturnoye Obozrenie* 3 (1992): 49–57.

24. Ibid., 57.

25. Even though some writers did have ambitions to be taken seriously as moral and political philosophers.

26. This is the subtitle of David Caute's well-known study, *The Fellow Travellers* (New Haven, Conn., 1988).

27. This thesis is eloquently stated in the most famous such tract: Lion Feuchtwanger, *Moscow 1937* (New York, 1937). For the prehistory and fate of this book, see Walter Laqueur, "Central European Writers . . ." *Partisan Review*, Fall 1992.

28. Thus Lvov wrote, "Even such a wise and sober thinker Herbert Marcuse wrote in 1968 . . ." ("Ne sotvori sebe kumira," 57). But on the subject of Communism and Russia, Marcuse was neither wise nor sober nor competent to express an opinion commanding respect.

29. Except for one official paper from each republic. These publications carried little information not found in *Pravda*.

30. Quoted in Rohrwasser, *Der Stalinismus und die Renegaten*, 345.

31. The very concept of the "fifth column" played a central role in the mentality of fellow travelers. Only after the war did it appear that the fifth column had been a figment of their imaginations, a misguided attempt to explain the reasons for Hitler's successes in the blitzkrieg. And Franco, who allegedly coined the term, did not do so.

32. "The differences between the (party) elite and the dissidents were not so much ideological as psychological and moral" (Dmitri Furman, "Nasha strannaya revoliutsiya," *Svobodnaya Mysl* 1 [1993]: 14).

33. The reform period (1987–1991) ought to be investigated in detail. Some interesting beginnings have been made in this direction, but it is too early for

definitive studies on the subject. The fullest available so far is John B. Dunlop, *The Rise of Russia and the Fall of the Soviet Empire* (Princeton, 1993). Among the personal recollections published so far, the most interesting are those written by Anatoli Tschernajew, *Die letzten Jahre einer Weltmacht. Der Kreml von innen* (Stuttgart, 1993).

Chapter 2

1. This figure is suspect. While considerable progress was made in the years before World War I to illiteracy in Russia, the Brockhaus-Efron encyclopedia notes that of every 1,000 new recruits in 1913, 617 could not read or write, compared with 6 in Switzerland and 33 in France.

2. Edmund Burke, *Reflections on the Revolution in France* (London, 1790).

3. The French author referred to is Edmond Terry, *La Russie en 1914* (Paris, 1914), who was rediscovered by the Russian right under *glasnost* and is frequently quoted.

4. H. Rogger, *Russia in the Age of Modernization and Revolution 1881–1917* (London 1983), chap. 6.

5. S. S. Oldenburg, *Tsarstvovanie Imperatora Nikolai II* (Moscow, 1991). A second small edition appeared in Munich in 1949. Since the original publication, the book has been reissued several times and apparently circulated in the right-wing *samizdat* (clandestine publications) in the 1970s and 1980s. It appeared in Moscow in 1991.

6. For an assessment of Oldenburg's view, see Jane Burbank, *Intelligentsia and Revolution* (New York, 1986), 178–184. Another, though much less weighty and more tendentious, source of information is a booklet by Boris Brasol, *Tsarstvovanie Imperatora Nikolaya II v tsifrakh i faktakh* (New York, n.d.).

7. Alexander Gerschenkron, "Problems and Patterns of Russian Economic Development," in *The Transformation of Russian Society*, ed. C. E. Black (Cambridge, Mass., 1960). "Germanization" refers to the paramount role played by the state in the industrialization process.

8. Some writers maintained that only an effective dictatorship, such as Lenin's or Stalin's, was capable of pushing through Russia's industrialization. Theodore von Laue, *Why Lenin, Why Stalin? A Reappraisal of the Russian Revolution, 1900–1930*, 2nd ed. (New York, 1971), presents an extreme form of this thesis, but with slight modification it was accepted by other historians.

9. Abraham Ascher, *The Revolution of 1905*, vol. 1: *Russia in Disarray* (Stanford, Calif., 1988), 11. For the volcano analogy, see Hans Rogger, "Russia in 1914," *Journal of Contemporary History* 4 (1966): 95–96.

10. S. S. Oldenburg, *Gosudar imperator Nikolai II* (Berlin, 1922).

11. It appears perhaps most clearly in Aleksander Blok's *Stikhia i Kultura* (1908). It pervades much of the writing of Andrei Belyi, Dmitri Merezhkovsky, Zinaida Gippius, and their contemporaries.

12. In Russia, the feeling of doom was far more pronounced in literature than in painting and music. But then there was hardly an expressionist trend in Russian art (except for the works of Chagall and a bit of Larionova), and literature had always been more important in Russian cultural life than the visual arts.

13. Georg Brandes, *Impressions of Russia* (London, 1889), 108.

14. An excellent survey of German attitudes toward Russia is the massive study edited by M. Keller, *Russen und Russland aus deutscher Sicht* (Munich, 1991).

15. Rafael Abramovich, *The Soviet Revolution, 1917–1939* (New York, 1962).

16. Dietrich Geyer, *The Russian Revolution* (Leamington Spa, 1987), 22.

17. E. J. Dillon, *The Eclipse of Russia* (London, 1918), 181.

18. J. P. Nettl, *The Soviet Achievement* (London, 1967), was a typical example for this trend, as were the books of E. H. Carr and Isaac Deutscher.

19. Among those who argued that a more democratic regime in Russia was not a priori ruled out were, in addition to Gerschenkron, Jakob Walkin, *The Rise of Democracy in Pre-Revolutionary Russia* (London, 1963), and Arthur Mendel, "Peasant and Worker on the Eve of the First World War," *Slavonic Review* 24 (1965). The opposite stand was taken by Leopold Haimson, Roberta Manning, Theodore von Laue, and others.

20. H. Norman, *All the Russias* (London, 1902).

21. Four hundred more books on the October Revolution were published between 1976 and 1985.

22. See, for instance, the controversy about the role of Martov, between A. Kostikov, in *Ogonek* 10 (1990), and I. A. Aluf, in *Voprosy Istorii KPSS*, December, 1990.

23. Pavel Volobuyev, in *Voprosy Istorii* 6 (1987).

24. For early Western comments, see various articles in *Radical Historians' Newsletter*, *Radical History Review* (1987–1989), and *Soviet Studies in History* (1988 and 1989), and by Stephen Wheatcroft, in *Australian Slavonic and East European Studies*. *Kommunist* became *Svobodnaya Mysl*; *Voprosy Istorii KPSS* became *Kentavr*; *Sovetskie Arkhivy* became *Otechestvennie Arkhivy*; and *Agitator* became *Dialog*.

25. See for instance, A. Aryutiunov, *Fenomen Vladimira Ulyanova* (Moscow, 1992).

26. Virtually every issue of *Nash Sovremennik* and *Molodaya Gvardia* during 1988 through 1991 devoted at least one article, usually more, to "research" on these lines.

27. Viktor Anpilov, in *Den*, 8 November 1992.

28. Papers by Pavel Volobuyev, V. D. Dmitrenko, V. P. Budlakov, and others, at Russian Academy of Science conference on the October Revolution, 26 November 1992; *Otechestvennaya Istoriya* 4 (1993).

29. This is the Burdzhalov thesis (*Vtoraya russkaya revoliutsiya* [Moscow, 1967], 120–21).

30. As D. Beyrau has shown, the Russian economy was probably in less critical shape than the German in 1916 and 1917, and the fall of the old regime has to be seen mainly in the light of the loss of political legitimacy (*Voprosy Istorii* 1 [1992]). See also M. Gorinov, in *Svobodnaya Mysl* 3 (1993): 104.

31. For this ill-fated decision and its execution, see Louise F. Heena, *Russian Democracy's Fatal Blunder: The Summer Offensive of 1917* (New York, 1987).

32. Abramovich, *Soviet Revolution*, 70; Victor Chernov, *The Great Russian Revolution* (New Haven, Conn., 1936), 193.

33. Jonathan Frankel et al., ed., *Revolution in Russia* (Cambridge, 1992), 11.

34. This movement had been described, critically in Walter Laqueur, *The Fate of the Revolution*, 2d ed. (New York, 1987), chap. 9, and (sympathetically) in Stephen F. Cohen, *Rethinking the Soviet Experience* (New York, 1985), chaps. 1, 2.

35. E. H. Carr was the only writer to whom a whole chapter was devoted in Laqueur, *Fate of the Revolution*. His history of the Soviet Union, now dismissed as almost useless by critics, was for many years considered a classic, a crowning achievement.

36. Was revisionism predominantly a generational phenomenon? This question remains to be investigated in greater detail. The revisionists of the 1970s and 1980s certainly considered themselves a generational cohort in deliberate opposition to their predecessors. There were a few exceptions; Carr and Moshe Lewin were held in high esteen by these younger Sovietologists. But by and large, those in the older generation were considered hopeless cold warriors, lacking sound theoretical grounding. The new generational cohort was preoccupied with one another's writings, and it was only natural that appointments were made on the basis of political and methodological affinity. "Cold warriors" were thought to be an anachronism and politically incorrect–there was no common language with them.

37. Edward Acton, *Rethinking the Russian Revolution* (London, 1990), 208.

38. David Mandel, *The Petrograd Workers and the Seizure of Power* (New York, 1984), 1; S. A. Smith, *Red Petrograd: Revolution in the Factories 1917-1918* (Cambridge, Mass., 1986). For other examples, see the writings of Sheila Fitzpatrick, Alexander Rabinowitch, William Rosenberg, Robert Service, and Diane Koenker. For a summary, see Acton, *Rethinking the Russian Revolution*.

39. A. Rabinowitch, *Voprosy Istorii* 2 (1985).

40. See Richard Pipes, "1917 and the Revisionists," *National Interest*, Spring 1993, 76.

41. John Keep, *The Russian Revolution* (London, 1976).

42. Robert B. McKean, *St. Petersburg Between the Revolutions* (New Haven, Conn., 1990). While the working class had been glorified in the publications of the revisionists, post-revisionist findings were less complimentary. See, for instance, Charters Wynn, *Workers, Strikes and Pogroms* (Princeton, 1992), and Wolf Zöller, "Der Bund des russischen Volkes" (M.A. thesis, University of Frankfurt, 1993.)

43. Robert Service, in Frankel et al., *Revolution in Russia*, 304.

44. As Pipes noted, it was one thing for social historians dealing with centuries of feudalism to downplay politics, and another to ignore politics when the subject was a single year and the issue at stake was gaining control of the government ("1917 and the Revisionists").

45. For a strong advocacy of "treating the Russian experience as that of a developing country," see Geyer, *Russian Revolution*, 12. For a critique of the modernization thesis, see the Introduction to Martin Malia, *The Soviet Tragedy* (New York, 1994).

46. Cohen, *Rethinking the Soviet Experience*, 5.

47. Acton, *Rethinking the Russian Revolution*, 209. The fullest available account of the "revisionist revolution," this work is highly sympathetic in approach, even though the author subscribes to the views of a subgroup, the libertarian (i.e., anarchist) approach. (There is no significant libertarian historiography of 1917, and the years after, other than contemporary writings by A. Berkman and Emma Goldman.)

48. I. I. Kanishsheva, in *Sovremennaya burzhuaznaya Istoriografia Sovetskovo Obshestva*, ed. I. M. Volkov et al. (Moscow, 1988), 39. The volume was published under the auspices of the Soviet Academy of Sciences.

49. Among them, Keep, *Russian Revolution*.

50. Richard Pipes, *The Russian Revolution* (New York, 1990); Pipes, *Russia Under the Bolshevik Regime* (New York, 1994); Malia, *Soviet Tragedy*.

51. Malia, *Soviet Tragedy*, pp. 26, 516.

52. Pipes, *Russia Under the Bolshevik Regime*, chap. 5.

Chapter 3

1. A.H.M. Jones, *The Later Roman Empire*, 2 vols. (Oxford, 1964), was the standard work for many years. See also Ramsey MacMullen, *Corruption and Decline of Rome* (Cambridge, Mass., 1988).

2. The literature on the subject is immense. Detailed bibliographies are in Jones, *Later Roman Empire*, vol. 2, and Joseph Vogt, *The Decline of Rome* (London, 1964).

3. *Monumenta Germaniae Historica*, X. *Auctores Antiquissimi*; Amianus Marcelinus, in V. Gardthausen (Leipzig, 1874).

4. For a review of certain analogies between the decline of Rome and the Soviet empire, see Vasili Rudich, "Senat Rimskii i Sovietskii narod," *Strana i Mir* II (1984), reprinted in *Novoye Vremya* 48 (1992). Earlier, in the 1970s, the analogy with the decline of the Roman Empire had occurred to Soviet poets and bards. Okudzhava was singing a ballad that opened "Rimskaya Imperiya vremeni upadka" (The Roman Empire at the time of its decline . . .), and there is the same motif in Joseph Brodsky's poems.

5. See the essays by C. R. Boxer and J. Hamilton in *The Economic Decline of Empires*, ed. Carlo Cipolla (London, 1970).

6. Dietrich Geyer, *Der russische Imperialismus* (Göttingen, 1977); William C. Fuller, *Strategy and Power in Russia, 1600–1914* (New York, 1992), 512. Too little attention has been paid in the West to the ideas of Rostislav Fadeyev, an eccentric, perhaps the most influential advocate of Russian imperial expansion at the time. He was an uncle of Sergei Witte, the future prime minister. Eccentricity seems to have been endemic in the Fadeyev family; Fadeyev's niece was Madame Blavatsky of theosophical fame.

7. An example of this school of thought is a collective work (probably the last to be published) edited by V. V. Zhuravlev on behalf of the Institute of Marxism-Leninism of the Central Committee of the CPSU: *Na poroge Krizisa. Narastanie zastoinikh yavlenii v partii i obshshestve* (Moscow, 1990).

8. Dostoyevsky's *The Diary of a Writer* contains many such *obiter dicta*. It might be blasphemy to mention it, but Zhirinovsky's short memoir *Poslednyi brosok* . . . (Moscow, 1993) is a link in the same chain.

9. Solomon Schwartz, in *Sotsialisticheskii Vestnik*, 6 September 1945.

10. Walter Kolarz, *Myth and Realities in Eastern Europe* (London, [1946]), 63.

11. See, for instance, Alec Nove and J. A. Newth, *The Soviet Middle East: A Communist Model for Development* (New York, 1967), and Charles K. Wiber, *The Soviet Model and the Underdeveloped Countries* (Chapel Hill, N.C., 1969).

12. Mary McAuley, "Nationalism and the Soviet Multi-ethnic State," in *The State in Soviet Society*, ed. Neil Harding (London, 1984). Timothy Colton wrote in 1987 that Soviet ethnic relations were too often described by foreigners in apocalyptic language, as if the Soviet multinational state were on the verge of collapse like a house of cards (*The Dilemmas of Reform in the Soviet Union* [New York, 1987]).

13. Edward Gibbon, *The Decline and Fall of the Roman Empire* (New York, n.d.), 1:762.

14. See A. E. Medunin on the alleged omnipresence of the Stalin cult in A. A. Kara Murza, *Totalitarianizm kak istoricheskii fenomen* (Moscow, 1990), 312.

15. The best known works of this genre of "official" (i.e., anti-intelligentsia) working-class literature at the time were V. Kochetov, *The Erzhov Brothers* (1958), and K. Lvova, *Elena* (1961).

16. *SSSR v. tsifrakh, 1985 g* (Moscow, 1986), 50.

17. Philip Hanson, *From Stagnation to Catastroika* (New York, 1992), 16–17.

18. Abram Bergson, ed., *Soviet Economic Growth* (Evanston, Ill., 1953), 32.

19. Alec Nove, *The Soviet Economy* (London, 1966); Harry Schwartz, *The Soviet Economy Since Stalin* (London, 1966).

20. Central Intelligence Agency, *Organization and Management in the Soviet Economy* (Washington, D.C., 1977), 21.

21. Vladimir Kontorovich, "The Economic Fallacy," *National Interest*, Spring 1993, 44; Michael Ellman and Vladimir Kontorovich, eds., *The Disintegration of the Soviet Economic System* (London, 1992).

22. Grigorii Khanin, "Economic Growth in the 1980s," in *Disintegration of the Soviet Economic System*, eds. Ellmann and Kontorovich, 73.

23. Abram Bergson and Herbert Levine, eds., *The Soviet Economy Towards the Year 2000* (London, 1983), 445–46.

24. Edward Hewett, *Reforming the Soviet Economy* (Washington, D.C., 1988), 37. See also Central Intelligence Agency, *Handbook of Economic Statistics, 1985: A Reference Aid* (Washington, D.C., 1986), 39.

25. Vasilii Selyunin and Grigorii Khanin, "Lukavaya tsifra," *Novy Mir* 2 (1987). An earlier article by the same authors in *Pravda*, 30 December 1985, did not, however, attract remotely as much attention. There had been other earlier papers, such as the famous report by Academician Tatyana Zaslavsky, but they did not frontally assault official statistics. Some of Khanin's assessments had been published even earlier in *samizdat*.

26. It has been reported that even Gorbachev, when he became a member of the Politburo in 1983, was not aware of the state of the Soviet economy–outside the field of his specialization (agriculture) (*Pravda*, 10 December 1990). Brezhnev, however, beginning in the late 1960s in his annual reports to the Central Committee, made many admissions about the poor performance of the economy–and these were read by all party members.

27. Charles Wolf, "The Costs and Benefits of the Soviet Empire," in *The Future of the Soviet Empire*, ed. Henry S. Rowen and Charles Wolf (New York, 1987); David F. Epstein, "The Economic Cost of Soviet Security and Empire," in *The Impoverished Superpower*, ed. Henry S. Rowen and Charles Wolf (San Francisco, 1988); more recently, Dimitri Steinberg, "The Soviet Defense Burden," *Soviet Studies* 4 (1991).

28. *Washington Post*, 16 November 1992.

29. It could be claimed that while détente had no immediate ill effects for Soviet power, there were long-term negative consequences. Soviet society was opened up at the time to foreign influences that helped to undermine the Communist raison d'être. This question remains to be explored, but the ease with which the détente policy was reversed tended to show that the party was still in full control. Myron Rush argues that if military expenditure had been halved, the economic situation would have substantially improved ("Fortune and Fate," *National Interest*, Spring 1993). But in this case, it would have been difficult to sustain the state-of-siege mentality.

30. D. R. Kelly, K. R. Stunkel, and R. R. Westcoth, *The Economic Superpowers and the Environment* (San Francisco, 1987).

31. A Soviet doctor, quoted in Murray Feshbach and Alfred Friendly, *Ecocide in the USSR* (New York, 1992), 262. See also Mark Field, "Medical Care in the Soviet Union," in *Quality of Life in the Soviet Union*, ed. H. Herlemann (Boulder, Colo., 1987).

32. These facts were noted by Western observers well before *glasnost*. See Murray Feshbach, "Between the Lines of the 1979 Soviet Census," *Problems of Communism*, January 1982, and, more recently, Feshbach and Friendly, *Ecocide*, chaps. 8 10. About fifty countries had a lower rate of infant mortality than the Soviet Union (*Narodnoye Khoziaistvo SSSR za 70 let* [Moscow, 1988], 405–6).

33. Y. Lysitsyn and N. Kopyt, *Alkogolism* (Moscow, 1978), 95. Alcohol consumption between 1950 and 1980 probably increased tenfold. See also Vladimir Treml, *Alcohol in the USSR* (New Brunswick, N.J., 1982), and Boris M. Segal, *The Drunken Society* (New York, 1990). But there still are some mysteries in this context, for total alcohol consumption was apparently smaller in the Soviet Union than in France and Italy.

34. *Na poroge Krizisa*, 164; *Kommunist* 14 (1989): 50.

35. If a party leader was honest and incorruptible–and there were some in this category, such as Masherov, party boss in White Russia–he acquired the reputation of a saint. Such were the moral standards of the times.

36. Widespread corruption, of course, antedates the Brezhnev era. Concerning corruption in Moscow in the early 1960s, see the recollections of German Karakozov, a leading Soviet prosecutor, in *Kuranty* 42 (1992). For a sociological attempt to assess the role of corruption in the late Brezhnev period, see Ken Jowitt, "Soviet Neotraditionalism: The Political Corruption of a Leninist Regime," *Soviet Studies*, July 1983.

37. For instance, in Viktor Astafiev's *Tsar Fish* (1976) and the novels of Alexander Yashin, Boris Vasiliev, and V. Tendryakov. For a general discussion of this trend, see Rosalind J. Marsh, *Soviet Fiction Since Stalin: Science, Politics and Literature* (London, 1985), chap. 5.

38. On the problem of poverty in the Soviet Union, see Mervyn Matthews, *Poverty in the Soviet Union* (Cambridge, 1986). On the various forms of popular discontent, impossible to measure statistically but very real and infectious, see Peter Reddaway, "The Role of Popular Discontent," *National Interest*, Spring 1993, 57.

39. About 200 years ago, when the great historian Karamzin was asked what was going on in Russia, he is said to have replied laconically, "Kradut" (stealing).

40. Wolf, "Costs and Benefits of the Soviet Empire," 121. These figures, by necessity, can be only estimates.

41. Franklyn Holzman, Letter, *New York Times*, 22 November 1992.

42. Valentin Falin, in *Die Zeit*, 13 March 1992.

43. Steven Sestanovich, "Did the West Undo the East?" *National Interest*, Spring 1993, 26. G. Arbatov claims at one and the same time that Reagan's hard line did not alter Soviet policy and that the Soviet high command, with its ever-growing demands for resource allocation, went out of control and caused serious tensions (*The System: An Insider's Life in Soviet Politics* [New York, 1992]).

44. Grigorii Zinoviev, *XIII s'ezd RKP(b)* (Moscow, 1963), 42.

45. Leonid Brezhnev, *Leninskim Kursom*, vol. 4 (Moscow, n.d.), 63.

46. *Der Spiegel*, 1989.

47. One study on the nationality problem is Helène Carrère D'Encausse, *Decline of an Empire* (New York, 1978). Similar views were expressed by Theresa Rakowska-Harmstone, R. G. Suny, and a few other students of Soviet nationality problems. However, while these authors rightly emphasized the crucial importance of national conflict, in contrast to most mainline Sovietologists, who played it

down, not one of them predicted a total breakdown on these lines in the near future. Ludmilla Alekseeva, a Soviet dissident, mentioned the possibility.

48. D. M. Wallace, *Russia* (New York, 1905).

49. Marc Raeff, "Patterns of Russian Imperial Policy Towards the Nationalities," in *Soviet Nationality Problems*, ed. E. Allworth (New York, 1971), 22.

50. Alexander Dallin, "Causes of the Collapse of the USSR," *Post-Soviet Affairs* 8 (1992): 279–302.

51. Thomas F. Remington writes about a "concentration of grievances" and the "discontent of modernization" ("Regime Transitions in Communist Systems: The Soviet Case," *Soviet Economy* [1990]: 6). But earlier on, Soviet experts had put the stress on the benefits of modernization (urbanization, educational attainments, and so on, which had led them to a very positive assessment of the prospects of the Soviet system.

52. For instance, John Bushnell, "The New Soviet Man Turns Pessimist," *Survey*, Spring 1979.

53. Ibid., 12.

54. As the result of the declining birthrate, alcoholism, antireligious feeling, general decline in mores, and many other factors.

55. I follow the arguments developed in some detail by Vladislav Tsipko, "Territoriya," *Rodina* 8–9 (1992). Curiously, Tsipko does not mention Central Asia in this context.

56. Aleksander Yakovlev, in *Vechernaya Moskva*, 6 November 1991.

57. Mikhail Gorbachev, in *Nezavisimaya Gazeta*, 11 November 1992.

58. My own book on *glasnost – The Long Road to Freedom* (New York, 1990) – was perhaps the last to be translated in this series. In a short preface, the anonymous Russian editor noted that my views on the prospects of the success of *perestroika* were gloomy. Soon afterward, the Central Committee ceased to exist and the translations were discontinued.

59. Some of the seminal contributions to this debate are in B. M. Peternande, ed., *The Russian Revolution*, vol. 2 of *Articles on Russian and Soviet History, 1500–1991* (New York, 1992).

60. Martin Malia, *The Soviet Tragedy* (New York, 1994), 497. On the Chinese transformation period, see Merle Goldmann, *Sowing the Seeds of Democracy in China* (Cambridge, Mass., 1994), and Richard Evans, *Deng Xiaoping* (New York, 1994), chaps. 14, 15.

61. Buildings collapse and machines break up because of basic faults of construction or metal fatigue, sometimes without any forewarning. A Russian writer has used the term *samoraspad* (self-collapse, or disintegration) (Viktor Bondarev, "Samoraspad," *Rodina* 4 [1993]). Could the totalitarian or post-totalitarian system have been dismantled without at the same time destroying the Soviet empire?

Elsewhere I have been dealing with the thesis of the extreme Russian right and the neo-Communists that the Soviet system collapsed not as the result of its own ineffectiveness, but because of the intrigues and the sabotage of foreign enemies: democrats, freemasons, Jews, and the West in general (Walter Laqueur, *Black Hundred* [New York, 1993]). There are degrees of paranoia. Even Academician Igor Shafarevich was attacked for not realizing that all the resources – economic, political, and spiritual – of the so-called civilized world were devoted to war against the Soviet Union and the destruction of the Soviet system (Tatyana Glushkova, in *Molodaya Gvardiya* 9 [1993]).

62. Richard Pipes, *Russia Under the Bolshevik Regime* (New York, 1994), 473.

Chapter 4

1. There still are basic differences of opinion between various schools of taxonomy, such as numerical phenetics and cladistics. One leading ornithologist counts fifty-one orders of birds; most other experts, twenty-seven or twenty-eight (Ernst Mayr, *Towards a New Philosophy of Biology* [Cambridge, Mass., 1988], 273).

2. I follow in this section thoughts developed in an earlier essay, "Is There Now, or Has There Ever Been, Such a Thing as Totalitarianism"? *Commentary*, October 1985, reprinted in Walter Laqueur, *Soviet Realities* (New Brunswick, N.J., 1990). In the light of the debate following publication of my article, and of subsequent events on the world scene, I have modified my views in certain respects. I first discussed the de-totalitarianization of Communist parties and systems as a highly probable development in 1962 (Walter Laqueur, "The End of a Monolith," *Foreign Affairs*, April 1962, 372).

3. Domenico Fisichella, *Analisi del Totalitarismo* (Messina, 1976), quoted in André Liebich, "Marxism and Totalitarianism," Occasional Paper 217, Kennan Institute, 1986.

4. Hilferding's article was first published in the Paris-based Menshevik journal *Sotsialisticheskii Vestnik*. Its first publication in English was in *Modern Review* 4 (1947). Hilferding perished in Nazi-occupied Europe during World War II.

5. Friedrich's thoughts were published *in nuce* a few years earlier ("The Unique Character of Totalitarian Society" in *Totalitarianism*, ed. Carl Friedrich (Cambridge, Mass., 1954) .

6. For instance, L. Schapiro, *Totalitarianism* (London, 1973).

7. Juan Linz, "Totalitarianism and Authoritarian Regimes," in *Handbook of Political Science, Macropolitical Theory*, vol. 3, ed. Fred Greenstein and Nelson Polsby (Reading, Mass., 1975) .

8. But the use of the term "Nazism" was also discouraged by the New Left; it became "German fascism" or simply "fascism." Thus the important differences between Nazism and Italian fascism (let alone other fascisms) were ignored, and the far more pronounced element of violence and terrorism inherent in Nazism was played down.

9. For some of the early criticism of the totalitarianism concept in the field of Soviet research, see Alfred G. Meyer, *The Soviet Political System* (New York, 1965); the conference reports in *Slavic Review* 1, 2, 4 (1967) (Midwestern Political Science conference); Frederic Fleron, ed., *Communist Studies and the Social Sciences* (Chicago, 1969); A. H. Brown, *Soviet Politics and Political Science* (London, 1974), as well as the writings of Jerry Hough and H. Gordon Skilling.

10. See, for instance, Hans Kaiser, in *Neue Politische Literatur* 18 (1973); Erik Hennig, "Zur Kritik der Totalitarianismustheorien," *Neue Politische Literatur* 21 (1976); Hella Mandt, "Ist der Totalitarismus Begriff überholt," *Trierer Beiträge* 11 (1982); and Stephen Cohen, *Rethinking the Soviet Experience* (New York, 1985), chaps. 1 and 2.

11. This term had first been used by political scientists about 1915 with regard to Britain and the United States.

12. Lucian W. Pye, in his presidential address to the American Political Science Association, stated that he considered the Marxist-Leninist regimes a

subspecies of "all types of authoritarian systems" ("Political Science and the Crisis of Authoritarianism," *American Political Science Review*, March 1990) This in the Russian context would have meant that there was no decisive difference between the tsarist and the Soviet regime.

13. Irving Howe, "Totalitarianism Reconsidered," *Dissent*, Winter 1991; Seymour Martin Lipset and Gyorgy Bence, "Anticipation of Communism" (manuscript, 1992–1993); Giovani Sartori, "Totalitarianism, Model Mania and Learning from Error," *Journal of Theoretical Politics*, January 1993.

14. Bracher's categories were certainly shorter, simpler, and more up to date than Friedrich's. See K. D. Bracher, *Die totalitäre Erfahrung* (Munich, 1987), and *Zeitgeschichtliche Kontroversen* (Munich, 1984), as well as *Wendezeiten der Geschichte* (Stuttgart, 1992).

15. This point had been made very strongly by the Mensheviks, the Russian Social Democrats in exile, first by Potresov and later by most others.

16. For critical reviews of the debates on totalitarianism, see Ernest A. Menze, ed. *Totalitarianism Reconsidered* (Port Washington, N.Y., 1981); Walter Schlangen, *Die Totalitäre Theorie* (Stuttgart, 1976); and B. Seidel and S. Jenkner, *Wege der Totalitarismus Forschung* (Darmstadt, 1974).

17. Richard Löwenthal, "Beyond Totalitarianism," in *1984 Revisited*, ed. Irving Howe (New York, 1984).

18. Laqueur, *Soviet Realitics*, 120.

19. Richard Löwenthal, Letter to the Editor, *Commentary*, January 1986. Löwenthal correctly analyzed the new trend; but since many of the totalitarian institutions continued to exist, he found it as difficult as others to define this interim period with any kind of precision. While he did not subscribe to any alternative model, he showed perhaps excessive readiness to ponder them.

20. As expressed in the writing of Alexandre Bennigsen, Theresa Rakowska, Helène Carrère d'Encausse, and others.

21. It put an end to the discussions on the left, before and after World War II, as to whether the Soviet Union was a progressive regime and its economy socialist or state-capitalist.

22. Michael Walzer, "On Failed Totalitarianism," in *1984 Revisited*, ed. Howe, 103.

23. For this reason, Soviet political scientists such as Andronik Migranyan and Igor Klyamkin had argued early on under *glasnost* that it was illusory to expect a transition from totalitarianism to democracy; an authoritarian regime was an inescapable stage in between.

24. Francis Fukuyama, "The Modernizing Imperative," *National Interest*, Spring 1993, 13.

25. Giovanni Sartori, "Totalitarianism, Model Mania and Learning from Error," *Journal of Theoretical Politics*, January 1993.

26. For a survey of the main issues involved, see Ian Kershaw, *The Nazi Dictatorship: Problems and Perspectives of Interpretation* (London, 1985).

27. But then in Russia, too, the victory of Bolshevism has been explained with reference to a Russian *Sonderweg*, the fact that the country was most of the time outside the mainstream of European history. There is a great deal of literature on this subject, most recently A. A. Kara Murza, "Chto takoe russkoe zapadnichestvo?" *Polis* 2 (1993).

28. On this point, as on some others, there were differences of opinion. Thus Dahrendorf and Schoenbaum claimed that there had been far-reaching social

changes, something akin to a social revolution under the Nazis, almost a break-through toward modernity. Later research tended to show that economic facts and figures did not bear this out, whereupon Dahrendorf argued that Nazism had been in power for a relatively short time. For a survey of the early stages of the debate, see F. L. Carsten, "Interpretations of Fascism," in *Fascism*, ed. Walter Laqueur (Harmondsworth, 1979). Others have claimed, more realistically, that the guiding principle of Nazism was the racialist utopia, the idea of the superiority of the German race, and its vocation to expand and rule and that economic and social changes that occurred in the Nazi era were more or less incidental.

29. Especially Ernst Nolte, but also younger writers such as Eckhard Jesse, Uwe Backes, and Rainer Zittelmann.

30. James Joll, quoted in Cohen, *Rethinking the Soviet Experience*.

31. Hans Kaiser, in *Neue Politische Literatur* 18 (1973); Eckhard Jesse, "Renaissance der Totalitarismus Konzeption"? *Neue Politische Literatur* 28 (1983).

32. Herbert Marcuse, *One-Dimensional Man* (Boston, 1964).

33. O. Yartseva, "Totalitarianizm kak istoricheskii-kulturny fenomen" (manuscript, April 1989). The proceedings were published by the Academy of Sciences in 1989, 40.

34. *Bolshaia Sovetskaia Entsiklopediia* 3rd ed. (Moscow, 1977).

35. *Sovetskii Entsiklopedicheskii Slovar* (Moscow, 1986), 1347.

36. Particularly Kh. Kobo, ed., *Osmyslit Kult Stalina* (Moscow, 1989).

37. Thus Gozman and Etkind in the volume just mentioned invoked "totalitarianism" in the title of their essay, whereas M. Kapustin did not, but there were apparently no basic differences between the authors.

38. A. A. Kara Murza, ed., *Totalitarianizm kak istoricheskii fenomen* (Moscow, 1988).

39. A. M. Filitov, *Kholodnaya Voina* (Moscow, 1991), 101.

40. I. V. Zagladin, "Totalitarianizm i Demokratia," *Kentavr* (formerly *Voprosy Istorii KPSS*), May–June 1992.

41. Yu. I. Igritsky, "Snova o totalitarizme," *Otechestvennaya Istoriya* 1 (1993). On the Andreski scale, Nazi Germany was 85 percent totalitarian at the beginning of World War II, and 95 percent at its end, with fascist Italy a mere 55 percent (Stalin's Russia being 100 percent yardstick) (S. Andreski, *Max Weber's Insights and Errors* [London, 1984], 44).

42. See, Yu. I. Igritsky "Kontseptsia totalitarianizma," *Istoriya SSSR* 1 (1990); "Perioda totalitarnoi vlasti," *Sotsiologicheskie Isledovaniia* 5 (1989); K. S. Gadzhiev, "Totalitarizm Kak fenomenon 20 ogo veka," *Voprosy Filosofii* 2 (1992); and A. Fursov, "KratoKratiia," *Sotsium* 8 (1991).

43. Igritsky, "Snova o totalitarizme," 10.

44. S. I. Lunev, "70 let istorii i tri etapa totalitarizma v. SSSR," in *Totalitarianizm*, ed. Kara Murza, 136.

45. Russian political figures were more outspoken in this respect than the academics. When asked in an interview how he defined Bolshevism, A. A. Yakovlev replied "Ordinary fascism" (*Moskovskie Novosti* 5 [1994]). *Ordinary Fascism* (1966) was the title of a well-known Soviet movie by Mikhail Romm.

Chapter 5

1. E. Domar, "Appraisals," in *The Soviet Economy in the Year 2000*, ed. A. Bergson and H. Levine (London, 1983), 446.

2. John Bushnell, "The New Soviet Man turns Pessimist," *Survey* (Spring 1979).

3. Marshall I. Goldman, *The USSR in Crisis* (New York, 1982).

4. Emmanuel Todd, *La Chute final* (Paris, 1976). The work was welcomed by Raymond Aron, Emmanuel Le Roy Ladurie, and Jean François Revel, but received hardly any attention outside France. It was dismissed as of no consequence by the Sovietological fraternity.

5. Milovan Djilas (1975) and others had argued even earlier that Communism was a spent force. More cautious pessimism was expressed by the Norwegian journalist and politologist Nils Morten Udgaard, who worked in Moscow from 1971. He saw clearly that the nationality problem was crucial for the survival of the regime, and stressed in detail that while far-reaching reforms were needed, they would lead to unrest and the party might lose control (*Sovjet Unionen, dem räville Kjempe* [Oslo, 1977]).

6. Domar, "Appraisals," 445–46.

7. Introduction to "Gorbachev's Economic Plans," vol. 1 (study papers submitted to the Joint Economic Committee, Congress of the United States, November 1987).

8. Dollar estimates for Soviet Russia and East European governments are notoriously difficult to make and potentially misleading. The newest figures undoubtedly understate the potential of the successor states of the Soviet Union.

9. Edward A. Hewett, *Reforming the Soviet Economy* (Washington, D.C., 1988), 2, 33.

10. Seweryn Bialer, in *After Brezhnev*, ed. Robert F. Byrnes (Bloomington, Ind., 1983) 85.

11. Which, in fact, they were in the United States and in Germany.

12. Stephen F. Cohen, *Rethinking the Soviet Experience* (New York, 1985), 29.

13. Ibid., 6–7.

14. Moshe Lewin, *The Gorbachev Phenomenon* (Berkeley, 1987) 4–9, 153.

15. Walter Laqueur, "What We Know About the Soviet Union?" *Commentary*, February 1983, reprinted in Laqueur, *America, Europe and the Soviet Union* (New Brunswick, N.J., 1983).

16. A reference to the charges against William Casey and others on the occasion of the Senate nomination hearings of Robert M. Gates to be director of Central Intelligence in September and October 1991. The revelations about Soviet, East German, and other East European support for various terrorist groups came in 1991 and 1992.

17. The first two attempts in this direction are Cohen, *Rethinking the Soviet Experience*, written from an enlightened revisionist point of view, and my own *The Fate of the Revolution*, 2nd ed. (New York, 1987), chaps. 9 and 10. See also Edward Acton, *Rethinking the Russian Revolution* (London, 1990).

18. Martin Malia, "From Under the Rubble–What?" *Problems of Communism*, January–April 1992, 105.

19. "What Is Happening in Moscow?" *National Interest*, Summer 1987.

20. According to Richard Pipes, "Those who expect an erosion of ideology vastly underestimate the fervor of the Russian ruling elite" (*Survey*, April 1963, 70).

21. According to Malia, the Mensheviks in the Western emigration were "Marxists and revolutionaries," their chief quarrel with the Communists, their *frères enemies*, was that the latter had spoiled a good proletarian revolution (*Na-*

tional Interest, Fall 1993, p. 112). They remained, of course, socialists, but such a characterization is about as correct as branding, say, Leon Blum and Ernest Bevin as fiery Marxist revolutionaries. While some Western social democrats collaborated with the Communists in a variety of popular fronts, most were their sharpest and best informed opponents, precisely because they knew them so well, whereas conservatives had seldom, if ever, any dealings with Communists on the political scene. From the early 1920s, the Mensheviks-in-exile were among the most consistent critics of Soviet Communism, and they had enormous influence on Western Sovietology in its heyday, in the late 1940s and the 1950s.

22. I. Shafarevich, "Dve Dorogi–k odnomu obryvu," *Novy Mir* 9 (1989): 148–49. Similar views were expressed by Vadim Kozhinov, one of the most influential writers of the Russian right. Solzhenitsyn's familiarity with Western Sovietological writing also seems spotty.

23. Shafarevich is also the author of a history of socialism from the time of the Incas; it is explained as the collective death wish of individuals and communities.

24. *The World Fact Book* (Washington, D.C., 1989).

25. Stephen Cohen et al., *The Soviet Union Since Stalin* (Bloomington, Ind., 1980), 222.

26. *Sevodnya,* 18 June 1993.

27. Ibid.

28. Tai-chun Kuo and Ramon H. Myers, *Understanding Communist China* (Stanford, Calif., 1986), 10. This study observed that the record of the Taiwan China watchers was in retrospect better than that of the Americans, who paid scant attention to the views of embittered people motivated by bias. This attitude strikingly resembles the approach of American Sovietologists toward the Russian émigrés.

29. John Fairbanks, *Chinabound* (New York, 1982), 317.

30. For a systematic study of changing American views, see Steven M. Mosher, *China Misperceived* (New York, 1990).

31. *New York Times,* 19 June 1966, quoted in ibid., 124.

32. But the radical *Bulletin* continues to appear even now–twenty-five years later. Francis Bacon compared those unwilling to acknowledge or retract error to an unruly horse that will neither stop nor turn.

33. Mosher, *China Misperceived,* 188–89.

34. A detailed, critical review of Cuban studies in the United States (and elsewhere) could also be of considerable interest in the context of the fate of Soviet studies. See Irving L. Horowitz, *The Conscience of Worms and the Cowardice of Lions* (New Brunswick, N.J., 1993).

Chapter 6

1. This is the line taken by the Russian right and the neo-Communists.

2. I would like to quote an example from personal experience. In a book I edited some years ago, I did mention the possibility of the total disintegration of the Soviet Union but concluded that this was an unlikely contingency (*Soviet Union 2000* [New York, 1990]). This struck a reviewer of this book as far too pessimistic and reflecting a cold war bias: "The intellectual dilemmas and mental blinkers that confronted readers of *Encounter* over several decades still seem to underline this symposium's assumptions and conclusions. The USSR cannot survive as it is, but it is totally unreformable" (G. Sanford, in *Journal of Communist*

Studies [1992]). This prescient review was published nine months *after* the Soviet Union had ceased to exist.

3. Robert C. Tucker, "Sovietology and Russian History," *Post-Soviet Affairs*, July–September 1992, 175.

4. Ibid. Michel Confino, a distinguished student of Russian history, has taken issue with the belief that Russian history can shed much light on the understanding of Stalinism (*Me St. Petersburg Leleningrad* [Tel Aviv, 1993], 30). According to Confino, it is a "groundless stereotype . . . to explain with reference to Russian history the dynamics of Soviet politics following the failure of the various Sovietological theses and models."

5. Robert Tucker, Foreword, in *Post-Communist Studies and Political Science*, ed. F. J. Fleron, Jr., and Eric P. Hoffmann (Boulder, Colo., 1993).

6. For instance, Martin Malia, "From Under the Rubble–What?" *Problems of Communism*, January–April 1992; Richard Pipes, "Russia's Chance," *Commentary*, March 1992; Walter Laqueur, ed., *A World of Secrets* (New York, 1985); A. Przeworski, *Democracy and the Market* (Cambridge, 1991); Alex Alexiev, in *Problems of Communism*, January–April 1992; as well as the contributors to "The Strange Death of Soviet Communism," *National Interest* [special issue], Spring 1993, 68–123.

7. Peter Rutland, in *National Interest*, Spring 1993, 122.

8. The concept had been mooted by John Lukacs, *A New History of the Cold War* (New York, 1966), 281, but had not been picked up by the Sovietologists at the time.

9. George Breslauer, "In Defense of Sovietology," *Post-Soviet Affairs*, July–September 1992, 197–98.

10. T. Remington, "Sovietology and Systems Stability," *Post-Soviet Affairs*, July–September 1992, 200.

11. Seymour Martin Lipset and Gyorgy Bence, "Anticipations of the Failure of Communism" (Paper submitted at the annual meeting of the American Sociological Association, Pittsburgh, August 1992), 2, 11.

12. Jack Snyder, "Science and Sovietology," *World Politics*, January 1988, 193, reprinted in *Post-Communist Studies*, ed. Fleron and Hoffmann, 105.

13. Alfred C. Meyer, "Politics and Methodology in Soviet Studies," *Studies in Comparative Communism*, June 1991, 127. As Sidney Monas put it, there was a "paralysis of imagination caused by an obsessive concern with methodology" (*Times Literary Supplement*, 2 July 1993). Elsewhere, Meyer wrote that it is "safe to assert that every important event that has taken place in the Communist world within the last few years or so has come as a surprise to the professional i.e. to students of the USSR and its client states" ("Politics and Methodology in Soviet Studies," *Post-Communist Studies*, ed. Fleron and Hoffmann, 169).

14. The books and essays of Western authors such as Klaus Mehnert, Mary Seton Watson, Michael Heller, and Vera Dunham ought to be mentioned, among others.

15. Alec Nove, ed., *The Stalin Phenomenon* (New York, 1992).

16. "Rekviem po Sotsializm," *ONS* 1 (1992).

17. E. H. Carr, *The Soviet Union from Lenin to Stalin* (New York, 1979), 179.

18. R. H. Davies, in *Stalin Phenomenon*, ed. Nove, 62.

19. Sheila Fitzpatrick, *The Russian Revolution, 1917–1932* (Oxford, 1982), 161.

20. Ibid., 9.

21. Quoted in Richard J. Evans, *In Hitler's Shadow* (New York, 1989), 20.

22. Sheila Fitzpatrick, in *Stalin Phenomenon*, ed. Nove, 88.

23. J. Thomas Sanders, "Historical Consciousness and the Incorporation of the Soviet Past," in *Post-Communist Studies*, ed. Fleron and Hoffmann, 145.

24. J. Arch Getty, *Origins of the Great Purges* (Cambridge, 1985).

25. *Origins of the Great Purges* was called a seminal text and "something of a bombshell" (Chris Ward, *Stalin's Russia* [London 1993], 130, 150).

26. Davies, 66. Rudolf Schlesinger was an Austrian Communist who had the good luck to leave Russia for England in time to escape the purges but remained a committed Stalinist. He wrote several books in the immediate postwar period in which he tended to take Soviet publications, however absurd, at face value. See Walter Laqueur, *The Fate of the Revolution* rev. ed. (New York, 1987).

27. According to Getty, "without the participation of professional historians, the process of glasnost will remain dangerously inchoate" (*Stalin Phenomenon*, ed. Nove, 110). Getty complained about "undervaluated and undocumented rumors," seeming to prefer the pre-*glasnost* publications. According to Getty, the purge of the 1930s was a chaotic wave of voluntarism and revolutionary puritanism, a "radical even hysterical reaction to bureaucracy" (*Origins of the Great Purges*, 206).

28. F. Fleron and E. Hoffmann, "Post Communist Studies, and Political Science," in *Post-Communist Studies*, ed. Fleron and Hoffmann, 371.

29. Ibid., 381.

30. Laqueur, *Fate of the Revolution*, chaps. 9, 10.

31. S. Gross Solomon, ed., *Pluralism in the Soviet Union* (New York, 1982), 27. For a critical retrospective review of the "evasions of pluralism," see William Odom, "The Pluralist Mirage," *National Interest*, Spring 1993, 99.

32. Malia, "From Under the Rubble," n. 6.

33. Martin Malia, "Apocalypse–Not," *New Republic*, 22 February 1993.

34. Malia, "From Under the Rubble," 100.

35. Ibid., 101.

36. *United States–Soviet Relations 1991*, Joint Hearings of the Sales Committee on Arms Control and the Joint Economic Committee (Washington, D.C., 1992), 236. See also Jerry Hough, *Soviet Economy* 7 (1991): "The belief that the Soviet Union may disintegrate as a country contradicts all we know about revolution and national integration throughout the world"; and "Anyone who sees him [Gorbachev] as a tragic transitional figure has little sense of history."

37. Richard Löwenthal clarified his position in an exchange with the present author (*Commentary*, February 1986). He preferred the term "post-totalitarian dictatorship" for the regimes that had emerged in the Soviet Union and elsewhere in Eastern Europe. But this did not entail the end of dictatorial single party rule. See Chapter 4.

38. W. Odom, "The Pluralist Mirage," *National Interest*, Spring 1993, 101. In a subsequent communication Odom slightly modified his claim but still argued that the Mensheviks had been a revolutionary party (*National Interest*, Fall 1993).

39. Malia, "From Under the Rubble," 15.

40. Walter Lippmann, *The Cold War* (New York, 1947).

41. The main figures in revisionist historiography on the Cold War were Isaac Deutscher (as a precursor), Gabriel Kolko, Ger Alperowitz, Donald Fleming, B. Bernstein, Thomas Paterson, W. A. Williams, Richard Barnet, Noam Chomsky. Lloyd Gardner, and David Horowitz. See, among many other publications, T. G. Paterson, ed., *Cold War Critics* (Chicago, 1971), and Richard A. Mellanson, *Writing History and Making Policy* (Lanham, Md., 1983).

42. A good example of revisionist thinking is H. W. Brand, *The Devil We Knew: Americans and the Cold War* (New York, 1993). Students of logic in ancient Rome were given the following classical definition of a fallacy: "Post hoc ergo propter hoc" (After this, therefore because of this). There has been no end to logical fallacy: since Hitler failed in the end, he must have been a weak dictator, and so on. This book does not contain a single reference to a Soviet source.

43. "Soviet Bloc Had Detailed Plan to Invade W. Germany," *Washington Post*, 16 March 1993; "Russia Says Soviet Atom Arsenal Was Larger Than West Estimated," *New York Times*, 25 September 1993. The stockpile of highly enriched uranium seems to have been twice as large as believed by Western analysts.

44. Strobe Talbott's views can be found most succinctly in *Reagan and the Russians* (New York, 1984), and *Deadly Gambits* (New York, 1984).

45. George Urban, ed., *The End of Empire* (Washington, D.C., 1993), 12.

46. Among them John Gaddis, M. Shervin, Melvin Loeffler, William Taubman, and L. E. Davis. But revisionism continued to have its strong advocates. *Glasnost* has brought a great many revelations concerning the conduct of Soviet foreign policy during the Cold War, but these are still very often ignored.

47. John Lewis Gaddis, "The Cold War . . . ," in *The End of the Cold War*, ed. Michael J. Hogan (New York, 1992), 23–28. Among radical theorists in Britain, a more self-critical approach could be detected than in the United States. See, for example, Mike Bowker and Robin Brown, eds., *From Cold War to Collapse* (Cambridge, 1993).

48. John Lewis Gaddis, *The United States and the Origins of the Cold War, 1941–1947* (New York, 1972), 360.

49. Ibid. Compare with the post–Cold War appraisal in John L. Gaddis, *The United States and the End of the Cold War* (New York, 1992), 58.

50. Walter Lafeber, "An End to Which Cold War?" in *End of the Cold War*, ed. Hogan, 13.

51. Ronald Steele, "The End and the Beginning," in ibid., 110.

52. Noam Chomsky, "A View From Below," in ibid., 138.

53. G. Lundestad and G. Alperowitz, in ibid., 195, 207.

54. Richard Barnet, "A Balance Sheet," in ibid., 126. This should be compared with the postmortem of a British political scientist on the performance of his radical colleagues: had they examined the structure of the Cold War a little more carefully, they might have been forced to the uncomfortable conclusion that the system to which they were so opposed had probably done more to contain conflict than unleash it. Michael Cox, "Radical Theory and the New Cold War," in *From Cold War to Collapse*, ed. Bowker and Brown, 53.

55. Ibid., 62.

56. The first edition appeared in the 1960s; the sixth, in 1990.

57. Walter Lafeber, *America, Russia and the Cold War*, 6th ed. (New York, 1990), 302. For an opposite view concerning the historical role of U.S. foreign policy under Reagan, see Steven Sestanovich, in *National Interest*, Spring 1993, 26–34.

58. George Kennan, in *New York Times*, 28 October 1992.

59. Talbott, *Reagan and the Russians*. An editor at *Time*, Talbott became coordinator of U.S. policy toward Russia under Clinton and later yet the deputy of the Secretary of State.

60. Ibid., 78. A similar line was taken even earlier by a young Soviet émigré turned Sovietologist who argued that the military balance had shifted against the

United States, that there had been a "worldwide slippage of U.S. positions" (Dimitri K. Simes, "The Anti-Soviet Brigade," *Foreign Policy*, Winter 1979-1980).

61. Seweryn Bialev, in *New York Review of Books*, 16 February 1984. A British expert on international relations referred in retrospect to the radicals' "inadequate understanding of three things, the Soviet Union, Reagan, and nuclear weapons" (Robin Brown "Introduction" to *From Cold War to Collapse*, ed. Bowker and Braun, 15).

62. "SDI, Chernobyl Helped End of Cold War, Conference Told," *Washington Post*, 27 February 1993. The reference is to a conference in Princeton, New Jersey, February 1993, on the end of the cold war.

63. When Foreign Ministry archives were opened under *glasnost* in Moscow and East European capitals, there was, of course, enormous curiosity among students of recent history. Access to these archives has not provided answers to all outstanding questions. But the work of American and Russian historians (such as Vladislav Zubok) is beginning to shed light on such specific issues as the origins of the Cold War, the outbreak of the war in Korea, the feelers put out by the Soviets in 1952 and 1953 aiming apparently at the reunification of Germany, the erection of the Berlin Wall, the Cuban missile crisis, the occupation of Czechoslovakia, and the invasion of Afghanistan. These and other issues were studied more or less systematically by working groups such as the Cold War International History Project at the Wilson Center, Washington, D.C., which published both a *Bulletin* and *Working Papers*. Their finding showed that the judgment of Western policy makers was sometimes at fault regarding Soviet intentions and that there still is room for controversy on specific issues. But for the basic assumptions of the revisionists no confirmation was found. The Cold War and its major crises could not have been prevented by a more conciliatory Western policy unless the West would have acceded all along to Soviet demands. Would a firmer, less ambiguous, line have prevented the Korean War? This, in the light of evidence, seems quite probable, for Stalin, like Mao, underestimated American readiness to intervene if need be on the Asian mainland. Hence their decision to encourage and support the North Korean invasion.

In later years, Khrushchev was willing to accept the risk of war (to quote his own words) when he decided to erect the Berlin Wall. The decisions to invade Czechoslovakia and Afghanistan were likewise based on the assumption that the West would refrain from using force. Whether a Western military response in these two cases had been wise is a different question. But in the light of what is now known, little remains of the original, revisionist assumptions concerning peaceful Soviet intentions, of measures that were not more than a reaction to bellicose Western policies. This should conclude a debate that has been going on for too long.

64. "Fourth Annual Report of the Board of International Broadcasting," 1978, 50, quoted in *End of Empire*, ed. Urban.

65. Barnet, "Balance Sheet," 126; Lundestad and Alperowitz, 216.

66. John Lewis Gaddis, in *Pravda*, 29 August 1988; for Colonel Rzhezhevsky's and also L. Bezymensky and V. Falin's answer, see *Stranitsy Istorii Sovetskovo Obshshestva* (Moscow, 1989) 346; and O. Rzhezhevsky, ed., *Pravda i lozh* (Moscow, 1988).

67. A further conference took place in Moscow in January 1993 and was mainly devoted to the question of access to the archives. Historians should be grateful for all the help they will get, but it is doubtful whether any sensational discoveries will be made and uncertain whether the crucial documents, those

pertaining to Stalin's initiatives and reactions, will become available in the fore-seeable future.

68. A. M. Filitov, *Kholodnaya Voina; istoriograficheskie diskussii na Zapade* (Moscow, 1991), 196. Filitov's book went to press shortly before the attempted coup in 1991; hence the unfortunate (but accurate) recommendation on page 1: "For historians and propagandists." The characterization by Filitov of a liberal such as Hugh Seton Watson (to give but one example) as an "ultra hawk" clearly belongs to the realm of propaganda.

69. Ibid., 197.

70. N. V. Zagladin, "Pochemu svershilas kholodnaya voina?" *Kentavr*, January 1992, 53.

71. It is, of course, too early to comment in detail on the strange new fronts that emerged among Sovietologists and the Western public at large following the breakdown of the Soviet Union. Stephen Cohen and others turned sharply against Yeltsin, whom they accused of antidemocratic behavior, whereas Martin Malia became a fervent Yeltsinite. Some Western writers found redeeming democratic features among the anti-Yeltsin forces, which, they argued, were not predominantly of the extreme right or neo-Communist. Similar arguments were adduced by Chinese Communists and Japanese conservatives, whereas the actress Vanessa Redgrave gave full backing to Yeltsin. Vladimir Bukovsky announced that there was no hope at all for Russia in the forseeable future. Richard Pipes though, saw reason for optimism.

Chapter 7

1. H. Krausnick and Hilt Wilhelm, *Die Truppe des Weltanschauungskrieges* (Stuttgart, 1981), 188. Even this seemingly exhaustive account is based on one source only, the report by the commander of the unit; there exist other figures, derived from the files of the territorial army command in Kiev. There is every reason to assume that the number given is no more than an estimate.

2. For some countries, such as France, Belgium, and Bohemia-Moravia, the figures are beyond dispute since lists of names exist. With regard to Poland, the estimates of the experts vary between 2.9 and 3 million victims out of a prewar Jewish population of 3.3 million.

3. *Voenno-Istoricheskii zhurnal* 3 (1992): 44.

4. G. V. Krivosheev, ed., *Grif Sekretnosti snyat* (Moscow, 1992).

5. A critical review of the Krivosheev book by B. Sokolov appeared in *Nezavisimaya gazeta*, 2 February 1993.

6. For estimates during early *glasnost*, see V. V. Tsaplin, in *Voprosy Istorii* 4 (1989), and M. S. Tolts, in *Rodina* 11 (1989). Among later publications based on archival material, see O. V. Khlebniuk, *1937ii, Stalin, NKVD i sovetskoye obschestvo* (Moscow, 1992), and V. V. Tsaplin, "Arkhivnye materialy o chisle zakliuchennykh v kontse 30kh godov," *Voprosy Istorii* 4–5 (1991).

7. J. Arch Getty, *Origins of the Great Purges* (Cambridge, 1985), 206.

8. Robert W. Thurston, "Fear and Belief in the USSR's Great Terror," *Slavic Review*, Summer 1986. Other revisionist estimates are quoted in Chris Ward, *Stalin's Russia* (London, 1993), 132. In Russia, this thesis has been propagated in considerable detail by the extreme right; see, for instance, Stanislav Kuzmin, "Lagerniki; gulag bez retushi," *Molodaya Gvardiya* 3–6 (1993).

9. For instance, Vadim Kozhinov in a series of articles in *Nash Sovremennik* that most recently appeared in *Narodnaya Pravda*, December 1992, in which he

argued that "under Stalin and Brezhnev our country was much more civilized than now."

10. Among the "dubious sources" were the memoirs of Boris Bazhanov, Stalin's private secretary in the 1920s, and Alexander Orlov, the KGB officer who had defected; the "Letter of the Old Bolshevik"; and the more recent novels of Anatoli Rybakov, such as *Children of the Arbat*; and the plays of Mikhail Shatrov (J. Arch Getty, in *The Stalin Phenomenon*, ed. Alec Nove (New York, 1993), 102.

11. Alec Nove, "How Many Victims in the 1930s?" *Soviet Studies* 4 (1990); S. G. Wheatcroft, "More Light on the Scale of Repression . . . ," *Soviet Studies* 2 (1990); Edwin Bacon, "Glasnost and the Gulag," *Soviet Studies* 6 (1992); René Ahlberg, "Stalinistische Vergangenheitsbewältigung," *Ost Europa* 11 (1992); Robert Conquest, in *Soviet Studies* 5 (1991).

12. Among the critical comments, see, for instance, O. Shatunovskaya, "Falsifikatsiya," *Argumenty i Fakty* 22 (1990), and V. Chalikova, "Arkhivny Yunosha," *Neva* 10 (1988).

13. See Vadim Bakatin, *Izbavlenie ot KGB* (Moscow, 1992), 133–65. For an excellent overall account of the state of Russian archives and the measure of access, see Mark Cramer, "Archival Research in Moscow," *Cold War International History Project – Bulletin*, Woodrow Wilson International Center, Washington, D.C., Fall 1953, 1, 18–39. For the fate of the KGB archives, see Amy Knight, in *Slavic Review*, Fall 1993, 582–86.

14. A. N. Dugin, in *Na boevom postu*, 27 December 1989; Dugin, in *Slovo* 7 (1990); Dugin and A. Malysin, in *Voenno-Istoricheskii Zhurnal* 7 (1991). An exception was V. N. Zemskov, in *Sotsiologicheskie Issledovanya* 6–7 (1991).

15. According to Dugin, in 1938 only some 12 percent of the inmates of the camps were there for political reasons, but he did not count "socially harmful and dangerous elements."

16. According to Zemskov, Khrushchev's vanity led him to emphasize his role as a "liberator" in his memoirs. The true explanation is probably that, while Khrushchev had no channels of information of his own, he knew from a lifetime of experience that NKVD/KGB figures were not to be trusted.

17. Ahlberg, "Stalinistische Vergangenheitsbewältigung," 937.

18. Inside the Soviet Union, the Dugin–Zemskov findings were questioned from the very beginning, partly because of the curious circumstances of the discovery and partly because they obviously served certain political interests (S. Cholak, in *Argumenty i fakty* 45 [1989]).

19. Anatoli Krayushkin, in *Rossiiskaya Gazetta*, 17 April 1993; *Rodina* 11 (1993).

20. There is a huge Russian literature, but most of it is neither systematic nor strong on facts and figures. The most detailed so far is Stanislav Kuzmin, "Lagerniki, Gulag bez retushi," *Molodaya Gvardiya* 3–5 (1993).

21. Ibid., 192.

22. J. Arch Getty, Gabor T. Rittersporn, and Viktor N. Zemskov, "Victims of the Soviet Penal System in the Pre-War Years," *American Historical Review*, October 1993, 1017–48; J. Arch Getty and Roberta T. Manning, eds., *Stalinist Terror: New Perspectives* (Cambridge, 1993).

23. Getty and Manning, "Introduction" to *Stalinist Terror*, ed. Getty and Manning.

24. Stanislav Kuzmin, "Lagerniki," *Molodaya Gvardiya* 4 (1993): 193.

25. J. Arch Getty and Roberta Manning, "Introduction" to *Stalinist Terror*, ed. Getty and Manning, 1019.

26. Kuzmin "Lagerniki," 193. According to Khlevniyuk, the figure was closer to 600,000 155.

27. But another Russian revisionist author (Dugin) mentions a death rate of 6 to 7 percent.

28. A. Roginsky and N. Okhotin, quoted in Knight, 584.

29. Alex Nove, "Victims of Stalin: How Many?" in *Stalinist Terror*, ed. Getty and Manning; Steven Wheatcroft, "More Light on the Scale of Repression," in ibid., 275–90.

30. Getty, Rittersporm, and Zemskov, "Victims of the Soviet Penal System," 1043.

31. Roger R. Reese, "The Red Army and the Great Purges," in *Stalinist Terror*, ed. Getty and Manning, 198–214. According to John Erikson, some 20–25 percent of the officer corps was affected; according to Robert Conquest, even more.

32. Kuzmin, "Lagerniki," 193–94.

33. The *Voenno-Istoricheskii Zhurnal* under General Filatov, whose views were close to those of Russian fascist circles, was the first to publish excepts from Hitler's *Mein Kampf*. Filatov became an embarrassment and was forced to resign. Under his successor, further documents about the size of the Red Army purge were published ("O masstabakh repressii v Krasnoi Armii v predvoennye gody," *Voenno-Istoricheskii Zhurnal*) beginning in January 1993, after Reese had concluded his research.

34. Wheatcroft, "More Light on the Scale of Repression," 280.

35. The mass murders in Nazi Germany took place, it will be recalled, during World War II.

36. Getty and Manning, "Introduction" to *Stalinist Terror*, ed. Getty and Manning.

37. Ibid., 14–15.

38. Getty, *Origins of the Great Purges*, 206.

39. Martin Malia, in *Stalinist Terror*, ed. Getty and Manning, 62..

40. R. Manning, "The Great Purges in a Rural District," in *Stalinist Terror*, ed. Getty and Manning, 197.

41. As far as the number of victims is concerned there is yet another source of which so far hardly any use has been made–aerial photography. The study and comparison of imagery makes it possible to corroborate evidence received from other sources, disturbed terrain points to the existence of mass graves. There are obvious limits to this approach; aerial photographs of European Russia are mainly from German World War II origin; at present, no such photographs are available with regard to Russia beyond the Urals. Furthermore, much of the evidence, as in the case of Solovetski Island and Babi Yar, has been systematically obliterated, in the first instance by the Russians, in the second by the Germans. Nevertheless, estimates are possible with regard to certain camps, execution, and burial grounds. According to an experienced interpreter of such evidence the number of victims who perished at Katyn, Vinnitsa, Solovetski, Kharkov, Kuropaty, Sukhoye, and other such sites was almost certainly considerably higher than hitherto believed, and the same is true with regard to the number of victims at Babi Yar (1941–1942) (Waclaw Godziemba Maliszewski, Society of Aero-Historical Research, personal communication, December 17, 1993).

42. M. Broszat, in H. Buchheim, *Anatomie des S.S. Staates* (Munich, 1965), 1:126.

43. *Encyclopedia of the Holocaust*, s.v. "Babi Yar."

44. In this connection, I ought to mention the work of W. Godziemba Maliszewski, to whom I owe a valuable summary of research.

45. An interesting example of gulag accounting concerning Siberia has recently come to light. Since a census in the 1930s would have shown an unnatural and implausible growth of population in certain Siberian districts, some of the "excess population" was simply transferred to other parts of Russia – 104,000 were added to Moscow, 76,000 to Leningrad, and so on. It is doubtful whether the knowledge that they were technically residents of Moscow would have been of much comfort to the inmates of the Gulag (V. A. Isupov, "Igra bez pravil," *Sovetskaya Istoriya* [1992]).

46. These comparisons are, by necessity, approximate. The figures for the Gestapo do not include the staff of other police organizations and intelligence units (such as the SD), and as for the KGB, no detailed breakdown is available.

47. Robert Gelatelly, *The Gestapo and German Society* (Oxford, 1990), 45.

48. W. O. Weyrauch, "Gestapo Informants: Fact and Theory of Undercover Operations," *Columbia Journal of Transnational Law* 24 (1986).

49. T. Ammer and H. J. Memmler, *Staatssicherheit in Rostock* (Cologne, 1991).

50. Guard duty in the camps was done by SS deathshead units, which were also quite small, counting a few thousand, as compared with the 300,000 NKVD guards. During the war, when the camp population greatly increased, other units were mobilized, German and non-German. But manpower was never a serious problem.

51. Sheila Fitzpatrick, "Impact of the Great Purges," in *Stalinist Terror*, ed. Getty and Manning, 247–60.

52. Vitaly Chenkalinski, *La Parole ressuscitée* (Paris, 1993).

53. This is true, to repeat once again, with regard to all losses of soldiers and civilians in time of war. A semiofficial German account written more than forty years after the end of World War II says that "there are no reliable figures about German losses" (Ruediger Overmans, "Die Toten des zweiten Weltkrieges in Deutschland," in *Der zweite Weltkrieg, Analysen, Grundzuege, Forschungsbilanz* [Munich, 1989], 858–59).

54. A recent example of "Holocaust denial" by the National Bolsheviks is Yuri Mukhin, "Mif o Katyne," *Zavtra* 2 (December 1993). *Zavtra* is the successor of *Den*, edited by Aleksander Prokhanov, which was banned after the insurrection of October 1993. The anti-Communists of the extreme right, on the other hand, have adduced truly staggering numbers of victims. According to Oleg Platonov, 87 million Russians, Ukrainians, and White Russians died between 1918 and 1955 as the result of mass repressions, war, starvation, epidemics, and other disasters, whereas the total demographic shortfall for this period was 156 million ("Russkaya Tsivilizatsiya," *Russkii Vestnik* 18–20 [1993]).

55. Ernst Nolte, *Der Europaeische Buergerkrieg, 1917–1945* (Berlin, 1987), 458; Nolte, *Streitpunkte* (Berlin, 1993).

56. François Furet, *Penser la Révolution française* (Paris 1978); Sunil Khilnani, *Arguing Revolution: The Intellectual Left in Postwar France* (New Haven, Conn., 1993), chap. 6.

Chapter 8

1. An early attempt to confront this issue was made in a lecture by Sergei Mikoyan at SAIS, Johns Hopkins University, Washington, D.C., June 1993.

2. G. Gleason, "The National Factor and the Logic of Sovietology," in *The Post-Soviet Nations*, ed. A. J. Motyl (New York, 1993), 17; A. J. Motyl, "Sovietology in One Country," *Slavic Review*, Spring 1989; Motyl, *Sovietology, Rationality, Nationality* (New York, 1990).

3. One of several exceptions was G. Simon, *Nationalismus und Nationalitäten-politik in der Sowjet Union* (Cologne, 1985). But Simon was writing in the mid-1980s.

4. James Critchlow, "Nationalities Studies: Where Did They Go Wrong?" *Journal of Soviet Nationalities* (1992).

5. See, for instance, Teresa Rakowska-Harmstone, "The Dialectics of Nationalism in the USSR," *Problems of Communism*, May 1974, reprinted in *The Soviet Nationality Reader*, ed. R. Denber (Boulder, Colo., 1982).

6. V. Tishkov, "Narody i Gosudarstvo," *Kommunist* 1 (1989): 51, quoted in Z. Gitelman, in *Post-Soviet Nations*, ed. Motyl, 234.

7. G. Gleason, "Nationalism and Its Discontents," *Russian Review*, January 1993, 79.

8. *Pravda*, 5 October 1977, quoted in Graham Smith, ed., *The Nationality Question in the Soviet Union* (London, 1990), 10.

9. Quoted in Walker Connor, in *The Post-Soviet Nations*, ed. Motyl, 43. There was no basic change in this respect in the early days of *perestroika* and *glasnost*. Gorbachev announced in 1987 that the nationalities question had been solved in the Soviet Union once and for all.

10. *Pravda*, 25 May 1982. Until the KGB reports from the republics are accessible, it will be impossible to say with any assurance how well informed the central leadership was. There is little doubt that they were aware of a great deal, but not the full extent of the ferment and the tensions.

11. If there were exceptions among Soviet officials, nothing is known about them at this time. Among some Soviet academics, there was greater awareness that the "nationalities crisis" was becoming more acute. See, for instance, G. Guseinov and D. Dragunsky, eds., *Ozhog rodnovo ochaga* (Moscow, 1990), 7–9, and E. A. Pain and A. A. Popov, "Mezhnatsionalnie Konflikty v. SSSR," *Sovetskaya Etnografiya* 1 (1990).

12. See, for instance, R. Szporluk, "The Ukraine and Russia," and A. Shtromas, "The Baltic States," in *The Last Empire*, ed. Robert Conquest (Stanford, Calif., 1986); L. Hajda and M. Beissinger, *Nationalities and Reform Soviet Politics*, (Boulder, Colo., 1990); G. Simon, *Nationalism and Policy Towards the Nationalities in the Soviet Union* (Boulder, Colo., 1991); and A. Motyl, *Will the Non-Russians Rebel?* (Ithaca, N.Y., 1987). B. Nahaylo and V. Svoboda mentioned in 1990 the gradual breakup of the Soviet empire as a possibility—"one out of at least four possible scenarios" (*Soviet Disunion* [New York, 1990]).

13. Conflicts included the attacks against the Meshket Turks in Uzbekistan (June 1989) and against Caucasians in Kazakhstan (June 1989), the fighting in Osh (June 1990), and the civil war in Tadzhikistan (beginning in 1991).

14. See Andrei Zubov, "Posleslovie K epoche etnicheskikh revoliutsii," *Znamya* 5 (1993).

15. Ibid., 161. On the "Second Caucasian War," see G. Vachnadze, *Goryachie tochki Rossii* (Marburg, 1993), 142–84.

16. Jedwiga Staniszkis, in *Dilemmata der Demokratie in Osteuropa*, ed. R. Deppe (Frankfurt, 1991), 326; Margarete Mommsen, Introduction to *Nationalismus in Osteuropa*, ed. Mommsen (Munich, 1992).

17. G. Gleason, *Federalism and Nationalism* (Boulder, Colo., 1990); Gail Lapidus, ed., *From Union to Commonwealth* (Cambridge, 1992); J. Bugajski, *Nations in Turmoil* (Boulder, Colo., 1993).

18. As Bennigsen and Wimbush wrote, the "critical issue determining the extent and degree of long-term commitment of Soviet Muslims to the Soviet Russian state is not 'socio-economics' but identity" (*Muslims of the Soviet Empire* [London, 1985], 3).

How can one explain the fact that the Muslim republics were the last to dissociate themselves from Moscow and the most eager to keep some ties even after 1991? Because they had been subsidized by the Kremlin and depended on Soviet skilled manpower. They did not want cultural and political assimilation, but they were certain that they could cope with this danger while maintaining their links with Moscow; they were apparently less confident about their capacity to confront Muslim fundamentalism.

19. Gerhard Simon, *Sowjet Union, 1986–1987: Ereignisse, Probleme, Perspektiven* (Munich, 1987), 80.

20. *Pravda*, 17 August 1989.

21. I. I. Krupnik, in *Sovetskaya Etnografiya*, 4 (1990): 5. Some other articles I found of particular interest are L. S. Perepelkin and O. I. Shkaratan, "Perekhod k demokratii v poliethnicheskom obshestve," *Polis* 6 (1991); Aleksei Miller, "Natsionalizm kak faktor razvitiya," *ONS* 1 (1992); A. M. Salmin, "Soyuz posle soyuza," *Sovetskaya Etnografiya* 6 (1992); V. A. Tishkov, "Samoubiistvo tsentra i konets soyuza," *Polis* 1–2 (1992); V. K. Volkov, "Etnokratiya," *Polis* 2 (1993); as well as an earlier work, Yu. Bromlei, *Nationalnye protsessy v SSSR* (Moscow, 1988).

22. Algis Prazauskas, "Mog li bit vechnim 'soyuz nerushimy' "? *Svobodnaya Mysl* 8 (May 1992): 13.

23. In an editorial statement in the first issue, the editors of the *Journal of Soviet Nationalities* stressed that "if we are to move the discussion and analysis of Soviet nationalities to a new level, we need to think about the subject with a more comparative and theoretical perspective" (2). It remains to be seen whether comparisons between, say, Esthonia and Tadzhikistan, or even between Ukraine and Kazakhstan, or between the former Soviet Union and India and Pakistan will improve understanding or create greater confusion.

24. Even the staunchest nationalists in Northern Ireland and the Basque country do not usually converse among themselves in Gaelic or Basque.

25. The literature on the subject is enormous. Much of the relevant literature is given in Anthony Smith, *The Ethnic Revival* (Cambridge, 1981); Anthony Smith, *Theories of Nationalism* (London, 1971); and Donald L. Horowitz, *Ethnic Groups in Conflicts* (Berkeley, 1985).

26. Written in 1961, John Armstrong's essay "The Soviet Ethnic Scene" was originally submitted as a paper at a conference at Brandeis University in May 1965. For a retrospective comment, see Armstrong, "The Soviet Ethnic Scene: A Quarter Century Later," *Journal of Soviet Nationalities* 1 (1990).

27. On the new Russian minorities, see Chauncy D. Harris, "The New Russian Minorities," *Post-Soviet Geography*, January and April 1993. On the "monster" of nationalist separatism in general, see V. K. Volkov, "Etnokratiya," *Polis* 2 (1993).

28. According to two leading American scholars, "De-Sovietization has left all fifteen republics in at least a predemocratic stage and committed, in one degree or another, to building democracy," and "the disintegration of the Soviet Union has

in part been a manifestation of creative disorder" (T. J. Colton and Robert Legvold, *After the Soviet Union* [New York, 1992], 179). For the time being, there is more disorder than creativeness, and the depth of the commitment to build democracy remains as yet to be tested. For the problems, partly self-inflicted, facing even the most advanced parts of the former Soviet Union, see Anatol Lieven, *The Baltic Revolution* (New Haven, Conn., 1993).

29. I have been dealing only in passing with the political and economic disasters that befell most successor states of the Soviet Union following the breakup. The politico-ethnic scene is so much in flux (and will remain so for a long time to come) that speculation along these lines seems unproductive. All that can be said with reasonable confidence is that things will not be the same again.

30. Debates on a new relationship between Russia and the Central Asian republics have become frequent. See, for instance, "Materialy diskussii zhurnala *Vostok*: Situatsiya v tsentralnoi Azii i Rossiya," *Vostok* 6 (1993): 63–131, and "Kruglyi stol: Rossiya i tsentralno-asiatskie respubliki, problemy i perspektivy," *Mirovaya Ekonomika i mezhdunarodnye otnosheniya* 12 (1993): 1–31. On Russia's vital interests in the "Near Abroad," see A. Migranyan, in *Nezavisimaya Gazeta*, 18 January 1994.

31. For a discussion of the foreign policy of the Russian extreme right, see Walter Laqueur, *Black Hundred* (New York, 1993).

Chapter 9

1. Egon Bahr, in *Frankfurter Rundschau*, December 13, 1988.

2. The fact that the representatives of the West German media in the DDR had to operate under stringent controls and that their offices were likely to be closed if they criticized the regime, beyond what was considered permissible, did probably have some effect. But so many West Germans visited the East that the journalists had no monopoly on information concerning the DDR. Although they may have engaged in self-censorship, conscious or unconscious, it was not a decisive factor.

3. Most prominent among them were Peter Bender and Egon Bahr.

4. The history of *Deutschlandforschung* has not yet been written, but there are many interesting details in Jens Hacker, *Deutsche Irrtümer* (Berlin, 1992), and a bibliography in Wilhelm Bleck, in *Handwörterbuch zur deutschen Einheit*, ed. Werner Weidenfeld and K. R. Korte (Bonn, 1991), 154. See also G. Glaessner and P. J. Winters, in *Deutschland Archiv* 10 (1990), and Eckhart Jesse, "Hat die DDR Forschung versagt?" *Frankfurter Allgemeine Zeitung*, 24 August 1990. Also H. P. Hamacher, *DDR Forschung und Politikberatung* (Cologne, 1991).

5. J. P. Ludz, *Parteielite im Wandel* (Opladen, 1968).

6. *DDR Handbuch* (Bonn, 1971, 1972, 1974).

7. It would have been interesting to have a comparative academic study of the Stasi and the RSHA, the chief internal security authority in Nazi Germany, but this was not the kind of research most Germanologists were interested in. It would have been considered a provocation.

8. The element of East German contentment was stressed in a widely read series of articles in *Die Zeit*, later published as Theo Sommer, ed., *Reise ins andere Deutschland* (Hamburg, 1986, 1989).

9. Kurt Sontheimer, *Die DDR, Politik, Gesellschaft–Wirtschaft*, 5th ed. (Hamburg, 1979); Sontheimer, "Real war nur der schöne Schein," *Rheinischer Merkur*, 23 February 1990.

10. Siegfried Mampe wrote authoritative comments on the constitution of the DDR. Brunner was the author of the standard work, *Einführung in das Recht der DDR* (Munich, 1979).

11. The study was undertaken on behalf of the Bonn Ministry of Inner German Relations. Quoted in Hacker, *Deutsche Irrtümer*, 448. For a similar report by Fred Klinger in mid-1987, see Wilfred von Bredow, *Entstehungstendenzen und Perspektiven der DDR Gesellschaft* (Erlangen, 1988).

12. See, for instance, Christian Lemke, *Die Ursachen des Umbruchs* (Opladen, 1991). Twenty-eight books on the fall of the DDR were mentioned in a single review (K. G. Riegel, in *Jahrbuch Extremismus und Demokratie* [Bonn, 1991]), and this is only a small part of the total literature.

13. This view was expressed by C. H. Janson, *Totengräber der DDR. Wie Günter Mittag den SED Staat ruinierte* (Düsseldorf, 1991). Many leading figures from inside the party apparatus and outside observers have since commented on the development of the DDR economy in the years prior to the collapse. Among them are G. Kusch et al., *Selbstbilanz DDR* (Berlin, 1991).

14. Erhard Crome, "Die SED," *Deutschland Archiv* 12 (1992): 1293.

15. H. Bortfeldt, "Die SED ihr eigener Totengräber?" *Deutschland Archiv* 7 (1991): 733.

16. Unpublished readers' letters to newspapers are an interesting source for the mood of the population in the Soviet Union as well. Some use has been made of this material, whereas letters to the party Central Committee have apparently not been made accessible so far.

17. Bortfeldt, "Die SED," 735–36.

18. Thomas Gensicke, "Mentalitätswandel und Revolution," *Deutschland Archiv* 12 (1992): 1266. Only people currently employed participated in these polls.

19. See also Walter Friedrich, "Mentalitätswandlungen in der Jugend der DDR," *Aus Politik und Zeitgeschichte* 16–17 (1990), and Walter Friedrich and Werner Nenning, *Jugend in der DDR* (Weinheim, 1990).

20. Karl Marxstadt, *Ich liebe euch alle! Befehle und Lageberichte des MFS* (Berlin, 1990), 188.

21. Ibid., 137.

22. Ibid., 148–49. The Stasi analysts drowned in an abundance of unimportant detail. See for instance, Bürgerkomitte Leipzig, *Stasi Intern, Macht und Banalität* (Leipzig, 1991); Joachim Gauk, *Die Stasi Akten* (Hamburg, 1991); Gisela Karau, *Stasi Protokolle* (Frankfurt, 1992); Tina Krone et al., *Wenn wir unsere Akten lesen* (Berlin, 1992); L. Wawrzyn, *Der Blaue* (Berlin, 1990); Spiegel-Spezial, *Stasi Akte "Verräter,"* January 1993. To give but two examples, the Stasi files concerning Lutz Rathenow, a DDR writer but by no means one of the most famous and not a dissident of many years standing, covered no fewer than 12,000 pages. Twenty agents were employed to keep track of the (nonpolitical) activities of an East German soccer trainer who had defected to the West.

23. Erich Honecker, Interview in *Wochenpost* 47 (1990).

24. A. Mittler and St. Wolle, *Untergang auf Raten* (Munich, 1993).

25. Gerd Meyer, "Die westdeutsche DDR und Deutschlandforschung im Umbruch," in *Deutschland Archiv* 3 (1992). For an answer to Meyer, see H. Kreutzer, in *Deutschland Archiv* 6 (1992). Kreutzer had been a senior government official. He argued that the true state of affairs inside the DDR could be observed from the window of a train crossing the "zone." Many Germanologists were so obsessed with stability and took so much for granted that they never asked

themselves what stability really meant. See Christian Fener, "Das Ende des realen Sozialismus und die Aporien vergleichender Politikwissenschaft," in *Jahrbuch Extremismus und Demokratie*, ed. U. Backe and E. Jesse (Bonn, 1991).

26. Meyer, "Die westdeutsche DDR," 279.

27. W. Hofer, "50 Jahre danach," *Geschichte in Wissenschaft und Unterricht* 34 (1983): 2.

28. *Die Zeit*, 13 March 1992.

29. It is only fair to add that in some cases there was willingness to admit mistakes. For the literature on finding extenuating circumstances, see Meyer, "Die westdeutsche DDR," 285–86, W. Thaa et al., *Gesellschaftliche Differenzierung und Systemverfall des DDR Sozialismus* (Tübingen, 1992).

30. Quoted in H. Jäckel, "Unser schiefes DDR Bild," *Deutschland Archiv* 10 (1990). As Peter Bender said in the same context: Wasn't there more to the DDR than the Stasi and the privileges of the nomenklatura?

31. B. Beitz in the preface to S. Larabee, ed., *The Two German States and European Security* (London, 1989), xiii.

32. *CIA Fact Book 1989* (Washington, D.C., 1990).

33. See A. James McAdams: "The GDR at Forty: The Perils of Success," *German Politics and Society* 17 (Summer 1989); McAdams, "Inter-German Détente: A New Balance," *Foreign Affairs*, Fall 1986; McAdams, "The Origins of a New Inter-German Relationship," in *The Two German States*, ed. Larabee, 53.

34. Martin McCauley, *The German Democratic Republic Since 1945* (London, 1983), 193–94.

35. A James McAdams, *Germany Divided* (Princeton, N.J., 1993), ix, 193.

36. Ivan Kuzmin, "Sekretnye Sluzhby mnogoe znali," *Novoye Vremya* 20 (1993), an answer to my article in *Novoye Vremya* 14 (1993). See also, in greater detail, I. N. Kuzmin, *Krushchenie D.D.R.* (Moscow, 1993).

37. Albert Hirschmann, "Exit, Voice and the Fate of the German Democratic Republic," *World Politics*, January 1993, 174, 198.

Conclusion

1. George Lichtheim, "From the Finland Station," in *Collected Essays* (New York, 1973), 311.

2. Pierre Pascal, born in 1890, was one of the leading French students of Russia at the time, and an early sympathizer with the Bolshevik revolution. See Boris Souvarine, "Pierre Pascal i Sfinks," *Kontinent* 34 (1982): 189–90.

3. *The World Hails Twentieth Anniversary of the Soviet Union* (Moscow, 1938), 117, 131, 171; Hewlett Johnson, *The Socialist Sixth of the World* (London, 1942), 89, 353. On his way back from Moscow, George Bernard Shaw told journalists that "if he were eighteen years of age he would settle in Moscow tomorrow." But since he was in his late seventies, he told his Russian hosts, "it is a real comfort to me, an old man, to be able to step into my grave with the knowledge that the civilization of the world will be saved" (Michael Holroyd, *Bernard Shaw* [New York, 1993], 3:247–248.) He had been convinced in Russia that the Communist system was capable of saving mankind from complete anarchy and ruin.

4. E. H. Carr, *The Soviet Impact on the Western World* (London, 1946), 109, 112. Carr also predicted that by the year 2000 two-thirds of Europe's population would be Slavs.

5. André Gide, *Back from the USSR* (London, 1936), 11.

6. Arkadi Volsky believes that there was no inevitability about the breakup of the Soviet Union right up to the coup of August 1991, and that those who had engineered the coup, intending to preserve the union, brought about the exact opposite. See *Nezavizimaya gazeta*, 18 June 1993. Otto Latsis likewise believes that there was a chance even in 1991 to save the union, whereas Andronik Migranyan thinks that by the end of 1989 or early in 1990 the leaders of some of the non-Russian republics were firmly resolved to settle for nothing less than full independence. Igor Klyamkin argues that democratization led by necessity to the downfall of the empire. See "Krugly Stol, Russkaya Idea . . . ," *Novy Mir*, January 1993.

7. A recent example of this approach is Chris Ward, *Stalin's Russia* (London, 1993). The subtitle of the conclusion is *"Tout comprendre c'est tout pardonner."*

8. One example from many is B. M. Pugachev, in *Kentavr* (formerly *Voprosy Istorii KPSS*) 2 (1993).

9. In the demographic field, the work of Murray Feshbach has been noted as well as the pessimistic assessments of the Soviet economy by Marshall Goldman, Igor Birman and, others. Other Cassandras included R. V. Burks, "The Coming Crisis in the Soviet Union," and Al. Shtromas, "How the Soviet System May End," both in *World and I*, January 1986.

10. Daniel Bell, "Ten Theories in Search of Reality . . . ," *World Politics*, April 1958, 358. A similar point on the dangers of extrapolation was made early on by T. H. Rigby: "One cannot predict the accidents of leadership and these may prove decisive" (*Survey*, April 1963, 29).

11. See for instance Mark Vishniak, "Pravda Antibolshevizma," *Novy Zhurnal* 2 (1949), an answer to Milyukov's "Pravda Bolzhevizma." See Chapter 1, n. 23.

12. G. P. Fedotov, in *Novy Grad* 6 (1932), reprinted in G. P. Fedotov, *Imperiya i Svoboda* (New York, 1989). This was a review of a book by S. Dimitrievsky, at the time a recent defector.

13. S. Zorin and N. Alekseev, *Vremya ne zhdet* (Frankfurt, 1970); Alexander Petrov-Agatov (manuscript), excerpts in Cornelia Gerstenmaier, *Die Stimme der Stummen* (Stuttgart, 1971), 156–67.

14. Eugene Lyons and Isaac Don Levine, in *Dilemmas of Change in Soviet Politics*, ed. Zbigniew Brzezinski (New York, 1969). In the same volume Brzezinski also considered the possibility that the Soviet political system would not be able to withstand a protracted rivalry with the United States (161). See also Michel Garder, *L'Agonie du régime en Russie Sovietique* (Paris, 1965).

15. Bernard Levin, in *National Interest*, Spring 1993, 64–65.

16. But Moynihan also expressed the view that liberal democracy, too, faced an uncertain future. Franz Borkenau and Wilhelm Staringer predicted the Sino-Soviet conflict even before Stalin's death.

17. Walter Laqueur, "Six Scenarios for 1980," *New York Times*, 19 December 1971, reprinted in Walter Laqueur, *The Political Psychology of Appeasement* (New Brunswick, N.J., 1980), 73.

18. As the best known Western economics textbook stated, it was a vulgar mistake to assume that the majority of people in Eastern Europe were miserable. See Paul Samuelson and William Nordhaus, *Economics* (New York, 1976), 881.

19. Some continued to do so right up to the end. See V. Alekseev and L. Walker, eds., *Estimating the Size of the Soviet Economy* (Washington, D.C., 1991).

For other examples, see Igor Birman, "Tupik v nauke i kak s nim borotsya," *Ekonomika i matematicheskie metody* 28, no. 4 (1992): 639.

20. Recent attempts to come to terms with the record of mainstream Sovietology in the 1970s and 1980s are not encouraging. It is conceded that the revisionists went too far, but at the same time it is argued that the "traditionalists" made the same mistake. The lessons drawn are that language should be used more carefully, that there should be no "concept stretching," and that greater attention must be paid to "objective factors." All this is very well but hardly touches the essence of the problem. Elsewhere in this all too gentle postmortem on Sovietology, an attempt is made to rethink Soviet Islam, inspired by gurus such as the paleo-Marxist Louis Althusser, Michel Foucault, and Raymond Williams. It is not readily obvious in what way these authorities can help explain the civil war in Tadzhikistan or the return to power of Haidar Galiev in Baku. See Edward W. Walker, "Sovietology and Perestroika: A Postmortem," in *Beyond Sovietology*, ed. S. Gross Solomon (Armonk, N.Y., 1993), 225, and Mark Saroyan, "Rethinking Islam in the Soviet Union," in ibid.

21. This could explain Alexander Zinoviev's turn to the right and neo-Communism after the breakdown. His anger now turned against those who had refuted his analysis of *Homo sovieticus*. In 1980, Zinoviev wrote: "One has to be totally blind in order not to see the general position of the Soviet Union vis-à-vis the West; by every means to penetrate the West, to use the West for its own ends, to sow disunity, to provoke destabilization, to demoralize, to deceive, to confuse, to threaten, in brief to prepare the West for utter military defeat" (Introduction to Kyrill Henkin, *Okhotnik verkh nogami* [Frankfurt, 1980]). In 1993 Zinoviev wrote exactly the same but now with the West as the malefactor and Russia as the victim.

22. For a survey of recent debates, see Vladimir Andrle, "Demons and Devil's Advocates. . . . ," in *Stalinism*, ed. N. Lampert and Gabor Rittersporn (London, 1992), and G. Rittersporn, *Stalinist Simplification and Soviet Complications* (Chur, 1991).

23. There was never a common front in the first place except in the imaginations of anti-anti-Communists.

24. This was by no means true with regard to all conservatives, some of whom were attracted by the great emphasis in the Soviet Union on law and order, patriotism, and other such values. The case of Enoch Powell in Britain could serve as an interesting illustration.

25. On this point, the likelihood of the long-term trend toward a mixed economy—that is, a social democratic system. See R. V. Daniels, "Is There Socialism after Communism?" in *The End of the Communist Revolution* (London, 1993). Unlike Daniels, I do not rate the chances of a "moderate revolutionary revival" (something akin to Gorbachevism) very high. The belief in the market and privatization as a panacea has gone too far: the "ugly face of capitalism" is so prominent that a backlash not only in Russia but also in the other successor states and even in Eastern Europe has become very probable. But there is a far cry from a populist-nationalist backlash to a second coming of socialism.

26. Boris Grushin, in *Nezavisimaya Gazeta*, 15 June 1993.

27. A. Lieven, *The Baltic Revolution* (New Haven, Conn., 1993), 337.

28. "Russia's search for a new identity" and "Russian Westernism" were the topics of conferences sponsored by the Institute of Philosophy of the Russian

Academy of Science in 1992 and 1993. See the report by A. A. Kara Murza, in *Polis* 2 (1993), and various contributions in *Voprosy Filosofii*, 1989 and 1993. On the search for a new identity, see also Liudmilla Belyaeva, "Rossiia pered istoricheskim vyborom," *Svobodnaya Mysl* 15 (1993): 56–66; Igor Klyamkin, "Politicheskaya sotsiologiya perekhodnovo obshshestva," *Polis* 5 (1993): 49–78; and "Mezhdu Rusiyu i rossiiskoi Federatsiei," *Rodina* 10 (1993): 13–17.

Index

228   *Index*